what is this thing called metaethics?

D1567232

Are moral standards relative to cultures? Are there any moral facts? What is goodness? If there are moral facts how do we learn about them? These are all questions in metaethics, the branch of ethics that investigates the status of morality, the nature of ethical facts, and the meaning of ethical statements. To the uninitiated it can appear abstract and far removed from its two more concrete cousins, ethical theory and applied ethics, yet it is one of the fastest-growing and most exciting areas of ethics.

What is this thing called Metaethics? demystifies this important subject and is ideal for students coming to it for the first time. Beginning with a brief historical overview of metaethics and the development of a "conceptual toolkit," Matthew Chrisman introduces and assesses the following key topics:

- Ethical reality: including questions about naturalism and non-naturalism, moral facts, and the distinction between realism and antirealism.
- Ethical language: does language represent reality? What mental states are expressed by moral statements?
- Ethical psychology: the Humean theory of motivation and the connection between moral judgment and motivation.
- Ethical knowledge: intuitionist and coherentist moral epistemologies, and theories of objectivity and relativism in metaethics.
- New directions in metaethics, including non-traditional theories and extensions to metaepistemology and metanormative theory.

Additional features such as chapter summaries, questions of understanding, and a glossary make this an ideal introduction to metaethics.

Matthew Chrisman teaches and researches ethics, epistemology, and philosophy of language at the University of Edinburgh, UK. He also works on action theory, political philosophy, deontic logic, and the ethics of climate change.

● WHAT IS THIS THING CALLED?

The Routledge *What is this thing called?* series of concise textbooks has been designed for use by students coming to a core and important area of philosophy for the first time. Each volume explores the relevant central questions with a clear explanation of complex ideas and engaging contemporary examples. Features to aid study include text boxes, chapter summaries, study questions, further reading, and glossaries.

What is this thing called Philosophy?
Edited by Duncan Pritchard

What is this thing called Knowledge? third edition
Duncan Pritchard

What is this thing called Philosophy of Language?
Gary Kemp

What is this thing called Metaphysics? second edition
Brian Garrett

What is this thing called Ethics? second edition
Christopher Bennett

● FORTHCOMING

What is this thing called Emotion?
Dorothea Debus

What is this thing called Global Justice?
Kok-Chor Tan

What is this thing called Metaphysics? third edition
Brian Garrett

What is this thing called Philosophy of Religion?
Elizabeth Burns

MATTHEW CHRISMAN

what is this thing called metaethics?

Routledge
Taylor & Francis Group

LONDON AND NEW YORK

First edition published 2017
by Routledge
2 Park Square, Milton Park, Abingdon, Oxon OX14 4RN

Simultaneously published in the USA and Canada
by Routledge
711 Third Avenue, New York, NY 10017

Routledge is an imprint of the Taylor & Francis Group, an informa business

© 2017 Matthew Chrisman

British Library Cataloguing in Publication Data
A catalogue record for this book is available from the British Library

Library of Congress Cataloging in Publication Data
A catalog record for this book has been requested

ISBN: 978-1-138-82760-8 (hbk)
ISBN: 978-1-138-82762-2 (pbk)
ISBN: 978-1-315-43833-7 (ebk)

Typeset in Berling and Arial Rounded
by GreenGate Publishing Services, Tonbridge, Kent
Printed in Great Britain by Ashford Colour Press Ltd

For my parents Sharon and Chris, who have supported me so much.

CONTENTS

✓ **List of figures and tables**   x
✓ **Preface**   xi

✓ **Introduction**   xv
   BACKGROUND   xvi
   FOUR KEY ISSUES   xvii
   FOUR MAIN THEORIES   xx
   CONCLUSION   xxii
   CHAPTER SUMMARY   xxii
   STUDY QUESTIONS   xxii
   FURTHER RESOURCES   xxiii
   ANSWERS TO QUESTIONS OF UNDERSTANDING   xxiii
   WORKS CITED   xxiv
   NOTE   xxiv

✓ **1 Four key issues**   1
   QUESTIONS ABOUT ETHICS AND METAPHYSICS   2
   QUESTIONS ABOUT ETHICS AND EPISTEMOLOGY   4
   QUESTIONS ABOUT ETHICS AND PHILOSOPHY OF LANGUAGE   6
   QUESTIONS ABOUT ETHICS AND PHILOSOPHY OF MIND   8
   CONCLUSION   11
   CHAPTER SUMMARY   13
   STUDY QUESTIONS   13
   FURTHER RESOURCES   14
   ANSWERS TO QUESTIONS OF UNDERSTANDING   14
   WORKS CITED   15
   NOTES   15

2 Nonnaturalism   16
   A MORE PRECISE CHARACTERIZATION   16
   THE CASE FOR NONNATURALISM   18
   ARGUMENTS AGAINST NONNATURALISM   23
   CONCLUSION   28

CHAPTER SUMMARY   29
STUDY QUESTIONS   30
FURTHER RESOURCES   30
ANSWERS TO QUESTIONS OF UNDERSTANDING   30
WORKS CITED   31
NOTE   31

3 Expressivism   **32**
ARGUMENTS IN FAVOR OF EXPRESSIVISM   33
VERSIONS AND OBJECTIONS   36
CONCLUSION   48
CHAPTER SUMMARY   49
STUDY QUESTIONS   50
FURTHER RESOURCES   50
ANSWERS TO QUESTIONS OF UNDERSTANDING   50
WORKS CITED   51

4 Error theory & fictionalism   **52**
MACKIE'S ARGUMENTS FOR ERROR THEORY   53
OBJECTIONS AND REPLIES   55
VERSIONS OF FICTIONALISM   58
CONCLUSION   61
CHAPTER SUMMARY   61
STUDY QUESTIONS   62
FURTHER RESOURCES   62
ANSWERS TO QUESTIONS OF UNDERSTANDING   62
WORKS CITED   63
NOTES   63

5 Naturalism   **65**
NEO-ARISTOTELIAN NATURALISM   66
RELATIVISM AS A FORM OF NATURALISM   71
A POSTERIORI NATURALISM   75
A PRIORI NETWORK NATURALISM   79
CONCLUSION   83
CHAPTER SUMMARY   84
STUDY QUESTIONS   85
FURTHER RESOURCES   85
ANSWERS TO QUESTIONS OF UNDERSTANDING   85
WORKS CITED   86
NOTES   87

6 Summary & chart   88
   THE FOUR MAIN AREAS   89
   COSTS AND BENEFITS   95
   CONCLUSION   96
   CHAPTER SUMMARY   96
   STUDY QUESTIONS   97
   ANSWERS TO QUESTIONS OF UNDERSTANDING   97

7 Theories that are hard to classify in traditional terms   99
   BELIEFS OR DESIRES—WHY NOT A BIT OF BOTH?   100
   ETHICAL FACTS—WHY DO THEY HAVE TO BE "OUT THERE"?   105
   PRAGMATISM   111
   CONCLUSION   113
   CHAPTER SUMMARY   115
   STUDY QUESTIONS   115
   FURTHER RESOURCES   116
   ANSWERS TO QUESTIONS OF UNDERSTANDING   116
   WORKS CITED   117
   NOTES   118

8 Outstanding issues   119
   FROM METAETHICS TO METANORMATIVE THEORY   121
   FROM METAETHICS TO METAEPISTEMOLOGY   131
   CONCLUSION   137
   CHAPTER SUMMARY   137
   STUDY QUESTIONS   137
   FURTHER RESOURCES   138
   ANSWERS TO QUESTIONS OF UNDERSTANDING   138
   WORKS CITED   138

Glossary   140
Index   151

FIGURES AND TABLES

• FIGURES

1.1	Four main metaethical theories	12
6.1	Traditional metaethical theories	88
7.1	Hard to classify metaethical theories	114

• TABLES

6.1	Four metaethical traditions with metaphysics	90
6.2	Four metaethical traditions with metaphysics and epistemology	91
6.3	Four metaethical traditions with metaphysics, epistemology, and philosophy of language	92
6.4	Four metaethical traditions with metaphysics, epistemology, philosophy of language, and philosophy of mind	94

PREFACE

Is morality a matter of objective fact or a subjective creation of the human mind? Do ethical statements express beliefs about how things stand in reality or emotive reactions to a value-free world? Assuming there are ethical facts, are they discoverable by empirical methods broadly contiguous with the methods of science, or does moral knowledge require a special form of intuition or wisdom? Does someone who is not at least somewhat motivated to do what they think is morally right not count as really understanding the phrase "morally right"?

These sorts of questions have been a part of the study of ethics since the beginning of philosophy, and they are as interesting and pressing today as they have ever been. They are the sorts of questions that lead one to do metaethics. This book is about metaethics.

The book has been written as a general introduction to metaethics suitable as a textbook for an undergraduate course on the subject matter, though it could also be used as part of a self-study or as groundwork for a graduate level course. (More on the study resources below.) In it you will be introduced to the way philosophers have sought to systematize their approach to metaethics and develop general metaethical theories capable of making progress on the sorts of questions above. We won't answer those questions once and for all here, but we will hopefully develop a much richer understanding of what's at stake in many of the answers that various philosophers have developed for them and intuitions about how we might answer them for ourselves.

One of the exciting things about metaethics is the way it is a crossroads for a lot of other areas of philosophy. The way I tend to approach metaethics, as I'll explain in more detail in the Introduction and Chapter 1, is by viewing the subarea as comprising questions in metaphysics, epistemology, philosophy of language, and philosophy of mind *as they apply to ethics*. Where a metaphysician might ask about which facts obtain and what they are like, in metaethics we ask about whether ethical facts obtain and if they do what they are like. Where an epistemologist might ask about the nature of knowledge, in metaethics we ask about the nature of moral knowledge. Where a philosopher of language might ask about how sentences get their meanings, in metaethics we ask about how paradigmatically ethical words contribute to the meaning of the sentences in which they figure. Where a philosopher of mind might ask about what happens in our psychologies when we perform an action, in metaethics we ask about the role of ethical judgment in motivating action.

As a result, metaethics can often be the place where general theories in these other areas of philosophy get tested on especially thorny terrain. And it can also help us to remember that all of the philosophical ideas we develop, be it about ethics, metaphysics, epistemology, philosophy of language, or philosophy of mind, must in the end hang together as an attractive package with the rest of the views we develop in these other areas (as well as with other areas of human knowledge).

To help you access this exciting subarea of philosophy, the book contains a number of study resources that have helped my students in their study of metaethics. First, there is a glossary of key terms. When a term is first used, if it's in the glossary, then it is in bold. And if it's not used for a while and then used again several chapters later in a way that might be unfamiliar to the beginning reader, I have placed it in bold again. Second, each chapter contains quick "questions of understanding" sprinkled throughout the text that I encourage you to try to answer when they occur in the text before you check my answers at the end of the chapter. This, I have found, helps to maintain a focus on reading the text closely. Third, each chapter is dotted throughout with text boxes containing "key points" and a "chapter summary" at the end that should be helpful for reviewing the material. Fourth, each chapter concludes with some "study questions" which are the sorts of questions that might make for anything from a short assignment to a full-fledged essay topic. If you're feeling confident with answering all of the study questions, you are probably pretty close to mastering the material. Fifth, each chapter also has a list of "further resources" where you can go to deepen the knowledge you acquire by reading the chapter. In some cases these are other introductory articles or encyclopedia entries that I recommend you read; in other cases there are videos or other multimedia that I think also help one to access the material.

I want to thank several people for helping me along the journey I have taken into metaethics. I had the great fortune to study metaethics as a graduate student at the University of North Carolina at Chapel Hill. My Ph.D. thesis was directed by Geoffrey Sayre-McCord, who was hugely influential on my interest in and knowledge of the topic. I also learned a lot during those years from Dorit Bar-On, Simon Blackburn, Thomas Hill, Jr., William Lycan, Ram Neta, Gerald Postema, Jesse Prinz, David Reeve, Michael Resnik, and Jay Rosenberg. Since graduate school I have been on the philosophy faculty at the University of Edinburgh, where I have benefited from interaction with many great colleagues and students. Material for this book grew out of lecture notes developed for an undergraduate metaethics course that I have taught many times with Michael Ridge. The first seven chapters were trialed on our metaethics class at the University of Edinburgh in autumn 2015. In addition to shaping my way of thinking of the subject matter, Mike generously read full drafts of all of the chapters and gave me extensive and extremely helpful feedback. Colleagues such as Selim Berker, Campbell Brown, Guy Fletcher, Graham Hubbs, Elinor Mason, and Debbie Roberts have generously discussed various elements of this material with me. In summer 2015, Samuel Dishaw and Silvan Wittwer formed a reading group to work through full drafts of most of the chapters with me, and they provided many useful and detailed comments. A good chunk of the manuscript was finalized while traveling in Costa Rica with my overly indulgent wife and our two lovely children. The cover art—"Opposing Quadrants"—is a painting by my talented father Chris Chrisman, who along with my mother Sharon Chrisman, has been extremely supportive. To all of these people, I say a hearty thank you.

Contemporary metaethics is an exciting and fast-changing area of philosophy. In its dark moments, it can seem like a series of sectarian skirmishes between proponents of various -isms representing vague and unfalsifiable theoretical persuasions rather than concrete philosophical doctrines. But in its light moments, the way the very terms of the ongoing debate come up themselves for regular review and revision indicates what I see as a healthy self-consciousness of the mutability of the theoretical terrain on which all philosophy is pursued. I wrote this book in an attempt to get down on paper my own map of the theoretical terrain I found when I started doing metaethics sixteen years ago. I did so because I hope it will be helpful for understanding how the terrain is shifting and new theories are quickly emerging. But I also hope that joining the evolution of metaethics—even if only for a semester or a year—will lead more and more people into thinking in philosophically careful ways for themselves about all sorts of topics.

Matthew Chrisman
Edinburgh, May 2016

INTRODUCTION

In 2003, George Bush, the President of the United States, ordered American troops to invade Iraq (alongside troops from the UK, Australia, and Poland). In 2010, Bradley Manning, an American Army intelligence analyst in Iraq, leaked hundreds of thousands of classified documents to Wikileaks, which then released them on the internet and to several high-profile newspapers, thereby exposing operations of the American military and intelligence services. In 2013, Denise Lind sentenced Manning to 35 years of confinement. Were these controversial actions ethically right or wrong? Did they have, on balance, morally good or bad consequences? Would you say that Bush, Manning, Wikileaks, the newspaper editors, or Lind exhibited moral virtue or vice in acting in these ways?

When we answer questions like these, we make **ethical judgments**. As a matter of course, we also make ethical judgments about less controversial issues every day. Should you keep your promise to meet a friend tonight, even if you really don't want to? Would it be good to give a regular donation to a local charity that helps the homeless? What would be the kind way to treat your parents when you disagree with them?

Ethics concerns these sorts of questions. The philosophical study of ethics can be divided into three areas. In **normative ethics** we seek general theories of right/wrong, good/bad, virtue/vice—that is, theories which might explain why, in general, some acts are right others wrong, some outcomes good others bad, some people virtuous others vicious. Utilitarianism and Deontology are two classic normative ethical theories. Moving towards the more particular and concrete, in **practical ethics** we seek to determine (often by reflecting on normative ethical theories) the correct ethical judgments relevant to our practical decisions in everyday life. For example, here we might inquire into whether things such as capital punishment, abortion, cognitive enhancement, or single-payer healthcare are right or wrong. Moving in the other direction towards the more theoretical and abstract, in **metaethics**, we seek to understand what we are doing when we make ethical judgments and to integrate this understanding with our other philosophical views about the nature of reality, the meaning of language, the psychology of action, the possibility of knowledge, and related topics. For example, are we making objective claims about the nature of reality, expressing evaluative attitudes like preferences, forming tacit agreements about how to live together, some combination of the above, or something totally different? If we lump normative ethics and practical ethics together as the "first-order" subject matter of ethics, we can think of metaethics as a "meta-level" or "second-order" investigation into the nature of this subject matter.

This book is about metaethics, which is a subdiscipline of the philosophical study of ethics, covering second-order questions about ethics.[1] It is what emerges when one reflects critically and carefully about the nature of one's own ethical opinions. This means that metaethics doesn't directly address questions like those above about what is right/wrong, good/bad, virtuous/vicious, etc. Rather it addresses questions about the status of the opinions we form when we answer such questions. It is an exciting area of contemporary philosophy, where perennial questions about the nature of morality are brought into contact with important and active debates in metaphysics, the philosophy of language, moral psychology, and epistemology.

> QU1: Which of the following is a metaethical question: (i) Is war ever morally legitimate? (ii) What does it mean for something to be morally legitimate? (iii) How common is war since the invention of guns?

• BACKGROUND

Many people, both now and for most of human history, have thought that morality comes from God. One way to appreciate the kinds of questions investigated in meta-ethics is to critically examine this idea. We might, of course, query whether God really exists. But even assuming there is a God and following his commands is morally right, we can ask, as Plato's *Euthyphro* encourages us to ask: are things morally right *because* they are commanded by God, or does God command things *because* they are morally right? That is to say, assuming there is a God, does his commanding something make it morally required, or does he make his commands because he thinks following them is required by morality? Both answers to this question represent metaethical views. On the one hand, morality might be viewed as a standard for judging actions, people, and institutions that is enacted by rather than independent of God's will. On the other hand, morality might be viewed as an independent standard for judging actions, people, and institutions (which God, if there is one, is good at discerning).

Neither answer is completely satisfying. If God's command *creates* morality, then doesn't that make morality seem somewhat arbitrary? If God had commanded self-ishness rather than charity, then on this view selfishness would be morally good rather than charity. To many, however, moral actions seem to be good in themselves rather than because of their relation to someone's (even God's) commands. On the other hand, if morality is a standard independent of God's command, then where does it come from, what grounds its authority?

This challenging question might lead one to skepticism about ethics. In book I of the *Republic*, Plato's character Thrasymachus argues that the things we generally view as ethically right are—as a matter of fact—whatever tends to promote the interests of the stronger people in society (e.g., paying our debts, respecting the property of others, not telling lies, etc.). His idea is that morality is essentially ungrounded because it is a sort of pernicious ideology, emerging in human societies because of its usefulness for controlling people. By contrast, in book II, Plato's character Glaucon defends a more optimistic view, arguing that morality is a human convention, grounded in its usefulness for solving the otherwise difficult problem of living together in a peaceful and cooperative society. Interestingly, however, Plato's main character Socrates rejects both of these viewpoints, arguing over the course of the rest of the book that morality is an objective and eternal standard for judging actions, people, and institutions.

This cluster of views we find in Plato represents one key historical antecedent to contemporary metaethics. Others can be found in Hume and Kant. Hume famously argued that reason is the slave of the passions, and he located the heart of morality in our natural human sentiments. Kant, by contrast, stressed reason and especially *practical* reason, which he thought to be the only possible route to universal truths about ethics.

• FOUR KEY ISSUES

By briefly considering some ancient ideas, we've already seen four broad metaethical viewpoints about the status of morality: (i) it comes from God; (ii) it is a pernicious ideology; (iii) it is the solution to a coordination problem; and (iv) it is a self-founding objective standard for evaluating actions, people, and institutions. We'll see remnants of each of these in the contemporary theories we discuss here. But to assess these theories properly, it will prove helpful to separate four different issues that are wrapped up in this question about the status of morality:

- Questions about the existence and nature of ethical facts and properties. # 1
- Questions about ethical knowledge and disagreement. # 2
- Questions about the meaning and use of ethical language. # 3
- Questions about ethical thought and reasoning towards action. #4

We will become much better acquainted with these questions in the following chapters, but I will introduce them briefly here.

The first set of questions is where ethics comes into contact with **metaphysics**. In #1 contemporary philosophy, it is G. E. Moore's *Principia Ethica* (1903) that is commonly credited with distinguishing second-order metaethical inquiry from first-order normative and practical ethics. In the first chapter of that book he set out to identify the subject matter of ethics, arguing that we need to determine what the word 'good' refers to—that is, what is *goodness?* Relatedly, of course, we might also ask: what is *rightness*; or what is *virtue*? These are questions about ethical properties.

We could, however, just as well ask about ethical facts: when we think that something, e.g., charity has the property of being good, we might put this by saying that it's a fact that charity is good. So, in the part of metaethics that's about metaphysics, we ask things such as: are there really such facts or is it possible that there's really no such thing as goodness (sort of like there's really no such thing as phlogiston)? If there are such facts and properties, are they natural, supernatural, or classifiable in some other way? Are ethical facts and properties mind-independent or somehow the product of human thought?

> QU2: True or false: If God doesn't exist, then there isn't a fact about whether murder is wrong.

#2 The second set of questions is where ethics comes into contact with **epistemology**. Many philosophers think ethical facts aren't knowable by **empirical investigation** of the world, so they suggest that we must have a special faculty of **intuition** whereby we come to know what things are good/right/virtuous, etc. However, other philosophers have turned this argument on its head arguing that, if ethical claims cannot be verified by empirical investigation, then there's no way to settle whose intuition is right when we disagree, so ethics must not really be in the business of discovering facts but rather of expressing our emotions. This theoretical dispute raises a host of interesting philosophical questions about the possibility and nature of ethical knowledge, and the status of moral disagreement.

#3 The third set of questions is where philosophical ethics comes into contact with the **philosophy of language**. Note that Moore asked what the word 'good' refers to, but this raises three questions in the philosophy of language and mind:

1. What is it for a word to refer to something?
2. What concept or idea does a word express?
3. Why should we even think that the word 'good' and the concept of goodness refer to something?

More generally, there is a tendency in some areas of philosophy to think that the main job of declarative sentences and the thoughts they express is to represent a way reality could be, and a sentence and the thought it expresses are true just in case reality is the way they represent it as being. This is especially plausible when it comes to a sentence such as, "The sun is shining in Edinburgh," which we might think of as expressing a belief about the weather and thereby being a partial description of the weather in Edinburgh. The key question then is whether we think of ethical language this way too. When someone says "Bush's invading Iraq was wrong," are they expressing beliefs about the wrongness of this action and thereby partially describing moral reality? Some philosophers have thought not. For example, A. J. Ayer (1946) claimed that they are expressing emotive reactions, and R. M. Hare (1952) famously compared ethical sentences to **prescriptions**, e.g., the kind of thing we often convey by using an imperative sentence. As we'll see, these ideas raise important issues about how to explain meaning, in particular the role of *use* in a comprehensive theory of meaning. They also raise important issues about the relationship between language and mind.

QU3: Which of the following might be said to represent something else: (i) a map of NYC, (ii) an x on the ballot, (iii) the play-by-play description of a basketball game?

Finally, the fourth set of questions is where ethics comes into contact with the **philosophy of mind**. #4 Whatever exactly our view is about the existence and nature of moral reality and the explanation of the meaning of ethical language, we might wonder what is going on in the minds of people making ethical judgments and how to think about the reasoning process which moves from ethical judgment to action. Unlike judgments about ordinary matters of fact (e.g., the weather yesterday), ethical judgments seem to be closely tied up with our motivations to act. This is true in at least two different senses. First, normally, when someone sincerely judges that they ought to do something, we can expect them to do it; if they don't do it, we'll long for an explanation (maybe they changed their mind, they succumbed to weakness of will, they were overpowered by emotions, etc.). Second, we tend to think that ethical facts (if such exist) provide us with *reasons* to act. That is, if something is the ethically right thing for you to do, that's a reason (perhaps even a conclusive reason) for you to do it; this is true, some philosophers have thought, even if you don't recognize that it's the right thing to do, or even if it doesn't connect in any way to things you want. There is considerable controversy in philosophy about what a reason to do something is, but plausibly it is connected to the way we reason from premises to conclusions about what to do. So this second connection between ethics and reasons raises an important question in the theory of practical reasons: what does it take for something to be a reason for someone to do something and how does that affect our reasoning to conclusions about what to do?

In Chapter 1, I'll present each of these four sets of questions in more detail, seeking to develop a sort of "conceptual tool-kit" that we can use to chart the theoretical terrain of metaethics. That is, we'll come to understand several different concepts deriving from metaphysics, epistemology, philosophy of language, and philosophy of mind and use these to explain some of the main theoretical viewpoints one finds in metaethics. Often a particular metaethicist's commitments regarding some of the key issues above are driven by her commitments regarding other issues, and we generally evaluate metaethical theories via a kind of **theoretical cost–benefit analysis**. Much like one might weigh costs and benefits of different family vacations, or the government might weigh costs and benefits of various taxation policies, we philosophers can weigh costs and benefits of different philosophical theories. These typically consist of positive reasons one might favor the theory (benefits) weighed against negative reasons one might use to critique the theory (costs), as well as further counter-arguments in both directions. In metaethics, different philosophers will attach different costs and benefits to theory's commitment in metaphysics, epistemology, philosophy of language, and philosophy of mind, and by outlining various theories in terms of their commitments across these four domains we will begin to understand what motivates philosophers to endorse and defend them.

> ***Key Point***: Metaethics is the study of metaphysics, epistemology, philosophy of language, and philosophy of mind as they apply to ethics.

• FOUR MAIN THEORIES

I have already mentioned some of the roots of metaethics in Plato, Hume, and Kant. Three of the more recent but still historical sources are Moore, Ayer, and Hare. All three were deeply influenced by the **linguistic turn** in philosophy, and accordingly they pursued analysis of the meanings of words, including ethical words, in the hope that such analyses might shed light on issues in metaphysics, epistemology, and the philosophy of mind. It is in this way that metaethics began to look like a freestanding subdiscipline around the beginning of the twentieth century. We'll discuss their views in the coming chapters. By and large, however, this book is going to be about contemporary metaethics. The theories we will explore are ones that metaethicists working today defend, although they are often inspired by historical figures (which I will often note in passing). In this regard, I find it illuminating to divide these into four main theories and then mention some other ideas that are somewhat harder to classify.

#1 We'll start, in Chapter 2, with **nonnaturalism** because the subsequent theories were often developed in reaction to early forms of nonnaturalism. In rough outline, this is the view that there are objective ethical facts and these facts are **sui generis** ("of their own kind"). More specifically, nonnaturalists deny that ethical facts are a species of natural fact, the sort that we might discover by empirical investigation; but they also deny that ethical facts are a species of supernatural fact, the sort that might be created by the commands of God. This view is often motivated by the ordinary thought that morality is important and objective, but also by particular commitments in the philosophy of language/mind or moral psychology. And as we have already seen, it can seem to require a special view about how we might come to have ethical knowledge, and how we can resolve moral disagreements.

> QU4:   If someone thinks that what it is for an act to be right is for it to be commanded by God, then what are they—a naturalist, supernaturalist, or nonnaturalist?

#2 **Expressivism** is the second theory. This will occupy us in Chapter 3. The basic idea begins in the philosophy of language and the philosophy of mind with the claim that the core job of ethical sentences is not to represent a distinctive piece of reality, but to express a distinctive kind of mental state—one with a peculiar profile in the psychology of human motivation. The idea is that ethical judgment serves as a kind of emotionally-laden spur to or constraint on action rather than a cool picture of how things stand in reality. For example, someone who thinks eating meat is wrong will typically be motivated not to eat meat. Some expressivists take this to encourage an "antirealist" stance regarding questions of the metaphysics of morality: since our ethical judgments don't purport to describe reality we are not committed to there being ethical properties as part of reality. Other expressivists take a "quasi-realist" stance regarding these questions: there's nothing wrong with saying, e.g., "It's a fact that leaking classified documents is wrong," but we'd be mistaken to think we learn much about ethics from metaphysical investigation into what the nature of such facts is (natural, supernatural, or nonnatural) or where they fit into the fundamental fabric of reality. Either way, considering this view raises important questions about the possibility of ethical knowledge and resolving moral disagreement.

QU5: Which of the following express mental states: (i) blushing, (ii) sleeping, (iii) some scribbles on the wall, (iv) a high five, (v) your answer to this question?

In Chapter 4, we'll cover **error theory** and **fictionalism**. These are two closely related #3 views that agree with the nonnaturalist (against the expressivist) in the philosophy of language/mind that ethical sentences represent an objective way reality might be. But because they agree with the expressivist (against the nonnaturalist) in metaphysics that there are no sui generis nonnatural facts as part of the fabric of reality, they argue that positive ethical claims are uniformly false. Perhaps this is because ethical thought and discourse rest on a fundamental error: we often think we know things to be right/wrong, good/bad, virtuous/vicious, but we're mistaken (as Thrasymachus argued). Or perhaps this is because ethical thought and discourse involve a kind of useful fiction. Compare: It can be quite useful to pretend that the Earth is fixed and the sun rises every day, even though strictly speaking that's false (because it's really the earth's rotating that determines when and where sunlight is visible). If either view is right, that has important implications for how we might think about settling moral disagreements. If either view is right, that has important implications for how we might think about settling moral disagreements.

The final main theory we'll discuss is **naturalism**. This is the topic of Chapter 5. The #4 basic idea is to start with a commitment to the reality of ethical facts (i.e. disagreeing with the expressivist, error-theorist, and fictionalist), but to argue that nonnaturalists were wrong to think that ethical facts are sui generis. In metaphysics we can "reduce" ethical facts to natural facts, or at least we can "locate" ethical facts among the other facts we believe in as part of a naturalistic worldview. If this is right, then maybe there is an empirical method to resolve moral disagreements, or perhaps ethical knowledge is always relative to a particular culture or moral community. Either way, naturalism is right, then ethical sentences can be construed as representational and not literally false in many cases where they seem true.

Key Point: The four main theories we will consider are nonnaturalism, expressivism, error theory/fictionalism, and naturalism.

• CONCLUSION

Discussing the four main issues and the four main theories will put us in a position (in Chapter 6) to summarize the core of metaethics by developing a chart whereby we outline each theory's stance on each of these issues. There are two points to doing this. First, it hopefully gives readers enough of an understanding of the main theoretical fault lines of metaethics to begin to apply a cost–benefit analysis to these theories. For example, you can begin to develop your own answer to questions such as, "Is the nonnaturalist's commitment to the existence of nonnatural properties worth the seamless treatment she can give of ethical and non-ethical language?" "Is the expressivist's position in moral psychology and metaphysics an attractive reason to embrace his commitments in the philosophy of language/mind and epistemology?" Second, the chart we develop will also expose some holes, leading us to ask whether there couldn't be more theories that take up a different constellation of commitments across the four main issues. In Chapter 7, I will briefly introduce some contemporary theories that are hard to classify within the four main theories precisely because they seem to do this. Then, in Chapter 8, I will outline several outstanding issues that the traditional focus of metaethics on "the status of morality" may seem to have wrongly neglected. These are areas where much of the most recent theoretical discussions are happening.

• CHAPTER SUMMARY

- The philosophical study of ethics can be divided into three main areas: normative ethics, practical ethics, and metaethics.
- Metaethics prescinds from first-order questions about what is right/wrong, good/bad, virtuous/vicious to ask second-order questions about the "status of morality."
- Four key areas of metaethical reflection are about metaphysics, epistemology, the philosophy of language, and philosophy of mind as each of these more general areas of philosophy apply to specifically *ethical* thought and discourse.
- This book will be organized around four main theoretical viewpoints: nonnaturalism, expressivism, error theory/fictionalism, and naturalism.

• STUDY QUESTIONS

1 Explain in your own words the difference between normative ethics and metaethics.
2 What is the difference between asking whether what Manning did was wrong and asking about the nature of wrongness?
3 What is metaphysics about, when it comes to morality?
4 What is moral psychology?
5 Do you think most declarative language is representational of reality? What are the alternatives?
6 Do you think there is always an objectively right answer about what is right and wrong?

• FURTHER RESOURCES

- Chrisman, Matthew. 2014. "Morality: Objective, Relative, or Emotive" in Chrisman, Matthew and Pritchard, Duncan, et al. *Philosophy for Everyone*, Routledge. [A chapter length introduction to questions about the status of morality, which forms the basis for the Introduction to Philosophy MOOC Lecture available here: www.youtube.com/watch?v=R7gHPXnVmac&index=15&list=PL wJ2VKmefmxqgjDHRppT_jnqEXuKLmKY6.]
- LaFollette, Hugh (ed.). 2013. *International Encyclopedia of Ethics*. Wiley-Blackwell, online, http://onlinelibrary.wiley.com/book/10.1002/9781444367072. [A very comprehensive encyclopedia of articles by top researchers in the field introducing topics in ethics.]
- Sayre-McCord, Geoffrey. 2014. "Metaethics," *The Stanford Encyclopedia of Philosophy (Summer 2014 Edition)*, Edward N. Zalta (ed.), http://plato.stanford. edu/archives/sum2014/entries/metaethics.
- Will Wilkinson interviews Geoffrey Sayre-McCord on Metaethics, http://bloggingheads.tv/videos/1562.

• ANSWERS TO QUESTIONS OF UNDERSTANDING

QU1: (ii) is a metaethical question because it is not about which particular ethical judgment would be correct but rather about what being correct amounts to. (i) is an applied ethical question, whereas (iii) is not a question in ethics but rather in history.

QU2: Some Divine Command Theorists think this is true, but one can consistently think it is false if one thinks ethical facts obtain independently of God's will. Just like an atheist can believe that facts about the color of grass obtain independently of God's will, an atheist can believe that the fact that murder is wrong obtains independently of God's will. An interesting and hard question for those who think this is what these facts are like—are they like facts discoverable by science, or like facts about our own subjective reactions to the world, or are they "facts" only in some lightweight sense?

QU3: They all represent something else, though in subtly different ways. Example (iii) is the closest to the way philosophers commonly think of declarative sentences as representing a way reality could be.

QU4: They're a supernaturalist. We might include supernaturalists within the category of nonnaturalists, as allied against the naturalist view that what it is for an act to be right is a matter of it having some natural property. However, Moore's very influential arguments that ethical properties are nonnatural works equally well against the view that what it is for an act to be right is a matter of it having some supernatural property (such as being commanded by God). So it is common to reserve "nonnaturalism" to refer to views that deny that ethical properties are natural or supernatural.

QU5:   (i), (iv), and (v) all express mental states though in interestingly different ways. If you made this or some other statement as your answer to this question, then that would be the best example for the way philosophers think of linguistic acts as expressing our thoughts. Expressivists think that when a statement is ethical in its content the mental state is interestingly different from the sorts of beliefs about reality we ordinarily express with our statements. It's worth noting that (iii) is ambiguous. If those scribbles were created with the intention of conveying something (either a feeling or a thought) they may be expressive, but if they were simply the result of an accident, they wouldn't express a mental state.

• WORKS CITED

Ayer, A. J. 1946. *Language, Truth and Logic*. 2nd edn. London: V. Gollancz Ltd.
Hare, R. M. 1952. *The Language of Morals*. Oxford: Oxford University Press.
Moore, G. E. 1903. *Principia Ethica*. Cambridge: Cambridge University Press.

• NOTE

1   In this book I will generally use the words 'ethical' and 'moral' interchangeably with a slight preference for the former over the latter. It's worth noting, however, that some authors mark a distinction between morality and ethics, where the former concerns maxims for human conduct based on a particular set of concerns such as respect for others and preventing harm, and the latter covers more general terrain for how to live one's life.

1
four key issues

In this chapter, we'll discuss in more detail the four key issues on which any complete metaethical theory would take a stand. In brief, these are:

- Questions in *metaphysics* about the existence and nature of ethical facts and properties.
- Questions in *epistemology* about the possibility of ethical knowledge and the nature of ethical disagreement.
- Questions in *philosophy of language* about the meaning and expressive role of ethical words and sentences.
- Questions in the *philosophy of mind* about the connection between ethical thought and action.

As I said in the Introduction, these are points where the philosophical study of ethics connects with other areas of philosophy. So, one way we might think of metaethics is as the subdiscipline of ethics that seeks to answer questions in metaphysics, epistemology, philosophy of language, and philosophy of mind *as they apply to ethics*. In the rest of this chapter I shall seek to explain the general issues and how they apply to ethics. Hence, by the end of this chapter, we will have a "conceptual toolkit" which we can use in future chapters to probe the interlocking theoretical commitments of various metaethical viewpoints.

Before we begin, a word of warning: this chapter contains a high number of technical terms which may sound rather jargony. I explain these terms as we move along, noting how they are commonly used in metaethics to mark key distinctions between competing views on some matter. However, any term in bold is also in the glossary at the end of this book. So while it will be helpful for future chapters to understand the distinctions these technical terms mark, you can always consult the glossary if you forget what a particular term means.

● QUESTIONS ABOUT ETHICS AND METAPHYSICS

Metaphysics is the area of philosophy concerned with the fundamental nature of reality. What kinds of things are real, what are they like, and how do they relate to one another? For example, metaphysicians may be interested in the difference between particulars (e.g., the Statue of Liberty) and universals (e.g., being a statue) and the composition of things (e.g., are statues more than a combination of their proper parts?). More relevant to metaethics, metaphysicians are also interested in whether every fact is reducible to a fact about the physical world or whether some non-physical facts obtain. Or, for another example, whether we might take it as obvious that we are conscious but then wonder whether our being conscious can be explained in terms of things that are purely biological. One more example: we all use mathematics everyday, but one might wonder whether numbers really exist. These are examples of the sorts of issues investigated in metaphysics.

That is to say that metaphysics might ask about the reality, nature, and interrelations of various things such as particulars, properties, numbers, and facts. When it comes to ethics, we may wonder about the reality and nature of particular ethical entities, such as virtues and vices. However, it's much more common to focus on metaphysical questions about ostensible ethical *properties* and *facts*. As we saw briefly in the Introduction, in one of the foundational texts of metaethics, G. E. Moore assumed that the property of goodness is real, and queried its nature (ultimately arguing that it is sui generis). Talk of properties can usually be translated into talk of facts. So, in what follows, to keep the discussion manageable, I'll generally focus on facts rather than properties, under the simplifying assumption that an ethical fact generally involves something's possessing an ethical property.

In response to this kind of question about the nature of ethical reality, metaethicists commonly draw three different distinctions; it's a matter of some theoretical controversy how exactly they are related:

- natural vs. supernatural vs. nonnatural
- reducible vs. irreducible
- mind-dependent vs. mind-independent.

The first distinction is born out of one of the key intellectual advances of the enlightenment: an increased acceptance of empirical science as the measure of what's real. The sorts of unifying, extendable, and falsifiable explanations of phenomena we experience provided by science have seemed to many to be better explanations than nonscientific appeals to unobservable forces, spirits, and gods. Because of this, some philosophers have gone so far as to argue that we should recognize the reality of only *natural* facts, where what it takes for a fact to count as "natural" is roughly for it to be the sort of fact that could in principle be discovered by science. In the context of metaethics, this allows us to ask: are ethical facts among the natural facts, or would they have to be supernatural facts (e.g., created by the will of God)? As I mentioned before, Moore argued that they are neither, which is what he used the (somewhat inapt term) "nonnatural" to capture.

The second distinction above comes from the idea that, for any kind of fact, we can ask whether it is "reducible" to facts of some other kind. It is not completely clear what it takes to reduce one kind of fact to another kind of fact, but the basic idea is that the target facts are constituted by or made up of facts of the other kind. For example, one might think that facts about how much money various goods are worth are reducible to facts about how much money consumers are willing to pay for those goods; or one might think that facts about the location of one's mind are reducible to facts about the location of one's brain. In metaethics, the key question is whether ethical facts are reducible to some other kind of fact. What other kind of fact? There are various options. Anyone who thinks that physical facts exhaust reality will want to know whether ethical facts, if any actually obtain, can be reduced to physical facts. More commonly, metaethicists are interested in whether ethical facts are reducible to *natural* facts, where it is an open question whether this includes biological, sociological, and psychological facts that are not themselves reducible to physical facts. However, some also follow Moore in thinking the interesting question about reduction is about whether ethical facts are reducible to *any* other kind of fact, even including *super*natural facts.

The final distinction above derives from wanting to know whether, assuming that there are some ethical facts, they are objective. Many people have thought that ethical facts, if there are such things, must be the creations of human thought rather than something obtaining independently of us like we typically assume the facts of physics do. By way of comparison, consider the question of whether there are facts about what's cool (in the sense of hip rather than slightly cold). It's tempting (though not unquestionable) to think that whether something is in fact cool depends in part on how certain people tend to react to it. Martian scientists couldn't discover what's cool by studying only the physics, chemistry, and biology of Earth; they'd have to do some social psychology. That's not to say that coolness is merely "in the eye of the beholder" (though it may be). Even if coolness isn't an objective property of things in reality, there could still be *intersubjective* standards. Nonetheless, were there no minds to react, there would—according to this view—be no coolness.

Similarly, some might think that ethical facts depend on the reactions of certain people. Indeed this is one way to understand Thrasymachus' view, which we encountered in the Introduction. On this understanding, what's right/wrong is largely a matter of what the powerful people in a society say is right/wrong. (Another and perhaps textually more accurate interpretation is that Thrasymachus thought that nothing is *really* right/wrong, but the things we call "right/wrong" are things we're taught to call this by structures supporting the powerful people in a society.) That's not to say that whether something is right or wrong is merely "in the eye of the beholder," as there could be intersubjective but not objective standards (as there seems to be with coolness).

On the other hand, others think that morality requires objective standards. Recall the Euthryphro problem: their idea is that morality requires an independent standard against which we can evaluate the correctness of ethical judgments (even the judgments of God), and so ethical facts must be objective.

As we'll see in what follows, one's views about whether there are any ethical facts depend a lot on what one thinks they are like. To a first approximation, **realism** is thesis that ethical facts obtain objectively. Importantly, there are competing views about what these facts are like and how exactly they are objective, but all of these views count as realist views because they conceive of ethical facts as "out there" as part of reality to be discovered rather than merely the product or shadows of our subjective or inter-subjective reactions.[1] **Antirealism** then can be understood as the rejection of realism. Metaethicists who are antirealists often think that, if there were any ethical facts, they would have to have certain features (e.g., be nonreducible to natural facts, generate rea-sons for action independently of people's desires, etc.). And they reject realism because they think—usually inspired by a commitment to a scientific worldview—that such facts are too weird to posit in our overall ontology. By contrast, realists often (but not invariably) argue that ethical facts, as they conceive of them, aren't really that weird.

> QU1: What does it take to be a realist about beauty?

● QUESTIONS ABOUT ETHICS AND EPISTEMOLOGY

Epistemology is the area of philosophy concerned with knowledge and justified belief. For example, epistemologists are interested in specifying what more is needed for a belief to count as knowledge. Almost everyone agrees that the belief must also be *true*, but if someone forms a true belief by simply guessing, then that doesn't seem to count as knowledge. It seems, rather, that the belief has to be true because it is based on good reasons or formed reliably, in order to count as knowledge.

When it comes to ethics, any realist view about ethical facts is going to need to develop an account of how we might come to know the ethical facts it is committed to as part of its worldview. For example, if we agree that it's really a fact that charity is good, what does it take to know this fact to obtain? How one answers this ques-tion will depend, in part on what one thinks this fact is like. Is knowing this fact like knowing some empirical matter such as what the average temperature of the world's oceans was in 2010? Or is it more like understanding some cultural norm such as what kinds of clothes a bank employee is supposed to wear?

However exactly the realist conceives of ethical facts, knowing that charity is good is going to require *believing* that charity is good but also that this belief is true because it's based on good reasons or formed reliably. How might our ethical beliefs achieve this? Some metaethicists think the answer to this question will be broadly like the answer we give to parallel questions about non-ethical beliefs, whereas other metaethicists think there will need to be a special story about the reasonableness of ethical beliefs. **Intuitionism** holds that we have a special faculty of intuition whereby we can reflectively access ethical facts. Anti-intuitionists seek to explain ethical knowledge without appeal to a special faculty.

Usually this is either by appeal to a **foundationalist** or **coherentist conception of knowledge**. The former seeks to show how all knowledge is built out of some small number of foundational beliefs that are hard to doubt. The latter seeks to show how knowledge emerges from the wide coherence of a whole system of beliefs.

In contrast to realist views, it may seem that antirealist views don't need a moral epistemology. Indeed, as I mentioned in the Introduction, one of Ayer's motivations for rejecting realism was his view that it is impossible to make sense of genuinely ethical knowledge. He thought this because he thought that ethical judgments cannot be verified by our senses or derived logically from reflection on the relations between our concepts. Because of this he was a **moral skeptic** about ethical knowledge. More recently, however, some antirealists have recognized that we commonly speak about knowing that something is right/wrong and good/bad. So even if they reject realism, they may need to explain this commonplace, which may require a moral epistemology.

One reason some philosophers reject realism is that they believe we can explain why people have the moral views that they do by conceiving of these views as products of the way we developed; and this explanation will be better than any that appeals to our cognitively accessing ethical facts. An original proponent of this view was Gilbert Harman (1977), who argued that the best explanation of our perceptual beliefs in ordinary matters of fact will appeal to some of those very facts and our cognitive access to them, but the best explanation of our ethical beliefs will appeal instead to things like our cultural development and the influence of our parents and teachers. More recently, others have argued that, while there might be evolutionary explanations for why humans have developed to be good at tracking ordinary matters of facts about their natural environment, the best evolutionary explanations for why we have developed the ethical beliefs we have will instead appeal to the beneficial effects for our genes of developing ethical feelings for one another rather than cognitive tracking of a supposed ethical reality.

It's important to figure out what the basis for our ethical judgments is, and not just for theoretical purposes in moral epistemology. One of the more practical reasons it is important to understand how ethical judgments can be justified is that morality is an area of heated debate among people all across the world. At the beginning of this book I mentioned Bush ordering the invasion of Iraq, Manning leaking classified documents, and Lind sentencing Manning to 35 years' confinement. It is highly controversial whether these acts were right or wrong, and even among those who agree, there is controversy over how good or bad each act is. These are cases of **moral disagreement**, and one thing we want an epistemological theory to do is to provide some resources for assessing disagreements and thinking about how to resolve them.

> **Key Point**: Metaphysical questions about ethics are largely about whether ethical facts objectively obtain and if so what their nature is; epistemological questions about ethics are largely about what ethical knowledge is like (if it is even possible).

• QUESTIONS ABOUT ETHICS AND PHILOSOPHY OF LANGUAGE

Philosophy of language is the area of philosophy concerned to explain the meaningful use of language to communicate. For example, philosophers of language are interested in how individual words refer to things in the world and how words and phrases express our ideas (and also which of these notions is more fundamental in the explanation of meaning). One of the fundamental questions of the philosophy of language is about where to draw the line between **semantics** and **pragmatics**—that is, which aspects of language are part of conventionally encoded meaning and which aspects are instead due to the ways language is used for various nonlinguistic purposes.

Grammarians commonly divide sentences of English into three classes: declarative, imperative, and interrogative; and by grammatical standards, an ethical sentence such as "Abortion is wrong" is clearly declarative. However, as I mentioned in the Introduction, there is considerable debate in metaethics about whether ethical sentences such as this one have the same job in our language as non-ethical declarative sentences. It is natural (though not wholly uncontroversial) to view sentences such as "Grass is green" as getting their meaning by being **representations** of a way reality might be. That's not to say that all such representations are correct. For instance, the sentence "Grass is purple" is also commonly thought to be a representation of reality. However, the difference is that the first sentence about grass *correctly* represents reality and so is *true* whereas the second sentence *incorrectly* represents reality and so is *false*.

Do ethical sentences such as "Murder is wrong" or "Charity is good" also get their meaning from being representations of a way reality could be, or do they perhaps (instead) prescribe a way reality *ought* to be (even if it isn't actually so)? It will prove useful to have a piece of terminology to mark this distinction in metaethical views, so I will use the term **representationalism** to refer to the affirmative answer to this question and **antirepresentationalism** to refer to the negative answer to this question.

> QU2:   Consider the imperative "Close the door!" Is representationalism or anti-representationalism more plausible about this sentence?

The majority of the main metaethical views we'll encounter here are representationalist, i.e. they hold that ethical sentences *do* represent reality. Accepting those views doesn't yet make one a *realist*. For one could argue that, although ethical sentences represent reality, simple positive ethical sentences—such as "Murder is wrong"—never succeed in *correctly* representing reality. That is to say, perhaps all such sentences are literally false. This is the foundation of error-theoretic and fictionalist forms of antirealism, which we will discuss more in Chapter 4. Moreover, one could argue that ethical sentences represent reality but the possible facts they represent don't obtain *objectively*. This possibility is relevant for considering some of the newer metaethical views we'll discuss in Chapter 7. However, as soon as one thinks that ethical sentences represent facts obtaining objectively *and some of these sentences do so correctly*, then one can be classified as a metaethical realist of some sort. We'll consider two such realist views in detail in Chapters 2 and 5.

In contrast, one prominent way to develop an antirealist view in metaethics is by arguing that ethical sentences simply aren't in the business of representing reality. If the job of ethical sentences in our language is to do something else like prescribe action or express emotions/preferences, then we can use them sincerely and endorse others' use of them without committing ourselves to the existence of pieces of reality to match them. This is the foundation of the expressivist view we'll explore in Chapter 3. This view raises two important issues in the philosophy of language.

First, in order to make sense of the view, we need some understanding of what is meant by "express." In one clear sense, everyone should agree that ethical sentences can be used to express something other than beliefs about reality. For uncontroversially descriptive sentences can be used to express something other than beliefs about reality (in addition to the beliefs they express about reality). For example, in the right sort of conversational context, I might say "It's sunny in Edinburgh" in order to express my commendation of Edinburgh as a place to visit. However, that doesn't mean that this sentence isn't *also* a representation of a way reality might be. That way for a sentence to express an attitude is generally thought to be explicable in terms of the pragmatic conventions of language use rather than the semantic rules about the meaning conventionally encoded in our language. So, the expressivist needs to motivate some more semantic understanding of "express" in working out the claim that ethical sentences aren't representations of reality because they are expressions of nonbelief attitudes.

> *Key Point*: To be an antirepresentationalist it isn't enough to think that ethical sentences are pragmatically used to express nonbelief attitudes, you have to think that the expression of such attitudes is somehow more fundamental than any expression of beliefs by normal use of the sentences.

Second, as we'll discuss more in Chapter 3, a famous challenge to this view has to do with what it says about the presence of ethical sentences in the context of more complex sentences. For example, the sentence "Murder is infrequent but it is wrong" isn't purely ethical or purely non-ethical. So how should we understand the contribution made by the ethical parts to the meaning of the overall sentence in which they figure? In semantics, philosophers and linguists seek to explain the systematic interaction of the meanings of individual words and the whole sentences of which they are a part. But if ethical words are claimed to have meanings of a wholly different sort from non-ethical words, it may become impossible to explain the meaning of mixed, partially ethical and partially non-ethical sentences. This is a crucial challenge to those who think that ethical sentences are distinctive in that they get their meaning in some other way than from what in reality they represent.

QU3: Among metaethical nonnaturalism, expressivism, error theory/fictionalism, and naturalism, which theories are representationalist and antirepresentationalist?

• QUESTIONS ABOUT ETHICS AND PHILOSOPHY OF MIND

The philosophy of mind is the area of philosophy that attempts to explain what it is to have a mind and how mental phenomena such as consciousness relate to other things. We won't be too concerned with these issues here, but one aspect of the philosophy of mind that intersects with the elements of philosophy of language relevant to meta-ethics concerns the nature of ethical thought. A common view among philosophers is that a normal statement such as "Grass is green" represents reality in virtue of its conventional role of expressing *beliefs* about the way reality is. So the key question when it comes to ethical thought is whether the state of mind expressed by an ethical statement is also a belief about the way reality is or rather some nonbelief attitudes towards things, such as outrage, condemnation, praise, commendation, and so on? Although an affirmative answer to this question usually goes hand in hand with representationalism, they might come apart and so we'll say that someone who holds that ethical thoughts are beliefs endorses **cognitivism**, to distinguish this from the contrary **noncognitivism**.

QU4: Are expressivists cognitivists or noncognitivists?

The reason this is important here is that it bears on two closely related aspects of the philosophy of mind that are relevant to metaethics: **action theory** and **moral psychology**. In action theory we are concerned with questions such as:

- When is an action done freely, such that one is morally responsible for it?
- What makes the difference between actions (e.g., someone nodding her head in assent) and mere bodily movement (e.g., someone's head nodding as she falls asleep)?
- What makes the difference between doing something intentionally (e.g., purposefully offending someone with what you say) and doing it unintentionally (e.g., saying something that happens to offend someone)?

In moral psychology we are interested in the psychology of motivation, asking questions such as:

- What mental states are involved in someone being motivated to act?
- When one makes an ethical judgment, how closely is this connected to being motivated to act in its accord?

When it comes to ethical issues, we should distinguish between two importantly different questions we might ask about an agent's reasons:

- What were the actual mental states and processes that led the agent to act?
- What considerations could be cited in an attempt to justify the agent's action?

Although the label is contentious, the former question is often referred to as a question about **motivating reasons**. The idea is that these are the facts about the agent's psychology which would offer a particular kind of retrospective explanation of why she did what she did after she has already acted (whether or not the action was ultimately reasonable or morally acceptable). Of course, there *might* be an explanation of why an agent did what she did in terms of the chemical interactions in her brain, but this is not the kind of explanation we are looking for when we ask about motivating reasons. The fact that the levels of serotonin in my brain are high does not rationalize my giving money to charity; rather what would rationalize it is something like my belief that giving money to charity would help someone and my desire to help someone. Hence, motivating reasons are often understood by metaethicists to be some combination of an agent's psychological states, such as beliefs, desires, intentions, inclinations, emotions, etc.

By contrast, the latter question above is often referred to as a question about **justifying reasons**. The idea is that these are the facts that the agent could have cited prospectively as reasons to act as she was going to act. In many cases, these won't be facts about the agent's own psychology but rather facts about what effects the action will have on herself and others. For example, the fact that it would help a person in need might be a justifying reason for my giving to charity.

Focussing on the first question about motivating reasons, a popular view is that action always requires the cooperation of two different kinds of mental states with different **directions of fit** with the world. Anscombe (1957/2000) famously illustrated this metaphor with a discussion of two different ways we might think of a list of groceries. If a woman gives her husband a list of groceries they need for dinner, the list is a collection of goals to be met—the husband is to change the state of his shopping bag so that it fits the list. By contrast, if a private investigator charged with reporting what the man does gives the woman a list of groceries the man bought, the list is an indication of what the husband is up to—the private investigator is to change the list so that it fits what the husband puts in his shopping bag.

More generally, the so-called **Humean theory of motivation** is the view that the motivating reason for action always consists in the cooperation of a mental state which sets a goal to be met (such as the desire to have some bananas) and a mental state which is supposed to fit the world (such as the belief that bananas are in aisle seven). Typically (though controversially), the former are called *desires* and the latter are called *beliefs*, which is why this is sometimes also called **belief–desire psychology of motivation**.

Not everyone accepts the belief–desire psychology of motivation, but many metaethicists do. This sets up the question: where do ethical judgments fit in? For example, when someone judges that giving to charity is good, does the resulting mental state fall on the "belief" or "desire" side of the division? As we already saw above, one way the term "cognitivism" is used in metaethics is as the view that ethical judgments are something like the formation of beliefs about how ethical reality is, which gives rise to the contrasting "noncognitivism" which is the view that ethical judgments are rather the formation of something like desires in the way they set goals rather than attempt to represent facts.[2]

What would lead someone to endorse cognitivism or noncognitivism, understood in this way? As we will see, there are many factors to be weighed, but here are two prominent ones to keep in mind.

First, think about knowledge. If one thinks that there's such a thing as ethical knowledge, and one thinks that knowledge of a fact requires belief in the fact, then one will want to say that ethical judgments are cognitive, i.e. on the belief side of the Humean division. So the possibility of ethical knowledge, it may seem, requires the truth of cognitivism.

Second, on the other hand, as I mentioned in the Introduction, many philosophers have had the intuition that ethical judgment stands in a special "internal" relation to motivation. More specifically, they have thought that you don't need to add any more desires, inclinations, or emotions to the description of someone's psychology—besides their ethical judgment that ϕing was the right thing to do—to explain why they ϕed. This view is sometimes called **motivational internalism**. If it is right, then ethical judgments would seem to belong on the desire side of the Humean division. Or if they don't, then one has to argue (contra the popular belief–desire psychology of motivation) that some actions can be motivated by beliefs alone. Alternatively, one has to insist that ethical judgment does not actually stand in any special "internal" relation to motivation, which is a view often referred to as **motivational externalism**.

> QU5: True or false: Being a cognitivist about ethical thought will incline you to accept motivational internalism.

Turning then to the second question above, about justifying actions, a common view is that a justifying reason for an agent acting in a particular way is a consideration that counts in favor of the agent acting that way. However, that vague characterization simply raises a difficult and interesting question: what kinds of considerations can count in favor of an action? Here we see an importantly different use of the internalism/externalism terminology. On the view sometimes called **internalism about justifying reasons** a consideration can count in favor of an agent acting only if it connects in some appropriate way to the agent's inclinations, desires, intentions, or values. In the simplest case, if an action (e.g., drinking some water) would satisfy one of the agent's current actual inclinations (e.g., the agent's thirst), then that's a reason for the agent to do it in the sense that it provides at least partial justification of her doing it. However, there are more complicated cases where an action does not promote an agent's actual and present inclinations, desires, intentions, or values but it promotes inclinations, desires, intentions, or values the agent would have were she more fully apprised of the facts or thinking clearly about them. Hence, a consideration that connects an action to the inclinations, desires, intentions, or values, which an agent would have were she more fully informed and thinking clearly, is generally still counted as a reason, according to internalism about reasons. However, if one thinks that a consideration could count in favor of an agent acting in a particular way even if it bears no connection to the inclinations, desires, intentions, or values she presently and actually has or even would have were she more fully informed and thinking clearly, then one counts as accepting **externalism about justifying reasons**.

This is relevant to ethics because one prime candidate for a justifying reason is an ethical fact. For example, the fact that giving to charity to save a child in some distant country from dying of dysentery is the right thing to do—assuming this is a fact—seems like it's the sort of thing that could justify one performing this act. But what if someone just doesn't care about the fate of children in distant countries; what if performing this act wouldn't promote the inclinations, desires, intentions, or values they actually and presently have or even would have were they more fully apprised of the facts and thinking clearly? The internalist about justifying reasons is committed to saying that, if this is truly possible, then this fact simply isn't a reason for that person to perform the act. By contrast, the externalist about reasons can claim that this fact could still be a reason for that person to perform that act. In this disagreement, we see two competing views about the nature of morality: whether or not it is intrinsically reason-giving. On the one hand, many want to say that morality could not float free of the ordinary concerns of people, and it has its grip on us because of the way it is an outcropping of these concerns. On the other hand, to many it seems that such ordinary concerns will be the product of natural selection and in-group/out-group dynamics that won't necessarily promote what's ethically best overall; so it might be the case that ethics can float free from particular people's concerns.

> ***Key Point***: The labels "internalism" and "externalism" get used in two different ways in metaethics—one is to characterize views about how ethical thought can motivate action, the other is to characterize views about how it might be that ethical facts could justify action.

• CONCLUSION

In this chapter, we have covered a lot of territory in an attempt to lay out many of the key theoretical distinctions we will use in what follows to assess metaethical theories. By discussing questions about ethics as it connects to metaphysics, epistemology, philosophy of language, and philosophy of mind, we have developed a conceptual toolkit that we will use in the rest of this book. The key distinctions to keep in mind are:

- realism vs. antirealism about ethical facts and properties
- naturalism vs. nonnaturalism about the nature of ethical facts and properties

- representationalism vs. antirepresentationalism about ethical language
- motivating vs. justifying reasons
- motivational internalism vs. motivational externalism about the role of ethical judgment in motivating reasons
- cognitivism vs. noncognitivism about the nature of ethical thought
- internalism vs. externalism about justifying reasons.

In the past hundred years or more, many interesting ideas have emerged about one or more of the four key issues outlined above. In the following chapters we will focus on four main theories. These can be divided first into:

- realist vs. antirealist views about the metaphysics of morality.

Then, among the *realist* views, we can divide further between:

- naturalist and nonnaturalist views about the nature of ethical facts.

Among the antirealist views, on the other hand, we can divide further between:

- representationalists vs. antirepresentationalists about ethical language/thought.

Realists are representationalist too, but some antirealists think ethical sentences represent a way reality could be but they involve some kind of metaphysical error or tacit fiction. Other antirealists base their view on an antirepresentationalist conception of ethical language found most prominently in the expressivist idea that ethical statements express nonbelief attitudes (see Figure 1.1).

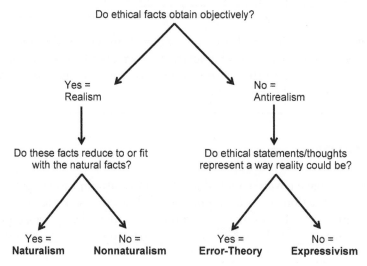

Figure 1.1 Four main metaethical theories

So, in this way of dividing up the theoretical terrain, we first use distinctions from metaphysics and the philosophy of language to divide up the four main families of theories. Then we can then add considerations from epistemology and the philosophy of mind to either provide further support for a theory or reveal some of its problems. It will prove helpful for understanding some of the main ideas to introduce these four theories in a different order from the one just given. So we'll start in the next chapter with nonnaturalism.

• CHAPTER SUMMARY

- Realists disagree with antirealists about the metaphysical question of whether any ethical facts objectively obtain.
- In moral epistemology, some philosophers are skeptics, and among the non-skeptics there is debate between intuitionist and coherentist conceptions of justification for ethical beliefs.
- One way to be an ethical antirealist and to avoid (or at least change) the question of how ethical beliefs are justified is to reject the representationalist view of ethical language in favor of a rival antirepresentationalism commonly found in expressivism.
- A belief–desire (or "Humean") psychology of motivation is commonly applied to metaethics in order to ask whether ethical judgments play the role of beliefs or desires in the motivating reasons for actions. One's view about this will be influenced by one's view about whether ethical judgments are internally connected to motivation in the way of motivational internalism.
- Justifying reasons are considerations that count in favor of an agent acting in a particular way. Internalists and externalists about justifying reasons disagree about whether a consideration has to connect to the agent concerns (actual or potential) in order to provide a justifying reason for action.

• STUDY QUESTIONS

1 You want to pass this course. Is that a natural or nonnatural fact? Does it reduce to some other sort of fact? Is it mind-dependent or mind-independent?
2 Considering something you believe to be morally wrong, what justifies this belief?
3 Does the sentence, "The sun rises in the morning" represent reality?
4 What is the difference between motivating reasons and justifying reasons?
5 What is a potential counter-example to motivational internalism?
6 Is the thought that the sun rises in the morning mind-dependent? Explain your answer.

• FURTHER RESOURCES

- Alvarez, Maria. 2016. "Reasons for Action: Justification, Motivation, Explanation," *The Stanford Encyclopedia of Philosophy* (Summer 2016 Edition), Edward N. Zalta (ed.), http://plato.stanford.edu/archives/sum2016/entries/reasons-just-vs-expl/. [Introduction to distinction between motivating and justifying reasons.]
- Blackburn, Simon. 1988. "How to Be an Ethical Antirealist," *Midwest Studies in Philosophy* 12 (1): 361–75. [A classic defense of an antirepresentationalist form of antirealism in metaethics.]
- Finlay, Stephen. 2007. "Four Faces of Moral Realism," *Philosophy Compass* 2 (6): 820–49. [Survey article going into more depth about the realism vs. antirealism distinction in metaethics.]
- Finlay, Stephen and Schroeder, Mark. 2015. "Reasons for Action: Internal vs. External," *The Stanford Encyclopedia of Philosophy* (Winter 2015 Edition), Edward N. Zalta (ed.), http://plato.stanford.edu/archives/win2015/entries/reasons-internal-external/. [Introduction to internalism about reasons and externalist alternatives.]
- Smith, Michael. 1987. "The Humean Theory of Motivation," *Mind* 96 (381): 36–61. [A classic statement and defense of the Humean belief–desire account of the psychology of motivation.]
- Tiberius, Valerie. 2014. *Moral Psychology: A Contemporary Introduction*. Routledge. [A book length introduction to moral psychology touching on recent scientific discoveries.]
- Zimmerman, Aaron. 2010. *Moral Epistemology*. Routledge. [A book-length defense of the possibility of moral knowledge, touching on many of the reasons for skepticism.]

• ANSWERS TO QUESTIONS OF UNDERSTANDING

QU1: Based on the definition in the text above, a realist about beauty holds that facts about what's beautiful obtain objectively. This means that beauty is not merely in the eye of the beholder, but rather a standard against which our judgments about what is beautiful can be judged correct or incorrect.

QU2: Imperative sentences seem to prescribe action rather than describe things in reality, so the antirepresentationalist view of "Close the door!" is more plausible. So, if you think ethical sentences are prescriptive rather than descriptive, you might be inclined to favor an antirepresentationalist view of them. However, read on to encounter some objections to this idea!

QU3: Nonnaturalism, error theory/fictionalism, and naturalism are the representationalist theories, as they all hold that ethical sentences represent a way reality could be, i.e. a possible fact. Expressivism is the antirepresentationalist theory, as it holds that ethical sentences express prescriptions or attitudes rather than beliefs about the way reality is.

QU4: Expressivists generally fund their antirepresentationalist stance in the philosophy of language with a noncognitivist view of ethical thoughts in the philosophy of mind.

QU5: False. One can be a cognitivist and motivational internalist, but one could also be a motivational externalist. In some cases, a commitment to motivational internalism leads one to accept *non*cognitivism. We'll explore the argument for this in more detail in the next chapter.

• WORKS CITED

Anscombe, G. E. M. 1957/2000. *Intention.* Cambridge, MA: Harvard University Press.
Harman, Gilbert. 1977. *The Nature of Morality: An Introduction to Ethics.* New York: Oxford University Press.

• NOTES

1 This is a first approximation for two reasons that will become clearer in later chapters where complications are relevant for understanding some nuanced contemporary metaethical views. (So you can mostly ignore the rest of this note till the end of Chapter 4.) The first reason is that most metaethicists would not count the radically subjectivist view that what is right is whatever you think is right as a form of realism. However, assuming psychological facts about what you think is right obtain objectively, this subjectivist view would seem to meet the definition of realism given above. This is because there is a sense in which "subjective" facts about our own attitudes obtain "objectively" and are thus matters for discovery. Avoiding this consequence of our definition of realism requires more care about what it takes for a fact to "obtain objectively." Relatedly, it's more controversial whether to count cultural relativist views, which say that what is right is whatever some culture treats as right, as a form of realism. Again, however, assuming there are objective facts about what a culture treats as right, this would count as a realist view on the definition given above. In Chapter 6, we'll encounter a view like this, and I'll treat it there as a form of realism, though with recognition that this is a controversial classification. The second reason the definition of realism in the text above is only an approximation is that some metaethicists are happy to claim that there are objective ethical facts, but they deny that in saying this they are attempting a metaphysical characterization of what reality is like rather than an attitude-laden evaluation of something. And although such metaethicists seem to be committed to realism as it is defined above, it is controversial in contemporary metaethics whether that's enough to count as a realist. Avoiding this consequence of the definition above requires more care about possible distinctions between ethical evaluations and metaphysical characterizations of what reality is like.

2 The terms "cognitivism" and "noncognitivism" are sometimes also used to mark the distinction between metaethical views about ethical language that hold that ethical sentences are or aren't **truth-apt**, i.e. properly evaluated as true or false. I think this is a confusing usage that is falling out of favor in contemporary metaethics, so I am going to avoid it here in favor of marking the crucial distinction in the philosophy of language, as I have done above, in terms of representationalist vs. antirepresentationalist views about the meaning of ethical sentences. But the reader may want to keep this alternative usage of *cognitivism* and *noncognitivism* in mind when reading other texts.

2

˙nonnaturalism

In this chapter, we begin to explore nonnaturalism. This theory starts in metaphysics with the claim that objective ethical facts really obtain (realism), and these are importantly different from natural facts (hence the name "*non*naturalism"). Proponents of the view are usually motivated by the thought that there is an objective fact of the matter about many ethical issues, and ethical modes of thought and inquiry about these facts are importantly different from the empirical modes of thought and inquiry that we use to know about the natural world. Characteristically, an ethical nonnaturalist will argue that, although empirical evidence might feed into ethical deliberation, the fundamental facts about what's good/bad, right/wrong, virtuous/vicious are not empirically knowable facts: ethical facts are their own sort of fact which we have to discover (when we can) in the special way characteristic of ethical thought and deliberation.

As I mentioned in previous chapters, this idea traces back to Moore's influential *Principia Ethica* (1903) (and before that to Plato's metaphysics of morality). I will describe Moore's ideas briefly below, but we won't spend much time here trying to interpret Moore; rather we'll focus on characterizing the view as it exists in contemporary metaethics, discussing some arguments for and against it, and explaining how its commitments in metaphysics bear on other issues in metaethics.

• A MORE PRECISE CHARACTERIZATION

The label "nonnaturalism" is potentially misleading and unfortunately imprecise. To see why it's potentially misleading recall from Chapter 1 that some philosophers argue that morality is the product of God's commands. If that's right, then ethical facts might be viewed as a species of *super*natural facts: they're facts about what God commands. However, as I already suggested above, the philosophers who embrace nonnaturalism—both canonically and in the contemporary literature—deny not only that ethical facts are natural facts but also that they are supernatural facts. So, the more precise characterization of the view is that ethical facts are sui generis in the sense of being neither part of nor reducible to natural or supernatural facts. If we wanted to be pedantic, we might have called the view "non-natural/ supernaturalism," but that's an ugly mouthful.

Unfortunately, however, we must qualify this slightly, because almost everyone would agree that ethics is a species of **normativity**, or something involving 'ought's, rules, and reasons; but there are potentially other species of normativity whose relation to ethical normativity is unclear. For example, just as we can ask about what someone *ethically* ought to do, we can also ask about what someone *prudentially* ought to do; just as we can ask about what is *morally* permissible, we could ask about what is *legally* permissible; just as we could seek to understand *moral* reasons for something, we could seek to under- stand *epistemic* reasons for something. These are other potential species of normativity (prudential, legal, and epistemic), and when nonnaturalists claim that ethical facts are sui generis, they do not mean to deny that they are a species of normative fact. In Chapter 8, we'll return to the interesting issue of how other species of normativity relate to ethical normativity, and what our main metaethical theories have to say about the broader genus of normativity. This is a topic of much current research. Until we get there, however, we can ignore this and think of nonnaturalism as the view that ethical facts are autonomous from other sorts of facts—supernatural facts, but more importantly natural facts.

What does it mean to say that ethical facts are sui generis? This is where a bit more precision would be helpful. If we had a criterion for what it takes for a fact to count as "natural," then we could say that nonnaturalists hold that ethical facts do not meet that criterion. Unfortunately there is simply no agreed upon criterion of "natural" in the relevant literature that we could use to characterize all forms of nonnaturalism.

There are, though, a handful of plausible candidates. Many philosophers characterize the natural in terms of science. For example, we might say that natural facts are the facts that (i) can in principle figure in scientific explanations, or similarly (ii) are in principle discoverable by scientific methods. In some ways, however, this just pushes the relevant question back to: what is *science*? Surprisingly, it is not trivial to answer this question. It's clear that physics and chemistry count as sciences, but what about economics, mathemat- ics, or anthropology? Perhaps we can ultimately define "science," but other philosophers prefer to characterize the natural in other terms. For example, we might say that natural facts are facts that (iii) figure in or are governed by the laws of nature, (iv) have causal powers, or (v) reduce to physical facts. Of course, these definitions also raise further ques- tions: What is a law of *nature*? What is a *causal power*? What is a *physical* fact? And again it is not trivial to answer these questions, but it is also not hopeless.

QU1: Which of the following *putative* facts are not plausible candidates for natural facts: (i) facts about the physical laws of the universe, (ii) facts about who is biologically related to you, (iii) facts about who has good karma, (iv) facts about what someone wants, (v) facts about conscious- ness, (vi) facts about mathematics?

These characterizations of the natural are related, but it is not completely clear how they are related or which is more basic. So, perhaps the best we can do in characterizing nonnaturalism's commitment to ethical facts being sui generis is to say that—in addition to holding that ethical facts are not supernatural facts—nonnaturalists hold that ethical facts are not natural in at least one and probably several of the senses of "natural" mentioned above. As it is sometimes put, ethics is an "autonomous" area of inquiry with its own distinctive subject matter: a realm of facts not reducible to facts of some other kind (such as the facts of physics).

As a rough analogy, consider a parallel issue from the philosophy of logic and mathematics. Here, many philosophers think that there are logical and mathematical facts, but they also think that these facts are not features of the natural world but rather more abstract facts that structure both the actual world and any other possible world. In this sense, logical and mathematical facts might be viewed as an autonomous realm of facts, discoverable (when they are) by some special mode of thought and inquiry distinct from empirical investigation of the natural world we experience. If so, these facts would count as nonnatural at least by failing to meet criteria (ii), (iv) and (v) above. Similarly, nonnaturalists in metaethics think that ethical facts are an autonomous realm of fact, though failure to meet criteria (i) and (iii) are also sometimes used to characterize this autonomy.

• THE CASE FOR NONNATURALISM

Ultimately the case for any metaethical theory is going to amount to a combination of:

- positive arguments for its specific commitments in metaphysics, epistemology, the philosophy of language, and the philosophy of mind;
- negative arguments against the competing commitments of other views about the same issues;
- attempts to respond to objections to one's own positive commitments and the arguments for them.

Hence, in order to decide which metaethical theory you find most compelling, you'll have to perform a complex theoretical cost–benefit analysis in full awareness of the competing theories. We won't be in a position to begin to do that until Chapter 6. In the meantime, however, we can develop some of these positive and negative arguments concerning the elements of the main theories we will consider. Here, we start with arguments in favor of nonnaturalism's metaphysical commitments. We'll start with the reasons some philosophers think that ethical facts (assuming they exist) are nonnatural. But we'll come later to the nonnaturalist's case for assuming that ethical facts obtain in the first place, and then consider some reasons other philosophers have been critical of nonnaturalism.

Hume's Law

A historical source of inspiration for nonnaturalism is Hume's famous suggestion that one cannot derive an 'ought' from an 'is.' This is commonly called **Hume's Law**. It is highly controversial how to interpret Hume on this point (as we'll see in the following chapter, expressivists also take inspiration from the attractiveness of Hume's Law). But here's how nonnaturalists understand it: no matter how many of the facts you know about what is the case, you still won't have enough evidence to settle how we ought to act. Facts about what someone ought to do are a separate and further issue from facts about what is the case.

For example, consider the position of Denise Lind whom we discussed above as the judge who had to decide how long to imprison Chelsea Manning. We might imagine she knew all of the relevant facts about what Manning did (copy classified files on to hard drives, transmit these files to Wikileaks, etc.); we might also imagine she knew all of the relevant facts about the actual and likely consequences of these actions (compromise military strategy, undermine faith in the military, inspire future leaks of classified information, etc.) and the likely consequences of various sentencing choices she might make (discourage leaks, ruin someone's life, etc.). Still, we might reasonably think, figuring out what Lind morally ought to do requires further reflection. Perhaps she needs to apply some abstract moral principle (e.g., about what in general one ought to do) to this particular case, or perhaps she needs to exercise practical wisdom in moving from the nonmoral facts of the case to a determination of what would be morally best. Because of this, if you think there is some fact of the matter about what she ought to do, then you'll probably think this fact is not one of the myriad of natural facts about what is the case but rather a special kind of fact: an ethical fact about what—given those other facts—someone ought to do.

Nonnaturalists often insist that ethical facts are ultimately about what one ought to do, and following Hume's Law suggests that these facts are importantly autonomous from other sorts of facts. That's not to say that other sorts of fact aren't *relevant* to determining what someone ought to do. But because they cannot settle this all by themselves, the ethical facts should be viewed as a different kind of fact: a nonnatural fact. In this we have an argument moving from moral epistemology (how we can or cannot come to know an ethical fact) to a conclusion in metaphysics (about what ethical facts are like).

> *Key Point*: One way to understand how ethical facts might be autonomous from natural facts is by claiming that they don't follow from natural facts because they involve 'ought's which cannot be derived from natural 'is's.

Moorean arguments

As I've already mentioned, another historical source for nonnaturalism is Moore, who introduced the **naturalistic fallacy** and the **open-question argument**. There is considerable scholarly debate about how exactly to interpret these ideas, which we won't go into here. (It also bears mentioning that Moore cites Sidgwick (1907) as an inspiration for both of these; and Reid (1788) and Ross (1930) defend nonnaturalist views with different arguments.) But you can begin to get the basic flavor of Moore's approach by noting that he wasn't focussed on questions about what someone *ought* to do but rather on a specific aspect of questions about what is *good*. He freely granted that we can make a plausible list of things that are good and begin to outline the natural properties these things have in common. For example, if asked to list some of the good things in life, we might say ice-cream, sunny afternoons, friendship, the loyalty of a dog, a warm bath on a cold night… Then, we might suggest that what all of these things have in common is that they cause pleasure. Even assuming this is right, however, Moore thought it would be a fallacy to go on to conclude that the property of goodness *just is* the property of whatever causes pleasure. This is what he called the "naturalistic fallacy." (Strictly speaking, as Frankena (1939) argued, it's not really a *fallacy*, but Moore is probably right that being good isn't the same thing as causing pleasure—just think of all the bad things that cause pleasure.)

In any case, Moore does give a famous argument for the claim that goodness is not identical to any natural property. This is the open-question argument. The core idea is that for any proposed analysis of the property of being good in terms of some natural property N, we can always sensibly, and without confusion about the meaning of the words we're using, say things of the form, "I know x is N, but is x good?" For example, we can sensibly and without confusion say, "I know eating meat causes pleasure, but is it good?" Since this question remains "open" even to those who understand the terms "causes pleasure" and "good," Moore concluded that causing pleasure must be different from being good (even if things that cause pleasure are often good).

> QU2: Which of the following are "closed" questions in the sense that one cannot sensibly and without confusion ask them: "Are bachelors unmarried?", "Is green a color?", "Does it rain a lot in Scotland?", "Does what goes up have to come down?"

Moore considered only a few possible analyses of goodness in terms of natural properties, but the best version of the argument contains an **inference to the best explanation** of many failed analyses. To start, we might extract various claims about what it is for something to be good (or right, or virtuous) from the history of ethics; most of these appeal to some natural commonality between things we evaluate the same way ethically. For each of these analyses, it seems that we can sensibly say, "I know x is N, but is x good (right, virtuous)?" (Shafer-Landau 2003, Chapter 3).

The fact that there is any debate at all about whether the analysis of some ethical property M in terms of some natural property N suggests that the question remains "open" in Moore's sense. This demands explanation: why haven't philosophers been able to analyze goodness (or rightness or virtue) in terms of some natural property? Well, Moore's hypothesis was that ethical properties are irreducible to natural properties. If this hypothesis is correct, that'd be one pretty good explanation of the longstanding failure to find any plausible naturalistic analysis of ethical facts. Here we have an argument from the semantics of ethical terms/concepts to a conclusion about metaphysics.

A further argument: deliberative indispensability

So far, we've discussed two prominent arguments for thinking of ethical facts as nonnatural facts. These arguments assume realism (i.e. that there ethical facts obtain objectively as part of reality), then they motivate a particular conception of what these facts are like (nonnatural). However, not all metaethicists agree with realism about morality. So we might also want some arguments for favoring moral realism in the first place.

One obvious starting point is the undeniable fact that our ethical predicates, such as "is wrong" or "is a virtue" seem to work in an isomorphic way in our language to other predicates we take to figure in descriptions of what reality is like, such as "is wet" or "is a chair." Also, we say things like, "It's an objective fact that torture is wrong," and "Everyone knows that kindness is a virtue." Moreover, we clearly recognize hard moral questions where it seems to take careful thought and reflection to determine the correct answers. For example, someone might wonder whether breaking the law is always morally wrong, or whether being selfish is ever morally permissible. If someone rejects moral realism, they owe us a pretty compelling explanation of what is going on with such statements and questions. As we'll see in Chapters 3 and 4, antirealists have attempted such explanations, but the burden of proof in the philosophy of language is clearly on their shoulders. We'd avoid this burden by accepting realism. And that's a prima facie reason to prefer realism.

Some philosophers have turned this starting point into a more substantive argument for nonnaturalism. When it comes to any kind of putative entity and facts involving it, we might wonder in our more philosophical moments what reason we have to believe in these entities and facts. For example, physicists say that there are quarks, chemists say that there are various elements differentiated by their configuration of protons and electrons, biologists say that different individuals have different genes—what reason is there to believe in facts about quarks, elements, and genes? Others say that there are witches with special evil powers, that astrological configurations indicate compatibility in love, and that telepathy is possible—what reason is there *not* to believe in facts about witches, astrology, and telepathy? These are metaphysical questions, more specifically questions about our **ontological commitments**, i.e. commitments to the reality of various entities and the facts involving them.

A popular answer in metaphysics and the philosophy of science is that we're justified in believing in whatever entities or facts figure in the best explanation of things we observe. The rough idea is that scientific explanations of things we observe in terms of (putative) facts about things such as quarks, elements, and genes are better than supernatural explanations in terms of (putative) facts about things such as witches, astrological configurations, or telepathic powers. That's why we're justified in believing in the former sort of facts but not in the latter; this is an inference to the best explanation.

> QU3: What's the difference between a logical inference and an inference to the best explanation?

We should ask, however: why does figuring in the best explanation of what we observe provide a reason for believing in the reality of something? How we should answer this question is a controversial issue at the interface of epistemology, metaphysics, and the philosophy of science. One prominent view is that it is rationally non-optional for us to try to figure out things about how the world is; and belief in entities/facts that figure in the best explanation of what we observe is a crucial part of doing this. So that's why we're justified in believing in the entities/facts that figure in the best explanation of what we observe.

As we saw in the previous chapter, Harman (1977) argues that the best explanation of our moral views will appeal to our cultural upbringing and the influence of our parents and teachers rather than specifically ethical facts. However, other philosophers have pointed out that there seem to be other rationally non-optional endeavors, and some of these might provide further resources for the nonnaturalist to argue that belief in ethical facts is indispensable.

More specifically, the project of deciding what to do seems to be rationally non-optional for beings like us. Often, of course, we act more on habit and instinct than deliberation; and sometimes we just pick among several equally attractive options. Additionally, however, we all face situations where we have to carefully deliberate on a difficult practical question. (Think of your decision of what to study, or whether to take a philosophy course.) In these cases, we weigh reasons for and against, attempting to reach the right answer about what to do. Enoch (2011, Chapter 3) argues that belief in normative facts (more specifically, facts about what is or isn't a reason for various practical decisions) is crucial for such practical deliberation. Otherwise it wouldn't seem to us that we were trying to reach the right decision.

If that's right (and this is the key "if" for this argument), then maybe reasons earn their ontological keep, so to speak, in a parallel way to quarks, compounds, and genes: belief in them is an indispensable part of a rationally non-optional thing we do. Instead of being parts of the best explanation of what we *observe* (as Harman claimed ethical facts are not), they may be crucial to our deciding what to do. As long as reasons (or facts involving them) are not "natural" (recall from above the many related things this might mean), this represents a further consideration in favor of nonnaturalism. (As far as indispensability by itself goes, we only get an argument for realism; but when combined with the open-question argument we get an argument for a nonnaturalist form of realism.)

The careful reader will have noticed that in the previous two paragraphs, we switched from talking about *ethical* facts to facts about reasons, which I characterized as "normative" facts. That switch is not innocent. As Enoch recognizes, this argument from indispensability for practical deliberation only gets us as far as recognizing facts abut reasons, which may not be specifically *ethical* reasons. However, if we go so far as to recognize the existence of nonnatural facts about reasons, one might think there's no further metaphysical objection to recognizing nonnatural ethical facts. After all, some reasons for doing things are ethical reasons.

We might also worry that indispensability for *practical* reasoning isn't enough to secure reasonable ontological commitment. After all, the indispensability arguments for believing in things like quarks, elements, and genes appealed to their role in explaining something philosophers typically think of as within the purview of *theoretical* reasoning about what is the case—which is often contrasted with *practical* reasoning about what to do. Moreover, some have even thought that there are arguments stemming from theoretical reasoning *against* the existence of ethical facts. For example, Kant famously argued that, as far as practical reasoning about what to do goes, we must assume that we are free to choose what we do. He also argued, however, that as far as theoretical reasoning about what is the case goes, we must assume that every event is determined by prior events in a way that seems to rule out freedom to choose what we do. So, it isn't obvious that indispensability for practical reasoning secures reasonable ontological commitment, all things considered.

• ARGUMENTS AGAINST NONNATURALISM

We've considered several positive arguments in support of nonnaturalism's commitments in metaphysics, the philosophy of language/mind, and epistemology. I turn now to critical arguments against the view. I'll briefly explain just four of the most prominent reasons some philosophers have been skeptical of these commitments. The works cited in Further resources below have discussion of many more.

Challenge from a naturalistic worldview

As we saw in the previous chapter, it is widely thought that one of the most significant advances ever in human thought came in the Enlightenment, and one key element of Enlightenment thought was an ever-increasing trust in *scientific* explanations of the way reality is. That's not the only key element, of course; recognition of the importance of individual freedom was perhaps even more important to the history of ideas and politics. But when it comes to explaining how reality is, many philosophers have come to think that the sorts of theories characteristic of science, i.e. falsifiable theories that can be extended arbitrarily to new cases, are the gold standard. The rough idea is that science discovers the natural laws of the universe and appeals to these to provide genuinely causal explanations of why things really happen the way that they do. Everything else (witches, astrology, telepathy, etc.) is pseudo-explanation.

This **naturalistic worldview** looks to be in stark tension with nonnaturalism in metaethics. And many philosophers deeply committed to the naturalistic worldview think that nonnaturalism about morality is a nonstarter. Nonnaturalists are aware of this: in insisting on the reality of nonnatural facts, they typically stress the autonomy of morality (or normativity more generally) in order to soften the blow of accepting the existence of something that doesn't fit within the naturalistic worldview. The idea is that, yes, ethical facts don't fit into the naturalistic worldview, but that's alright because they are special.

Proponents of the naturalistic worldview, however, tend to see this as one more psuedo-explanation that will eventually go the way of witches, astrology, and telepathy. Moreover, ontology is usually pursued with a **principle of parsimony** saying that all other things being equal it's better not to posit new entities into our overall picture of reality. So, if there are explanations of what we want to explain that don't posit the existence of witches or values, then we should prefer these over ones that do. That's not to say that these critics think we must give up on ethics as it is currently conceived. Some philosophers might think this (error-theorists), but there's also the possibility of arguing that ethical facts are in the end a species of natural facts (ethical naturalism) or that ethics is a fundamentally prescriptive rather than descriptive enterprise, one that seeks not to discover the way a particular region of reality is but to evaluate human actions and characters (expressivism).

A closely related challenge stems from the power of Darwinian explanations of the tendencies of human thought and behavior. Street (2006) argues that the evolutionary explanation of why we have the morality that we do will appeal to the way being disposed to care about others increases the likelihood that one will pass on one's genes to future generations. Crucially, this explanation does not seem like it will appeal to one's being good at tracking mind-independent ethical facts. By contrast, the evolutionary explanation of why we have the view of our natural surroundings that we do seems like it *will* appeal to one's being good at tracking mind-independent facts about our natural surrounding. This is related to Harman's inference to the best explanation mentioned above, but it takes it further, challenging the nonnaturalist to explain why we should have expected humans to evolve to be good trackers of nonnatural facts.

Objection from epistemology

The argument from a naturalistic worldview may seem to beg the question against the nonnaturalist. To avoid this appearance many philosophers locate the appeal of the naturalistic worldview in its epistemology. That is to say they suggest that the reason to believe only in natural entities and the facts in which they figure is that we have a pretty good theory of how we come to know such facts. Not that we know all or even most natural facts, but we have a pretty sophisticated understanding of how perception works to provide stimuli from outside our bodies to our brains, which we then use reason and other cognitive processes to organize into a conception of how reality is—at least the natural parts of reality. This is then amplified and refined in cooperation with other people through testimony, joint reasoning, and scientific theorizing to something like the naturalistic worldview.

Of course, not all parts of this are well understood; the perception-based conception of how we know the natural world is still under development at the intersection of the philosophy of mind, philosophy of science, and epistemology. More specifically, there is debate about how to make sense of epistemic justification for beliefs about the natural world. But the point is that someone urging us to recognize the reality of some realm of nonnatural facts faces a challenge to explain how we could possibly come to know such facts. On the face of things, they'll need to face this challenge without the resources of our sophisticated understanding of how perception and reasoning about the natural world works. So, if you think everything we know comes ultimately from perception, this will count against nonnaturalism.

There's a related further point at the intersection of epistemology and philosophy of language. Here one thing we want to be able to explain is how our words referring to things in reality get "hooked up" with their referents, such that we could even count as speaking and thinking about the things we take ourselves to know something about. For the words that refer to things we take ourselves to interact with causally, this explanation is relatively easy, at least as a first pass. The word 'water' refers to water because we come into contact with water. When it comes to nonnatural properties, however, the answer is much more difficult. If we don't causally interact with the nonnatural property of goodness, how does our word 'good' get hooked up with that referent (instead, say, with something else, or nothing at all)?

> ***Key Point***: Nonnaturalists face a serious challenge in their moral epistemology: if you think ethical beliefs don't "fit" with the other sorts of beliefs about our natural environment, which we typically take to be knowledge, then you'll need to explain how we could come to have ethical knowledge.

There are three routes nonnaturalists typically take in responding to objections from epistemology. First, some seek to develop a positive epistemology to explain how we come to know nonnatural facts. Moore famously argued that we have a special faculty of intuition, something akin to moral perception, and we can know the (nonnatural) ethical facts by using this faculty. But to make this response work, we need to develop a sophisticated theory of moral intuition. Second, others point out that even the standard story about our knowledge of the natural world appeals to the role of reason and other cognitive processes in organizing the input of perception into a coherent worldview. Hence, by embracing a coherentist epistemology, at least when it comes to ethical knowledge, we might be able to argue that these resources are already enough to explain how we could know nonnatural facts. For, by using our reason to think about how to live our lives, we might be able to form a broad and coherent web of beliefs about ethical facts. But to make this response work, we need to actually show how to reason from scratch to the existence of nonnatural ethical facts. Finally, some non-naturalists pursue a **partners-in-crime** response to the objection. This means that they argue that there are other sorts of facts that we take ourselves to be capable of knowing that don't fit well into the standard naturalistic story about knowledge of reality. For example, it's difficult to give a perception-based epistemology of mathematical, logical, and modal facts. Unless we want to throw out these babies with the bathwater of non-naturalism, perhaps we should be more liberal in our epistemology.

Argument from supervenience

Supervenience is a fancy name for the idea that one domain necessarily co-varies with another domain. There are various formulations, but the basic idea in the ethical case is that there cannot be a moral difference between two states of affairs without some underlying nonmoral difference.[1] Or more precisely, the ethical facts supervene on the natural facts. To see why many philosophers have thought this to be extremely plausible, imagine you're in the situation of a judge trying to decide the right punishment for two separate crimes. If all of the relevant nonmoral features of the two crimes are identical, on what basis could you possibly say, e.g., that five years' prison is the right punishment for one, but a slap on the wrist is the right punishment for the other? That would be completely arbitrary. Put differently, it seems that there would have to be some non-ethical difference between the two cases for there to be an ethical difference between the punishments deserved in each case. Taken more globally, philosophers sometimes say that there would have to be some non-ethical difference between two possible worlds for there to be an ethical difference between these worlds. This is the supervenience of the ethical on the non-ethical.

QU4: If fact 1 (e.g., that Lois kissed Superman) and fact 2 (e.g., that Lois kissed Clark) are identical, does fact 1 supervene on fact 2?

Critics of nonnaturalism have argued that the view has no good explanation of why the ethical seems to supervene on the non-ethical. After all, if ethical facts are sui generis in the way nonnaturalists think, that means that there are two separate realms of fact: the ethical facts and the non-ethical facts. So why shouldn't we be able to imagine two possible worlds which differ only in their ethical facts, and not in their non-ethical facts? If, by contrast, we thought that our ethical beliefs were about a species of natural fact (as naturalists do), we'd have a pretty good explanation of why supervenience seems true: everything supervenes on itself. Similarly, if we thought that our ethical statements were expressions of attitudes towards descriptive facts rather than themselves descriptions of ethical facts (as expressivists do), we'd be in a position to develop a different explanation of why supervenience seems true: these ethical attitudes one has towards non-ethical reality shouldn't be arbitrary. (The expressivist explanation of supervenience will be explained more in Chapter 3.) So the key issue here is whether nonnaturalists can mount a persuasive explanation of why the ethical seems to supervene on the non-ethical, or at least explain away the appearance that there's something important for them to explain in this regard.

Challenge from the practicality of morality

Above we saw that some philosophers attempt to argue from the premise that belief in normative facts is indispensable for practical deliberation to the conclusion that some nonnaturalist form of realism is true. However, others have viewed the practicality of morality to be an important liability for the nonnaturalist. Their idea is that our moral views play an importantly different role in the motivation and justification of action than beliefs about what is in fact the case. But, if nonnaturalism is true, then this difference is hard to make sense of.

There are two different ways to run the argument, depending on whether we're focussed on what we previously termed *motivating* reasons or *justifying* reasons and the corresponding versions of internalism (motivational internalism vs. internalism about justifying reasons).

QU5: What's the difference between motivating and justifying reasons?

Focussing first on the psychological states that actually motivate people to act, the internalist intuition is that our views about morality stand in a more intimate relation to motivations to action than our views about the natural world. As we noted before, it'd be very surprising if someone thought that giving to charity on a particular occasion was morally obligatory, but then when the time came to give, she had no motivation to do so. We could not say something similar about someone who thought, e.g., that giving to charity was rare. Motivational internalists stress this difference as important for determining the psychological role of our ethical thought.

This generates an explanatory challenge for the nonnaturalist. That is to say, since they think that our ethical views are beliefs about nonnatural facts, if they agree with the (motivational) internalist intuition, they need to explain why such beliefs would seem to have this intimate connection to motivation to action. Why do beliefs in natural facts not seem to move us in the same way as belief in (at least) these (supposedly) nonnatural facts seem to?

Switching our focus to the justificatory issue of what kinds of considerations can provide reasons for action, the internalist intuition is that a reason for someone to act must connect in some way to their concerns. This doesn't mean that it has to connect to their current desires, given their current knowledge. But if there were no connection between some consideration and what someone would care about were they to have full information and be thinking clearly, how could that provide a reason for them to act in any particular way? Internalists about justifying reasons say that it couldn't.

Again, this generates an explanatory challenge for the nonnaturalist. As long as we think morality sometimes provides reasons for people to act in particular ways, since nonnaturalists think that morality is about nonnatural facts, it seems that they owe us an explanation of how such nonnatural facts connect to our concerns. Why, that is, would those who have full information and are thinking clearly care about whether their action has the nonnatural property of rightness?

In both cases, nonnaturalists can deny the internalist intuition to get out of the explanatory challenge—that is, nonnaturalists can embrace some form of externalism. Then, however, they face a different sort of explanatory challenge: to explain why many philosophers have found the intuition compelling.

• CONCLUSION

In this chapter, we have been focussed on the first of our four main metaethical views: nonnaturalism. This is principally a view about the metaphysics of morality. It holds that ethical facts and properties really are part of reality, which is what makes it a realist view. Moreover, it holds that such facts and properties are autonomous from the natural facts and properties (but also the super-natural facts and properties), which is why it is called "nonnaturalism." There's no agreed upon definition of what counts as a natural fact/property, but several overlapping conceptions having to do with science and law-of-nature type explanations provide some sense of what nonnaturalists are denying when they deny that ethical facts and properties are natural.

This has epistemological implications. At the very least, it seems that nonnaturalists cannot say that we acquire ethical knowledge in the same way that we acquire knowledge of the natural world around us. Many nonnaturalists posit a faculty of moral intuition as the special way we come to know ethical facts, conceived nonnaturalistically.

Nonnaturalism also has implications in the philosophy of language. We haven't discussed these here because they don't distinguish nonnaturalists from error-theorists, fictionalists, and naturalists. By conceiving of ethical discourse as representational discourse, nonnaturalists share an advantage had by these views over expressivist views: an easy explanation of why ethical language seems to integrate seamlessly with other representational areas of discourse in terms of its semantics.

This is connected to the nonnaturalist's views in the philosophy of mind about moral psychology and action theory. Here, nonnaturalists would be classified as *cognitivists* because they take our ethical judgments to result in beliefs in facts (of a particular specification) rather than mental states with a desire-like direction of fit with the world.

The primary arguments for nonnaturalism come from:

- a particular interpretation of Hume's Law ("no ought from is");
- refinements of Moore's suggestion that there is always a gap between any set of ethical facts and the natural facts that might be proposed as reduction of those facts;
- the apparent indispensability of normative beliefs in practical deliberation about what to do.

The primary arguments against nonnaturalism come from:

- a deep seated commitment to the naturalistic worldview;
- an objection to its epistemology of morality;
- the very plausible supervenience of the moral on the nonmoral, which is difficult for nonnaturalists to explain;
- the way the nonnaturalist's metaphysics of morality makes it hard to respect various internalist intuitions in moral psychology and action theory.

As with all of the views we'll discuss in this book, the presentation here is necessarily brief and only scratches the surface of the potential philosophical debate that has happened and could happen about nonnaturalism. But hopefully it sets the stage for a comparative theoretical cost–benefit analysis that we'll pursue in Chapter 7.

• CHAPTER SUMMARY

- Nonnaturalists hold that reality includes objective ethical facts and these facts are irreducible to natural facts.
- Because there is no agreed upon definition of the "natural" and nonnaturalists also deny that ethical facts are reducible to supernatural facts, we think of nonnaturalism as the view that ethical facts are importantly *autonomous* from other sorts of facts, such as the facts discoverable by science or figuring in scientific theories and explanations.
- Hume's Law ("no ought from is") provides some initial support for this view.
- "Open-question" style arguments are one prominent source of positive support for the view.
- The claim that some facts are deliberatively indispensable provides further support for the view, but it can at best secure the existence of *normative* facts (rather than specifically *ethical* facts).
- Nonnaturalists typically endorse an intuitionist epistemology, a representationalist account of the meaning of ethical statements, and a cognitivist view about the nature of ethical thought.

- Resistance to the view comes from the naturalistic worldview, criticisms of the epistemology of nonnaturalism, an argument from the supervenience of the ethical on the non-ethical, and challenges to the nonnaturalist's ability to explain the practicality of morality.

• STUDY QUESTIONS

1 What is Hume's Law? Can you give an intuitive example?
2 Explain the difference between at least three things one could mean by "natural."
3 Why do some philosophers think that ethical properties aren't identical to natural properties?
4 What is an intuitive example of an inference to the best explanation?
5 Is belief in ethical facts indispensable for practical deliberation?
6 Why is it challenging for the nonnaturalist to explain the supervenience of the ethical on the non-ethical?
7 If there are nonnatural facts, how could we know them?

• FURTHER RESOURCES

- Enoch, David. 2011. *Taking Morality Seriously: A Defense of Robust Realism*. Oxford University Press. [A book-length defence of nonnaturalism, including a chapter on deliberative indispensability.]
- Finlay, Stephen. 2007. "Four Faces of Moral Realism," *Philosophy Compass* 2 (6): 820–49. [Survey article including a careful discussion of the claim that morality is "autonomous."]
- Ridge, Michael. 2014. "Moral Non-Naturalism," *The Stanford Encyclopedia of Philosophy* (Fall 2014 Edition), Edward N. Zalta (ed.), http://plato.stanford.edu/archives/fall2014/entries/moral-non-naturalism. [A longer introduction to nonnaturalism and some of the arguments against it.]
- Shafer-Landau, Russ. 2003. *Moral Realism: A Defence*. Oxford University Press. [A book-length defence of nonnaturalism, including a careful discussion of open-question style arguments and responses to many objections.]

• ANSWERS TO QUESTIONS OF UNDERSTANDING

QU1:   Since karma isn't something recognized by science, (iii) would not be a plausible candidate. (iv) is a plausible candidate as long as the "someone" is accepted as a part of the natural world (and not e.g., a god or angel). (v) and (vi) are interesting and difficult cases where philosophers have tried to "naturalize" these facts, but also where it can also be difficult to develop a plausible explanation of where they fit in the natural world.

QU2: The first two questions are "closed" in the relevant sense. One displays confusion with the meaning of the words 'green' and 'color' if one wonders whether green is a color. And one displays confusion in the relevant sense with the meaning of 'bachelors' if one wonders whether they are unmarried.

QU3: A logical inference moves from beliefs to a new belief because the new belief has to be true (given the logical structure of the original beliefs). The modus ponens form is most famous: from a belief in p and a belief in *if* p *then* q; one can logically infer q. By contrast, an inference to the best explanation moves from initial observations to a belief in some proposition because it would best explain the truth of those observations. For example, the conclusions detectives draw in murder mysteries are usually inferences to the best explanation and not logical inferences.

QU4: Yes, and fact 2 supervenes on fact 1. This is because any change to the one would necessitate a change to the other. Although identity entails supervenience, the entailment is not usually thought to go the other way around. Ethical facts might supervene on some set of natural facts without being identical to them.

QU5: Motivating reasons are the psychological facts or states that explain why someone was motivated to act in a particular way (even if the act is unjustified). Justifying reasons are the considerations that could be appealed to justify acting in some particular way (even if those weren't the considerations the agent actually acted for).

• WORKS CITED

Enoch, David. 2011. *Taking Morality Seriously: A Defense of Robust Realism*. New York: Oxford University Press.

Frankena, William. 1939. "The Naturalistic Fallacy." *Mind* 48: 464–77.

Harman, Gilbert. 1977. *The Nature of Morality: An Introduction to Ethics*. New York: Oxford University Press.

Reid, Thomas. 1788. *Essays on the Active Powers of Man*. Edited by Knud Haakonssen and James Harris. Edinburgh: Edinburgh University Press.

Ross, W. D. 1930. *The Right and the Good*. Oxford: Oxford University Press.

Shafer-Landau, Russ. 2003. *Moral Realism: A Defence*. Oxford: Oxford University Press.

Sidgwick, Henry. 1907. *Methods of Ethics*. London: Macmillan.

Street, Sharon. 2006. "A Darwinian Dilemma for Realist Theories of Value." *Philosophical Studies* 127 (1): 109–66.

• NOTE

1 Glossing supervenience in terms of an "underlying" difference suggests that philosophers who appeal to supervenience may have something stronger than co-variation in mind. Often in ethics, supervenience claims can be transformed into claims about "dependence" or "grounding" or "basing." The ethical facts seem to many to depend on or be grounded in some more basic non-ethical facts. Similarly, many metaethicists think our ethical beliefs must be based on beliefs about non-ethical matters. Understanding the subtle differences between all of these notions and how they affect the arguments given in metaethics is an active topic of current research.

3
expressivism

As we saw at the end of the previous chapter, nonnaturalists generally assume that ethical language is *representational* and ethical thought is cognitive. This assumption is common to realist positions. The basic idea is that ethical statements and the states of mind that they express represent reality as being a particular way, and they are correct when reality is indeed this way. Expressivist theories in metaethics start out from skepticism about this idea. In order to argue that a representationalist understanding of ethical statements is mistaken, expressivists typically encourage us to begin our metaethical enquiry by asking not about (i) the nature of some kind of supposedly real thing: ethical value, but about (ii) the nature of one of our practices: making ethical evaluations. Then, their answer to question (ii) typically claims some interesting disanalogy between ethical evaluations and representations of reality.

In their philosophy of mind, this typically leads expressivists to endorse some sort of *noncognitivism* about ethical thoughts. That is, they claim that the states of mind expressed by ethical statements have a desire-like rather than belief-like direction of fit with reality; they are something like desires, emotive reactions, preferences, or plans. By claiming that ethical sentences and the states of mind that they express are not in the business of representing reality, expressivists pave the way to an antirealist view, since they see no reason to commit to the reality of objective ethical facts. We call their view "expressivism" because the key claim that distinguishes it from the other main metaethical views is a claim about what kind of mental state is expressed by ethical statements.

In this chapter, we'll discuss several increasingly sophisticated versions of this view and the objections that lead to increased sophistication. But we start with a few of the general reasons some philosophers have favored this view.

> **Key Point**: Expressivism is a form of antirealism that understands ethical statements as expressions of evaluative attitudes rather than beliefs representing how reality is.

• ARGUMENTS IN FAVOR OF EXPRESSIVISM

The full case in favor of expressivism (or any other metaethical view) can only be pursued in comparison to the other theoretical options. So, in Chapter 7 we'll attempt to map many of the various dimensions of theoretical costs and benefits in metaethics. But before we get to that, it will prove helpful to canvass some of the initial motivations in favor of the view. Here, I start with three related motivations for expressivism.

Hume's Law and open-question intuitions + naturalistic worldview

As we saw before, Hume insisted on an important conceptual distinction between 'ought' and 'is,' and this has been pushed forward by various open-question style arguments in favor of the nonnaturalist view we encountered in the previous chapter that ethical facts are not reducible to natural facts. As Ayer (1936/1946, Chapter 6) pointed out, an equally valid response to Hume's Law and open-question intuitions is to argue that ethical thought and discourse aren't even in the business of representing aspects of reality. That is, rather than capturing the apparent difference in terms of the kinds of facts (natural vs. nonnatural) represented by ethical statements and the states of mind they express, one of the founding ideas of expressivism is that we can capture this in terms of the function of ethical statements and the states of mind they express. More specifically, assuming ordinary statements express beliefs about reality, expressivists claim that ethical statements express some noncognitive or non-representational state of mind—something like a desire, emotion, preference, or plan.

> QU1: What distinguishes a representational state of mind from a nonrepresentational state of mind?

As far as that goes, we have two competing explanations of Hume's Law and open-question intuitions: the nonnaturalist's and the expressivist's. Which should we prefer? Expressivism is usually motivated by a naturalistic worldview. If you find Hume's Law and open-question intuitions persuasive, and you're also committed to a naturalistic worldview, then the expressivist's explanation is likely to look pretty good. It's not that expressivists *have to* deny that there are nonnatural facts (and that ethical statements are about such facts). But they will argue that once we have recognized the fundamentally different function of ethical statements and the states of mind they express, there will be no explanatory or theoretical need to posit an autonomous realm of nonnatural facts. The principle of parsimony encourages us to do without them.

Argument from motivational internalism + Humean theory of motivation

The intuition behind Hume's Law and open-question style arguments is not just that ethical statements and the states of mind they express are different, but also that they are different *because of how they bear on action*. The basic idea stems from the Humean belief–desire psychology of motivation. Recall from Chapter 2 that many philosophers have found it convenient to think of action as the product of two distinct kinds of mental states—states that represent the way reality is and states that set a goal for the agent to change reality. These are commonly (though somewhat misleadingly) called *beliefs* and *desires*.

Someone who thinks the Humean belief–desire psychology is basically right isn't thereby committed to any specific metaethical view. However, if one is also attracted to some form of motivational internalism about ethical thought, expressivism becomes increasingly tempting. Motivational internalism, recall, was the view that there is some especially tight connection between ethical thoughts and motivation. For example, thinking that one ought not steal seems to be tightly correlated with one's being motivated not to steal. Of course, sometimes we do things that we think we ought not do. But often these can be explained by our being overpowered by the countervailing motivations of temptation, anger, envy, etc.; or they can be explained by our not fully comprehending what we were doing when we acted wrongly. It would be strange if someone thought that she ought not ϕ but had absolutely no motivation to refrain from ϕing.

This provides the resources for a prominent argument in favor of expressivism. If the distinctive feature of ethical thoughts is that they are internally connected to motivation, and one thinks that beliefs alone cannot motivate, then a natural conclusion is that ethical thoughts aren't beliefs about the way reality is, but instead some desire-like state of mind. That is to say that expressivists sometimes argue that the reason that motivational internalism is true is that ethical thoughts can play the goal-setting role in a Humean explanation of motivation unlike ordinary empirical thoughts; and if this is right, then ethical statements are plausibly thought to express desire-like states of mind rather than beliefs about the way reality is.

What does it mean to call these states "desire-like"? It means that they are goal-setting rather than reality-representing. It may be reasonable to distinguish several different species of goal-setting mental states: ordinary desires (e.g., wanting to have some oysters), comparative preferences (e.g., preferring living in New York to Sydney), moral stances (e.g., abhorring racism), conditional plans (e.g., planning to save a drowning child if one sees one). An important further question for expressivists is which of these is their more specific account of the nature of moral judgments. But as far as the argument from motivational internalism is concerned, it just has to be some "desire-like" state of mind.

> ***Key Point***: Expressivism would provide a plausible explanation of how moral judgments could be internally connected to motivation provided that the Humean theory of motivation is correct.

Argument from supervenience

The final general motivation for expressivism has to do with supervenience. Recall that a liability of nonnaturalist views in metaethics is that they have no easy explanation of the way the ethical status of actions seems to depend intimately on the non-ethical facts of the situation. It would be very strange indeed if two actions that were identical in all relevant non-ethical respects were nonetheless evaluated differently ethically. For one action to be permissible and another action to be impermissible, for example, it seems that there must be some underlying non-ethical difference. For this reason many philosophers say that the ethical supervenes on the non-ethical.

This objection to nonnaturalism was originally pressed by expressivists such as Hare (1952) and Blackburn (1971), and they thought that expressivism offers a fairly compelling explanation of supervenience. The idea is to reject the nonnaturalist's picture of two distinct realms of fact (ethical and non-ethical), whose relation must be explained in such a way to secure supervenience. In its place, expressivists suggest that supervenience intuitions reflect a natural consistency constraint on our desire-like reactions to the way we take the reality to be. If, for instance, there are two circumstances that are exactly the same in all relevant descriptive ways, then approving of one while disapproving of the other would be arbitrary. And holding and expressing such arbitrary attitudes would undermine the natural coordinative function of having these attitudes. Hence, over time there would have been pressure towards respecting this consistency constraint in these attitudes. So much so, in fact, that the constraint would have become part of the meaning of the relevant ethical terms. According to the expressivist, this manifests itself in the intuitions of supervenience.

To get the idea, consider a nonmoral example of choosing pieces of cake. If one believes that two pieces of cake are alike in all relevant respects (same size, same kind, same taste, etc.), then it'd be hard to make sense of someone preferring one of the pieces to the other. To put it differently, if someone said, "I know they are exactly alike in respects x, y, z, but I want piece A instead of piece B," we'd be inclined to think that there was some other respect in which they are different that explains this difference in desires. The preferability of pieces of cake, it seems, supervenes on a range of descriptive features (size, kind, taste, etc.).

If morality supervenes on the non-ethical facts in this way, and ethical thoughts are desire-like as the expressivist contends, then we could offer the same sort of explanation of why any difference in ethical evaluation must, on pain of irrationality, rest on the assumption that there is a relevant difference in non-ethical features. Again, we see an inference to the best explanation. The ethical seems to supervene on the non-ethical: expressivists argue that the best explanation of this is that ethical thoughts are desire-like reactions to how we take the non-ethical facts to be, not beliefs in some separate realm of nonnatural facts.

As far as that goes, however, the nonnaturalist might try to steal a leaf from the expressivist's playbook. She might argue that ethical beliefs are about nonnatural facts but then go on to insist that such beliefs are constrained by rational consistency in a similar way to the way expressivists think moral attitudes are constrained by rational consistency. That is to say that just like the expressivist holds that one's ethical view of two situations should not differ unless there is some underlying descriptive difference between the situations, perhaps the nonnaturalist could say something similar. In response, those sympathetic to expressivism will wonder why we should think that there are facts that are such that belief in them is constrained in this way. So this response on the part of the nonnaturalist would open them up to a metaphysical challenge, but they will think that this challenge can be met.

• VERSIONS AND OBJECTIONS

To appreciate the force of some of the objections that have been raised against expressivism, it will prove helpful to sketch a few more specific versions of the view. We'll use these sketches to explain the objections and then to explore the ways that expressivism has been refined to avoid the objections (though often with the consequence of inspiring new objections). Each subsequent view has been viewed as more plausible than the previous, in part due to reacting to objections, though some objections may remain.

Emotivism

Ayer's (1936/1946, Chapter 6) "Emotive Theory of Values" and Stevenson's "Emotive Meaning of Ethical Terms" (1937) are two key forbearers of more contemporary expressivist theories. Stevenson argued from ordinary language considerations that ethical words are primarily used to vent feelings, create moods, and incite people to action—rather than to record, clarify, and communicate beliefs. However, because it is not entirely clear whether to classify Stevenson as a proto-expressivist or a proto-relativist, I'll focus here on Ayer. Ayer's basic idea was that ethical statements should not be viewed as attempts to state matters of fact but rather to express emotive reactions to the facts (or at least what we take to be the facts).

To be more precise, we should say that Ayer argued that ethical words have at least two uses. First, they are used to describe the moralities of different communities of people; second, they are used to express one's own opinions about what is right, wrong, etc. According to Ayer, statements with ethical words used in the first way are sociological descriptions rather than expressions of normative judgments. For instance, we might say something like, "In Saudi Arabia, it's wrong for Muslim women to go bareheaded outside of their home," not meaning to *condemn* Muslim women going bareheaded while in Saudi Arabia but to *describe* the moral sensibility of Saudi Arabian society. Ayer thought statements with ethical words used in the second way, however, are not descriptions of a moral sensibility, nor even descriptions of our own moral sensibilities. Rather they are direct expressions of the emotions comprising these sensibilities. For example, if one uses an ethical word in the second way saying, "Stealing is wrong," Ayer's view was that this expresses one's negative attitude towards stealing rather than describing stealing or one's attitudes towards stealing.

> QU2: What's the difference between describing yourself as feeling some way and expressing that feeling?

One helpful way to conceptualize this theory is as the "boo/hooray! theory" of ethical language. Ayer thought that saying that something is wrong or bad is not describing it as having a particular property, but rather expressing a negative emotion towards it— like booing it. And, similarly, saying that something is right or good is not describing it as having a particular property but rather expressing a positive emotion towards it—like hooraying it.

To understand why many philosophers have been dissatisfied with emotivism, it's useful to delve into a bit of the history around the development of Ayer's metaethical view. He was largely concerned with issues in the philosophy of language, where he defended the **verificationist principle** of meaning. This says that the factual meaning of a sentence is the conditions under which it would be "verified" or confirmed as true. For example, the verification conditions of a sentence such as, "Crocodiles live in Florida" would be the conditions under which one could see or infer the existence of crocodiles living in Florida (presumably there is some range of experiences that would confirm this as true).

Ayer used the verificationist principle of meaning as a kind of philosophical weapon, arguing that various philosophers' views in metaphysics were unverifiable and so, strictly speaking, meaningless (since there would have to be some conditions under which they would be verified in order to have meaning, according to the verificationist principle of meaning). However, Ayer ran up against the fact that it often seems impossible to verify ethical claims. For instance, if someone says, "Manning's leak of the classified documents was morally wrong," how would we go about verifying this as true, or verifying its denial as false? It's not like there is some range of experiences which would settle the matter.

This may have led some philosophers to go back and reconsider the verificationist theory of meaning, but Ayer stood fast to this principle and embraced metaethical conclusions that seemed to him to follow from it. I'll mention four of these conclusions here.

First, Ayer argued that moral disagreement is senseless, unless it proceeds on the assumption of shared values. His idea was that there can be cases where two people share an ethical outlook, e.g., perhaps they both think economic conditions that lead to some people living in abject poverty are morally bad. Given such shared ethical values, there could be genuine disagreement about something like whether a particular governmental policy is morally bad. According to Ayer, however, this would actually be a factual disagreement and not a moral disagreement. True, we frame the disagreement as one about whether something is morally bad, but what the people disagree about is whether the governmental policy leads to abject poverty, not whether abject poverty is bad. But if the two parties to the disagreement didn't share ethical values, then it would be silly for them to disagree. In that case, according to Ayer, there's nothing really for them to disagree about—they simply have different ethical viewpoints. Accordingly, he thought that there is no such thing as genuinely *ethical* disagreement. Apparent ethical disagreements are either factual disagreements on the backdrop of shared values or simply people not sharing ethical values.

Second, Ayer argued that there's actually not much for moral philosophers to do, as there's not really a subject matter for them to figure out (remember he thought that there is no way to verify many ethical claims as true or false). He thought that different people have different values (which is something any anthropologist or sociologist could tell us), and all there is for the moral philosopher to do is to note that ethical words have no factual meaning. The remaining task of describing the different feelings ethical words are used to express, Ayer thought, is a matter for psychology not philosophy.

Third (and most famously), Ayer claimed that ethical statements "…do not come under the category of truth and falsehood" (1936/1946, 108). In contemporary jargon, he thought that they are not **truth-apt**, i.e. properly evaluated for truth or falsehood.

Fourth, he argued that ethical sentences do not express propositions but rather have only **emotive meaning** and not the sort of meaning normally associated with factual sentences.

As I'll explain below, these four striking tenets of Ayer's emotivism set the agenda for many of the criticisms of expressivism. In one way or another expressivists ever since Ayer have been trying to show how such conclusions are not forced by the basic expressivist idea—viz. that by focussing on what ethical statements do rather than on what they represent, we can come to appreciate that they express noncognitive attitudes towards the nonmoral world rather than describe moral properties of things, thereby avoiding ontological commitment to moral properties and facts.

Key Point: Emotivism is an early and extreme form of expressivism that conceives of ethical statements on the model of 'boo's and 'hooray's.

Disagreement and prescriptivism

Consider disagreement first. Whatever Ayer thought, intuitively speaking, it surely seems that there are genuine ethical disagreements. We are all familiar with disagreeing with someone about whether an action is wrong. Just think of the various opinions your friends and family may have about the ethics of Manning's leak of classified documents. And there seem to be deep-seated cultural differences that lead to some people favoring certain policies and laws that others oppose. To see this, just watch pundits discuss the pros and cons of a national referendum, or listen to a political debate in the lead up to a national election.

Of course, Ayer might put this appearance of moral disagreement down to disagreement about some underlying factual issue. For instance, consider two people who disagree about the value of same-sex marriage. Let's imagine the first person bases her objection to same-sex marriage on her belief that same-sex marriage decreases respect for marriage in society, leading to increased divorces and decreased well-being of children. The other person might think that if that were true, then same-sex marriage would indeed be bad. But let's imagine she doesn't agree about the factual issue about whether same-sex marriage leads to increased divorces and decreased well-being of children. If the apparently moral disagreement between these two people about same-sex marriage is based primarily on this difference of opinion about the consequences of same-sex marriage, then Ayer's description of the case looks pretty good. Their "moral disagreement" is really a disagreement about some underlying factual issue.

> QU3: Which of the following are topics of factual disagreement that might underlie differences in moral opinion: (i) Whether certain symbols such as the Confederate flag or the swastika are disrespectful, (ii) Whether universal access to primary healthcare leads to lower overall healthcare costs than private insurance systems, (iii) Whether the death penalty is an effective deterrent of serious crime?

However, if you've ever been in an argument with someone who disagrees with you about same-sex marriage or any other heated ethical topic, you will surely have had the impression that even after clearing up all factual disagreements you'd still disagree with the other person. As we sometimes say: some people seem to have fundamentally different values from us. But, if that's right, then it seems that there can be genuinely *moral* disagreements, which is a serious problem for any view that implies—as Ayer's emotivism seems to—that there cannot be.

The main response to the objection about disagreement among expressivists is to back away from Ayer's suggestion that ethical statements express *mere* feelings—attitudes that two people may fail to share but which they cannot sensibly disagree about—by arguing that there are other ways to disagree than two people having inconsistent beliefs. Stevenson already appealed to the idea of a "disagreement in attitudes." For example, if you prefer we go out for dinner and I prefer we stay at home for dinner, then there's a sense in which we disagree in preferences: we can't both get what we prefer. (It's important that these are preferences for what *we* do.) Similarly, imagine that your mother tells you, "Buy your miserable aunt a birthday present!" and your father says, "No, don't do that! She'll hate it no matter what." Surely your mother and father have disagreed in what they told you to do. It's impossible to follow both of their commands. Here we have a disagreement in prescription rather than a disagreement in belief.

Appreciating the relevance of prescriptions to explaining ethical thought and discourse, R. M. Hare (1952) defended **prescriptivism** as a theory of ethical language. The basic idea is that ethical statements are like commands in being prescriptive rather than descriptive, but they are unlike typical commands in embodying a "universalized prescription," i.e. a sort of prescription that is supposed to go for everyone in similar circumstances.

With a much-discussed example, the **missionary and cannibals example**, Hare argued that expressivists not only have an explanation of genuine moral disagreement but this explanation is better than representationalist theories. In the example, he asks us to imagine that a missionary has landed on a distant island, equipped with a dictionary translating the local language into English. Observing the things they call "good" (in their language), the missionary notices two things. First, they seem to approve of the things they call "good," striving for and promoting them. Second, the class of things they call "good" is radically different than the class of things the missionary would call "good": the cannibals think people who are bold and collect a large number of scalps are good, whereas he thinks meek and gentle people are good.

Hare argues that if we thought that the word 'good' describes things as having a property, we'd have to conclude that the missionary's word 'good' and the cannibal's word for 'good' simply have different meanings. It's like when British people use the word 'football' for a game played with a round ball and mostly the feet, and American people use this word to refer to a game played with an oblong ball mostly carried and thrown with the hands. If they don't apply the word to the same things, that's not because they disagree; rather it's because they are using the words with different meanings.

But Hare thought it was pretty clear that the missionary and cannibals *do* disagree in their use of 'good.' Because of this, he thought that their disagreement couldn't be about whether being bold and collecting lots of scalps has the property of being good but rather must be a disagreement in attitude and prescription. It's not exactly clear what state of mind is expressed by a prescription, but it's probably some desire-like attitude such as a preference. Hence, we might say that the cannibals prefer that people be bold and collect scalps, and using 'good' to express this preference they make (on Hare's view) a universalized prescription to act boldly and collect lots of scalps; the missionary prefers something incompatible with this, and using the term 'good' to express this preference he makes (again, according to Hare) a universalized prescription to do something different.

If that seems like a plausible analysis of the example to you, then you might be inclined to agree with Hare that ethical language is prescriptive, and genuinely *moral* disagreement is a disagreement in attitude/prescription rather than in belief. However, others have worried that, although ethics and prescription seem intimately related, the prescriptive does not exhaust the ethical. For example, consider the idea that it'd be good if there were less people in the world (as that'd decrease the stress humans put on the natural environment). This seems like an ethical evaluation, but it is not obvious that it is making any particular prescription. (It surely doesn't prescribe individual people not to have children.)

Blackburn and Gibbard on taking ethics seriously

To see a way forward for expressivists, let's turn now to Ayer's idea that there's not much sensible work to be done in moral philosophy because moral language is really the expression of feelings rather than a way to report facts. When he made it, you can imagine that moral philosophers weren't too impressed with this suggestion! And there appears to be no reason the expressivist has to endorse it.

Ever since Hume, we've had the idea that some of our thought and discourse may initially seem as if it is representing reality even though it really involves some sort of projection onto reality of stuff that's actually in our minds. In Hume's colorful terms, we "gild and stain" reality with our sentiments.

To see what he has in mind, consider first a nonmoral example: thought and discourse about what's *delicious*. At first it might seem that a cone of Belgian chocolate ice-cream has the following two properties (among others): it is frozen and it is delicious. However, upon reflection we should start to see a difference here. The frozenness of the ice-cream is a product of the microphysical interactions of its atomic parts, something that would remain were no sentient beings to be around to consider it. By contrast, its deliciousness seems to be, at least in part, something we project onto the ice-cream. Indeed, it's not hard to imagine someone who finds Belgian chocolate ice-cream disgusting rather than delicious (perhaps they once ate enough of it to make themselves royally sick). Is it *really* delicious or disgusting? Probably neither, "really." This is different from the question of whether it is *really* frozen or liquid. This difference may hold, of course, without undermining our concern for figuring out which things are delicious and which are disgusting. After all, the fact that their deliciousness/disgustingness is in part "gilded and stained" by us doesn't change the fact that we find them delicious/disgusting, which involves taking pleasure/pain in consuming them.

> QU4: Which of the following are plausible candidates for features we project onto reality as opposed to find there independently of our tendency to "gild and stain": (i) The humor in a joke, (ii) The distance between New York and Sydney, (iii) The temperature of the earth's atmosphere, (iv) The beauty in modern art?

There are two ways this idea has been used by expressivists to develop a version of the view that rejects Ayer's contention that moral philosophy is mostly empty. First, Blackburn (1984) argued for a **projectivist** form of expressivism, according to which our ethical evaluations involve a kind of projection of our values onto the world around us. In his view, this actually aids the function of ethical thought and discourse. If, rather than seeing ethics as mere booing and hooraying, we see it instead as "gilding and staining" reality for the purpose of our own practical deliberation but also to influence others, we can start to understand how ethical discourse works to influence action and preferences within our moral community. Second, Gibbard (1990) argued for a version of expressivism he called **norm-expressivism**. One of the key ideas of this was that in making ethical statements we are expressing not a mere feeling but rather our commitment to systems of norms or general rules. His suggestion, then, was that these provide guidance on how to act when they are combined with specific beliefs about how reality is. (This is an answer to the question raised above about what specific desire-like state of mind is expressed by ethical statements.) Because of the social utility of being committed to similar rules for living together, Gibbard argued, there is good evolutionary reason to think that humans would have developed a way to voice their commitment to norms, as this provides a means for coordinating on basic rules for behavior. And this seems to be very important for finding a way to live together and improving it by continued dialogue and collective practical deliberation.

So, what we see in early work by both Blackburn and Gibbard is the possibility of an expressivist-friendly explanation of why moral philosophy is very important. This is not because it is aiming at a correct representation of some objective piece of reality. Ethics is different from physics. Rather, it's because ethical discussion is a place where we express our values and commitments in order to coordinate and refine ways of living together. Moreover, as long as we think of these values and commitments as something meant for groups of people rather than individuals, Blackburn and Gibbard also develop resources to handle the challenge of disagreement discussed above. However, their idea about what ethical statements express leaves some important questions about ethical language unanswered. We turn to these next.

Truth-aptness and quasi-realism

While it may be a common thought that there is no objective truth in ethics only opinion, Ayer's suggestion that ethical sentences are not truth-apt raises certain problems in the philosophy of language having to do with the way we use the word 'true' and its relatives in ordinary discourse. Just consider the following mini-dialogs:

(A) Lying is wrong.
(B) That's true, but this is a case of not telling the whole truth, not lying.
(C) Torture is okay in extreme circumstances.
(D) No, what you believe about torture is false. In fact, torture is always wrong.

These are ordinary things to say. But, if Ayer is right that ethical sentences aren't even capable of being true or false, then how can it make sense for B to say "That's *true*"? And if ethical statements express noncognitive attitudes rather than beliefs, then shouldn't it seem nonsensical what D says about what C *believes* about torture? Moreover, if there are no ethical facts, how could torture in fact be always wrong?

Even if you're inclined to say that ethical thought and discourse "gilds and stains" reality rather than represents it, you should worry about expressivism's ability to make sense of these elements of ordinary ethical discourse. Using 'true' and 'believes' and 'fact' in conjunction with ethical statements doesn't seem like nonsense. Moreover, as we'll see in the following chapter, one of the main antirealist competitors to expressivism is the error theory, which says that our ordinary ethical discourse embodies an ontological error. So, unless expressivists can legitimate the use of these and related terms within ethics, it will seem that they avoid claiming that ordinary use of ethical terms is in error only at the cost of committing to the claim that ordinary use of terms like 'true,' 'believes,' and 'fact' is in error.

> QU5: What does it mean to say that ethical sentences are truth-apt?

Blackburn (1984, 1993) pioneered the response to this worry that has become standard among expressivists. He argued that the difficulty is not with the expressivist's view about ethical terms but rather with a common assumption philosophers make about 'true,' 'believes,' 'fact,' and related terms. The common assumption is that they apply only to areas of discourse and thought that are representational. This assumption stems from the **correspondence theory of truth**, which says that a proposition is true just in case it corresponds with reality. Importantly for Blackburn's purposes, that is a highly controversial view about truth, and a competing view is the **minimalist theory of truth**, which says that 'is true' is a kind of linguistic or logical device which allows us to talk about (possible) statements or belief to which we assent. And since we can assent to ethical statements just as much as we can assent to descriptive statements, if one adopts minimalism about truth, there's no reason the expressivist has to deny that ethical statements are truth-apt. Similarly, we might have thought that the word 'believes' refers to a mental state that represents reality as being some way. But if we instead think of it as referring to *whatever* mental state is involved in assenting to a statement, then there will be no reason expressivists have to say that the mental states expressed by ethical statements aren't beliefs. Moreover, there seems to be little difference between believing or saying, e.g., that it's *true* that torture is wrong, and believing or saying it's a fact that torture is wrong. So minimalism about 'truth' and 'belief' seems to support minimalism about 'fact.'

Hence, by adopting minimalism about 'truth' and 'belief' and 'fact' (which admittedly are controversial views in their own right), it looks as if expressivists can avoid the worry generated by our mini-dialogs above. Blackburn referred to this line of thought as the beginning of **quasi-realism**, the program of winning back for the expressivist right to use terms, such as 'true,' 'believes,' and 'fact' that were previously thought to be the providence of only realists. The resulting expressivist view is *quasi*-realist in freely saying that ethical statements are truth-apt and that they express ethical beliefs which may in fact be true, but then explaining why that doesn't commit the expressivist to realism.

Key Point: A minimalist theory of truth lets the *quasi-realist* expressivist say that ethical statements are truth-apt without undermining his commitment to the view that ethical statements do not represent reality.

Even if one goes this far with expressivists, one might worry that the view still entails that what's right and wrong depends on what we happen to think is right and wrong. As we'll see in Chapter 8, there are some metaethicists who accept some form of this mind-dependence claim about ethics. However, part of the continuation of the quasi-realist program for expressivists like Blackburn is to argue that once they have earned the right to use terms, such as 'true,' 'believes,' and 'fact' within ethical discourse, there's nothing to prevent them from denying claims of mind dependence. Consider, for example, the following mini-dialog:

(A)   Torturing people is wrong.
(B)   Sure, but it wouldn't be wrong if we all didn't disapprove of it.
(A)   No, that's not right; even if we all failed to disapprove of torture, it'd still be wrong.

You may agree with A or B, but the present point is that expressivism as a metaethical view is neutral on this issue, and most expressivists tend to agree with A. How could they do that if they think A's first statement is primarily an expression of an evaluative attitude? It's because they'll insist that A's second statement is *also* the expression of an evaluative attitude. It's something like the expression of a negative evaluation of the possible state of affairs where we all fail to disapprove of torture.

As I mentioned in Chapter 1, it is not entirely clear how we should characterize realism. There, I proposed to use, as a first approximation, a definition of it as the view that ethical facts obtain objectively. I mentioned (in note 1), however, that this definition is imprecise because some philosophers might say, e.g., it's an objective fact that torture is wrong, but go on to deny that in saying this they are metaphysically characterizing what reality is like. The philosophers I had in mind are quasi-realist expressivists such as Blackburn and Gibbard. Their minimalist positions about 'truth,' 'belief,' and 'fact' put them in a position to say things about ethical facts without obviously committing to ethical facts as part of a full and final metaphysical characterization of what reality is like. If we want to continue with tradition and characterize their view as a form of ethical anti-realism, we'll need to define moral realism as the view that a full and complete metaphysical characterization of reality will include objectively obtaining ethical facts.

However, there are two difficulties about quasi-realism we might continue to worry about. First, if we "go minimalist" about 'truth,' 'belief,' and 'fact,' where do we stop? These concepts seem tied up with concepts like reference, property, representation, obtaining, objectivity, etc. And if we adopt minimalism about all of these terms, we might have no stable way to draw the distinction between expressivism and realism. Second, it's not even clear this "go minimalist" move works for all elements of ordinary ethical discourse which might have tempted us to think of it as representational. For instance, consider the term 'knows'; it's perfectly ordinary to say something like, "I know that I ought to conserve energy, but I always forget to turn off the lights." But how could one claim to have ethical *knowledge* if the expressivist is right that one's judgment that she ought to conserve energy isn't a representation of reality? Regardless of one's stance on minimalism, most views of propositional knowledge require that there be some fact that-*p* that is tracked by one said to know that-*p*. But the expressivist doesn't seem to be in a position to appeal to a tracking conception of ethical knowledge, since he's an antirealist about ethics.

Frege–Geach

Let's turn now to the most famous challenge to expressivism. It is widely assumed in the philosophy of language that the meaning of a whole sentence is a function of the meaning of its parts and the way they are put together. This **compositionality assumption** seems to offer the only plausible framework for explaining the amazingly quick speed with which humans learn their first language and how we understand indefinitely many novel sentences with ease. If this is right, then there must be some stable content that is contributed by any part of a sentence to the meaning of all of the sentences in which it figures.

For example, consider the sentences "Roses are red" and "Fire engines are red." Both contain the word 'red.' So, according to the compositionality assumption, there's likely to be something common to both occurrences—the meaning of 'red'—which this word contributes *systematically* to the meaning of the whole sentences in which it occurs. Likewise with the other words in these sentences (and any other sentence we can understand). If that's right, then we can think of language learners as cottoning on to a finite number of word meanings and a finite number of principles for combining these meanings into meaningful whole sentences. And, with these two abilities, they should be able to understand an indefinite number of sentences.

Unfortunately, that much of modern semantics already stands in tension with early versions of expressivism, such as Ayer's emotivism. This was first noted by Searle (1962) and Geach (1965) and it rests on a point made by Frege; it has come to be called the **Frege–Geach problem**. The point made by Frege was that simple sentences could occur in more complex contexts, such as under negation ("It's not the case that…"), in a question ("Is it the case that…?"), under a propositional attitude report ("Sarah believes/doubts that…"), or in the antecedent or consequent of a conditional ("If…, then…").

To see how the objection goes, grant for the sake of argument that the following simple ethical sentences have no factual meaning and, as Ayer thought, only express negative moral sentiment:

> "Tormenting cats is wrong."

> "Getting little brother to torment cats is wrong."

QU6: How might we translate these two statements into the language of 'boo's and 'hooray's?

Then ask yourself what the emotivist would say about the meaning of more complex sentences which embed those sentences as parts. For example, consider the following conditional:

> "If tormenting cats is wrong, then getting little brother to torment cats is wrong."

It doesn't seem that the emotive "meanings" of the simple sentences can be the content these sentences contribute to the more complex conditional sentence. For one needn't have any negative moral sentiment at all towards tormenting cats in order to endorse the conditional sentence. This is because one who asserts a conditional—if p, then q—can remain neutral about each of its components. For example, one could consistently say, "If tormenting cats is wrong, then getting little brother to torment cats is wrong," but "Tormenting cats is not wrong."

Geach pressed this point by arguing that expressivists make a **fallacy of equivocation** out of what appears to be a clearly valid inference. The clearly valid inference is this one:

(1)   Tormenting cats is wrong.
(2)   If tormenting cats is wrong, then getting little brother to torment cats is wrong.
(3)   *Hence*, getting little brother to torment cats is wrong.

His idea was that expressivists hold that the simple sentence in premise 1 has emotive meaning by virtue of expressing a negative moral sentiment. But, as we have just seen, they must hold that the antecedent of the conditional sentence in premise 2 has some other kind of meaning. This implies that one who infers from these sentences to the conclusion 3 has equivocated in the course of the argument. But that's clearly not what's going on in this argument.

Because of this way of pressing the point, many expressivist responses to the Frege–Geach problem have sought to vindicate the inference and ones similar to it. For example, some have followed Hare in the idea that the ethical sentences convey prescriptions of some sort and noted that there are independently motivated logical properties of prescriptions. Perhaps someone who asserts 1 and 2 is committed to the prescription contained in 3. (However, it's not entirely obvious what this prescription is.) Others such as early Blackburn have suggested that conditionalized ethical sentences are used to express a higher-order attitude towards the simultaneous possession of two lower-order attitudes. In this way we may see premise 2 as expressing disapproval of anyone who would have the negative sentiment expressed by 1 but not have the negative sentiment expressed by 3. (However, there seems to be a difference between disapproving of combinations of attitudes and thinking an argument is logically valid.) And still others such as Gibbard have developed more complex expressivist accounts on which the content of ethical sentences can be represented as combinations of factual commitments and planning commitments, where the logical constraints on planning help to explain the validity of the inference Geach considered. And more recently Blackburn has developed another view according to which the logical connectives help to keep track of the way various statements commit us to other statements, sometimes "tying us to a tree" of other commitments, whether they are evaluative or factual.

It would take a chapter of its own to discuss the ins and outs of these proposals. However, I want to close this section by suggesting that the validity of the inference is not the core problem. The core problem is how expressivists can develop an account of the content of sentences that treats an ethical sentence as having the same content whether it is asserted or embedded in a more complex linguistic construction. Just consider the way we could embed the simple ethical sentences above under under the predicates, "It is doubtful that…" or "It might be the case that…". Because we can also embed any other declarative sentence in these contexts, the compositionality assumption puts strong pressure on us to think that there is some uniform account of the meanings of the sentences that embed in these ways. The standard account in the philosophy of language has been that declarative sentences (both ethical and non-ethical) express *propositions*, and its these propositions that remain the same across simple and embedded contexts. As a result, much recent work on expressivism has been about whether it can countenance such propositions for ethical sentences without giving up on the contrast it seeks to draw between ethical sentences and sentences that represent reality; and, if not, whether it can offer some general alternative that applies in both the ethical and non-ethical cases.

Motivational internalism

One last kind of objection I want to mention stems from the motivational internalist view that ethical thoughts can motivate action (though not infallibly) all on their own. As I mentioned above, this is a plank in one of the core arguments in favor of expressivism. Because of this, however, some have worried that challenges to motivational internalism are prima facie problems for the expressivist. For example, throughout history philosophers have puzzled over the phenomenon of **akrasia**, wondering how it is possible that one could think one ought to ϕ but when the time comes fail to ϕ. Indeed, even strong forms of this seem possible: where one thinks one ought to ϕ, forms a fully committed intention to ϕ, but when the time for ϕ-ing comes one's will turns weak; without changing one's mind about the ethical issue one nevertheless has no motivation to ϕ. There's naturally a lot of debate about whether this is really possible, but if it is, then it may seem to put pressure on the expressivist's view that these ethical thoughts are desire-like attitudes. For desire-like attitudes are simply the sorts of attitudes one needs in one's psychology to be motivated; so how could one simultaneously have them (in thinking that one ought to ϕ) but not have them (in suffering from akrasia)?

In response, expressivists might challenge the possibility of such an extreme akratic situation, arguing that even if one's will is weak, that's not because one has *absolutely* no motivation to perform the relevant action. It's rather because one's motivation (i.e. the attitude expressed by the ethical statement) is outweighed or undercut by countervailing motivations. Still some have worried that we can imagine someone who is seriously depressed, so much so that they have lost all evaluative affect. Nonetheless, remembering their previous ethical views, such a person might still make ethical statements. And the expressivist's view of these statements is that they function to express evaluative attitudes. Should we say that the seriously depressed cannot really make an ethical statement? It is not clear the expressivist *has* to say that, but this sort of case does pose a further challenge to expressivism. In evaluating how convincing you find it, you'll want to think about what it means when expressivists claim that ethical statements "express" evaluative attitudes.

• CONCLUSION

Expressivism in metaethics is a tradition that seeks to replace the representationalist and cognitivist assumption common to most other metaethical viewpoints with the idea at the interface of the philosophies of language and mind that ethical sentences express nonrepresentational states of mind. There's no agreement about what this state of mind is, but it's supposed to be the sort of state of mind that might explain the distinctive motivational or action-guiding character of ethical discourse. Some candidates are emotive reactions, preferences, desires, or plans. These show up in Ayer's emotivism, Hare's prescriptivism, Blackburn's projectivism and quasi-realism, Gibbard's norm-expressivism, and a number of more recent views developed within the tradition.

In any case, the view can be motivated in several different (and compatible ways) drawing on:

- Hume's Law and open-question arguments combined with naturalism;
- motivational internalism combined with the Humean theory of motivation;
- supervenience.

Yet expressivism faces a number of serious objections, including objections about:

- disagreement
- truth-aptness
- seriousness of ethics
- semantics
- mind-independence
- motivational internalism.

These objections have forced expressivists to refine their view in several significant ways. The jury is still out on whether the refinements meet the challenges in a way that maintains the core motivations for expressivism, especially on whether the compositionality assumption at the heart of the Frege–Geach problem can be respected by expressivists.

• CHAPTER SUMMARY

- Expressivists typically encourage us to begin our metaethical enquiry by asking not about (i) the nature of some kind of supposedly real thing: ethical value, but about (ii) the nature of one of our practices: making ethical evaluations. Then, their answer to question (ii) typically claims some interesting disanalogy between ethical evaluations and representations of reality.
- If you're attracted to the naturalistic worldview, expressivism can be motivated by the thought that ethics is different than description of the natural world (this is expressed in different ways in Hume's Law and the open-question argument).
- If you're attracted to motivational internalism about ethical judgments, then expressivism can be motivated by arguing that ethical judgments play a distinctive motivational role in a Humean psychology of motivation, suggesting that they must be "desire-like" rather than "belief-like."
- The apparent supervenience of the ethical on the natural provides one further way to argue for expressivism.
- Ayer's emotivism was an early predecessor to modern expressivism; he held that ethical statements have no factual meaning and only express positive or negative sentiments, which he took to mean that they are not truth-apt and that moral philosophy and ethical disagreement is mostly empty.
- Hare argued for a more nuanced prescriptivist view which had the resources to explain some moral disagreement as disagreement in prescriptions.
- Blackburn and Gibbard have argued for even more sophisticated forms of expressivism that make sense of the seriousness of ethics and the truth-aptness of sentences that express attitudes rather than representations.
- The most famous objection to expressivism is the Frege–Geach objection. Blackburn, Gibbard, and others have developed proposals for meeting it.

• STUDY QUESTIONS

1 If the open-question argument is an argument for nonnaturalism, then how could it also support expressivism?
2 Can you think of any counter-examples to motivational internalism about ethical judgments? How do these affect the case for expressivism?
3 Do the missionary and cannibals in Hare's example mean the same thing by their words 'good'?
4 What is "Frege's Point" in the Frege–Geach problem for expressivists? Why does it cause a problem for expressivists?
5 Do expressivists agree that ethical issues are important issues and that there can be true ethical judgments?
6 Explain supervenience.
7 What's the difference between expressivism and the subjectivist view that ethical statements are about what their author likes and dislikes?

• FURTHER RESOURCES

• Bar-On, Dorit, and Sias, James. 2013. "Varieties of Expressivism," *Philosophy Compass*, 8 (8): 699–713. [Covers more forms of expressivism, also as applied in domains besides ethics.]
• Chrisman, Matthew. 2011. "Ethical Expressivism," in *The Continuum Companion to Ethics*. Continuum. [Covers more forms of expressivism.]
• Glanzberg, Michael. 2014. "Truth," *The Stanford Encyclopedia of Philosophy* (Fall 2014 Edition), Edward N. Zalta (ed.), http://plato.stanford.edu/archives/fall2014/entries/truth/. [Comprehensive discussion of many different theories of truth, including correspondence theory and minimalism.]
• Schroeder, Mark. 2010. *Noncognitivism in Ethics*. Routledge. [Provides a book-length introduction to noncognitivist views which include contemporary versions of expressivism.]

• ANSWERS TO QUESTIONS OF UNDERSTANDING

QU1: In Chapter 1 we appealed to the idea of "different directions of fit" with the world to distinguish descriptive attitudes from directive attitudes. The idea was that beliefs try to fit the way the world is (in order to be true) whereas intentions, desires, plans, etc. try to make the world (come to) fit them (in order to execute or satisfy them). Maybe there are some nonrepresentational attitudes that are not directive, but the main nonrepresentational attitudes we'll be concerned with here are directive rather than descriptive.

QU2: Describing yourself as feeling some way (e.g., as sad) expresses a belief about the way the world is, it's just that this particular way the world is involves you and your feelings. This description could also be given third-personally by someone else observing you. By contrast, expressing your feeling (e.g., your sadness) conveys it to your audience. This is something you could do with a facial gesture, a cry, or an exclamation. It is somewhat controversial what to say about explicit avows such as "I'm feeling so sad!"—do they describe oneself as feeling sad or do they express the sadness, or perhaps both?

QU3:   Issues (ii) and (iii) are plausibly factual issues, whereas issue (i) involves a moral issue about what constitutes "disrespect."

QU4:   Features (i) and (iv) are the most plausible candidates for features which we project onto reality rather than find there, although note that some philosophers would argue that even (ii) and (iii) are in some sense mind-dependent.

QU5:   It means that they are normally either true or false. Notice how the sentence "It's sunny today" is something that we can normally evaluate as being either true or false, but "Take some sunscreen!" is not something we can really claim to be true or false. (In case you're wondering, the "normally" is a hedge to allow for cases of vagueness and presupposition failure where some philosophers want to argue that the relevant statement is neither true nor false, but for different reasons and in a different way from the emotivist's claim that ethical statements are neither true nor false.)

QU6:   We'd say something like "Boo for tormenting cats!" and "Boo for getting little brother to torment cats!" Notice how the if–then sentence which follows next in the text is not so easily translated into the language of 'boo's and 'hooray's.

• WORKS CITED

Ayer, A. J. 1936/1946. *Language, Truth and Logic*. 2nd edn. London: V. Gollancz Ltd.

Blackburn, Simon. 1971. "Moral Realism." In *Morality and Moral Reasoning*, edited by J. Casey. London: Methuen.

———. 1984. *Spreading the Word: Groundings in the Philosophy of Language*. New York: Oxford University Press.

———. 1993. *Essays in Quasi-Realism*. New York: Oxford University Press.

Geach, P. T. 1965. "Assertion." *The Philosophical Review* 74 (4): 449–65.

Gibbard, Allan. 1990. *Wise Choices, Apt Feelings: A Theory of Normative Judgment*. Cambridge, MA: Harvard University Press.

Hare, R. M. 1952. *The Language of Morals*. Oxford: Oxford University Press.

Searle, John R. 1962. "Meaning and Speech Acts." *The Philosophical Review* 71 (4): 423–32.

Stevenson, Charles L. 1937. "Emotive Meaning of Moral Terms." *Mind* 46: 14–31.

4

error theory & fictionalism

So far we have discussed nonnaturalism and expressivism. If you thought that the nonnaturalist's philosophies of language and mind were on the right track but the expressivist's metaphysics was roughly right, then you might be on your way towards endorsing some kind of error theory or fictionalism. The basic idea is to agree with the nonnaturalist that basic ethical statements[1] *purport to* represent a special sort of fact that is not plausibly construed as part of the natural world, but then also to agree with the expressivist's antirealist stance towards such putative facts. This means that you think all basic ethical statements are literally false. A similar way to get to this conclusion is if you think that morality presupposes the commands of a divine being but you come to think there is no such thing as a divine being. Then you might conclude that basic ethical statements are *trying* to say something true but they systematically fail. Similarly, error-theorists about ethical discourse think there are no ethical properties and so basic ethical statements are all erroneous. That is to say, error-theorists think ethical discourse presupposes an erroneous view about what kind of facts there are. In this it's like seventeenth-century discourse about Salem witches casting spells or eighteenth-century discourse about phlogiston.

The examples of discourse about witches and phlogiston suggest that the error-theorist will adopt an eliminativist stance about ethical discourse: we should stop talking in ways that presuppose a false metaphysical view about what's real. However, a softer stance is available in fictionalism, which has been imported from the philosophy of mathematics (and also applied in other areas). In metaethics, the core idea is to argue that basic ethical sentences are literally false but also that ethical discourse should be interpreted on the model of a **convenient fiction**. For example, one might think that the sun doesn't literally rise over the horizon and objects moving down an inclined plane never do so frictionlessly; but it is still convenient for many purposes to talk as if these things are true. In effect, discourse about these things may contain a lot of literally false sentences but as long as we realize this, it can be convenient for various purposes to pretend these sentences are true. Metaethical fictionalists think something similar about ethical discourse.[2]

> ***Key Point***: Error-theorists and fictionalists in metaethics agree with realists that ethical thought is cognitive and ethical language is representational, but they argue that it never succeeds in correctly describing reality and so is erroneous or part of a false but convenient fiction.

In this chapter, I'll introduce some famous arguments for error theory due to J. L. Mackie and consider some possible objections. Then I'll canvass some different forms of fictionalism, explaining why their proponents think they are better than eliminativist forms of error theory and how proponents of other metaethical views might object to them.

• MACKIE'S ARGUMENTS FOR ERROR THEORY

Any error theory must have two parts:

1 A positive conceptual/semantic claim: ethical discourse purports to be about objective ethical values or facts.
2 A negative metaphysical claim: objective ethical values or facts don't exist or obtain.

> QU1: Which of the following is a positive conceptual/semantic claim about mathematics: (i) there are no numbers, (ii) mathematics is a merely symbolic exercise not even trying to represent objective facts?

Philosophers such as Plato (via Thrasymachus in *Republic I*) and Nietzsche introduced error-theoretic ideas about morality, but Mackie is widely credited with providing a contemporary and systematic defence of the view in the first chapter of his book *Ethics: Inventing Right and Wrong* (1977). He provides several arguments but separates them under two headings: the **argument from relativity**, the **argument from queerness**.

The argument from relativity proceeds from the observation that there is widespread ethical disagreement around the world. For example, in some cultures, one must bury the dead, in others the dead are burned. Some cultures require women to wear headscarfs in public, others forbid it in certain professional contexts. Mackie claims that the best explanation of this variation of ethical opinion is that people participate in different ways of life; and they tend to approve of those ways of life in which they participate. If this is right, then it would seem that people disagree about ethics not because one culture is getting it right and others are getting it wrong, rather the disagreement is simply a manifestation of different cultural norms.

By itself, however, this argument doesn't establish the error theory. This is because— even if we agree that it is sound—it only supports the negative metaphysical claim, not the positive conceptual/semantic claim needed for an error theory. To see this, notice that expressivists such as Ayer could agree that people disagree about ethics not because one culture is getting it right and others are getting it wrong, rather the disagreement is simply a manifestation of different cultural norms. But they would argue that ethical discourse doesn't even purport to be about objective ethical values or facts, but rather is an expression of our commitment to our own values. Moreover, as we'll see in the following chapter, some naturalists in metaethics argue that there are ethical facts but they are facts about the customs and practices in different cultures, which means that they are relative not objective. Such a relativist could agree with Mackie's argument from relativity. Because expressivism and relativism are equally natural responses to Mackie's argument for relativity, in the discussion about error theory, his second argument—the argument from queerness—has received much more attention.

There are several versions of the argument we might glean from Mackie's text. They all begin by arguing for the positive conceptual/semantic claim mentioned above— viz. that ethical discourse purports to be about objective ethical values or facts. Here's roughly how the argument goes:

First, Mackie suggests that commonsense morality presupposes that ethical values are **intrinsically motivating** in the sense that someone recognizing that an action is good/bad would be drawn towards doing/avoiding it. That is to say, we do things to promote the good and avoid the bad—at least in part—*because* we know they are good/bad and not because of some antecedent desire we happen to have (e.g., to be seen in a certain light by our community or to be in a position to claim moral superiority over others). (This is related to the motivational internalist view I introduced in Chapter 1.)

Second, Mackie suggests that commonsense morality presupposes that ethical facts are **objectively prescriptive** in the sense that they generate universal reasons for people to do things, reasons which are independent of people's particular desires, cares, or concerns. For example, many people agree that torture is bad, and not just bad for satisfying someone's desires or concerns, but *really* bad irrespective of people's particular desires, cares, or concerns. In this case, for example, Mackie would suggest that we are presupposing that the badness of torture gives everyone an objective reason for action (of e.g., not torturing, preventing others from torturing) and not just a reason that is relative to this or that contingent set of desires, cares, or concerns. (This is related to the externalist thesis about justifying reasons that I introduced in Chapter 1; and it will be relevant for understanding relativist forms of naturalist realism that I will discuss in Chapter 5.)[3]

Those two claims pertain to the positive conceptual part of Mackie's error theory. Next, he turns to the negative metaphysical part of the theory, arguing that careful reflection reveals that there aren't facts that could intrinsically motivate and/or objectively prescribe. One reason he gives for this is epistemological in character. He thinks that if there were such facts and sometimes we know them, then we would have to possess a special faculty by which we come to perceive/recognize them—what Moore called the "faculty of moral intuition." But Mackie thought it was very implausible that we have such a faculty: it'd be nothing like vision, hearing, smell, or even our faculty of reason. This doesn't show that there are no ethical facts, but it puts the burden of proof on someone who claims that there are such facts. Another reason he gives for doubting the existence of ethical facts is metaphysical in character. He thinks that if there were intrinsically motivating and/or objectively prescriptive facts, then they would be wholly unlike any other kind of fact whose existence we recognize. As he puts it, objective values would have to have "to be doneness" built into them, but in light of our modern scientific worldview we should view that putative feature of reality as "queer."

QU2: What gives Mackie's first reason an "epistemological" character and his second reason a "metaphysical" character?

A final reason he gives for thinking would-be objective ethical facts are queer is based on the concept of supervenience, which we encountered in the previous chapter. Like many other metaethicists, Mackie assumes that ethical value (were it to exist) would as a matter of necessity have to be distinct from but supervene on the natural features of an action. Recall the intuition that there could be no *mere* difference between the value of two actions; to differ in their ethical properties, there would have to be some underlying difference in their natural properties. However, Mackie thought it would be a very queer fact that could be distinct from the natural and yet necessarily supervene on it. (This is essentially the objection from supervenience against nonnaturalism we encountered in Chapter 2.)

• OBJECTIONS AND REPLIES

There are not many philosophers who agree with the error theory. The simplest and perhaps most pervasive reason for this is that they are strongly convinced of their mostly deeply held ethical beliefs—e.g., that genocide is wrong, that charity is good, etc. and the error-theorist's position seems to imply that these beliefs are all false because based on a metaphysical error. Surely, one might think, no theoretical argument in metaethics could convince us that genocide is not wrong or that charity is not good! (This is similar to the Moorean response to radical external world skepticism: surely, no theoretical argument in epistemology could convince us that we know *nothing* of what we think we know about reality!)

It's important, however, to avoid a common mistake. True, error-theorists deny that genocide is objectively wrong and that charity is objectively good, but they also don't think that genocide is objectively *right* or that charity is objectively *bad*. That's because they deny that any actions have any such basic ethical properties whatsoever.

Moreover, they typically share our moral sensibilities. That is, they find genocide abhorrent, charity laudable, etc. They are not amoral; and they are generally no more immoral than the rest of us. So, we shouldn't confuse our feelings about things like genocide and charity with reasons to disagree with the error theory.

Nevertheless, the error-theorist's position can seem to do violence to ordinary discourse. Just as much as we talk as if statements about the external world are often true, we talk as if statements about morality are often true. And many philosophers think we should theorize under a **principle of charity**, which suggests that we should start out from the assumption that most of what people assert is true, and if it seems as if someone is making lots of false assertions, then we should reconsider whether we properly understand the meaning of what they are saying. Error-theorists think that ethical statements purport to be about facts that are intrinsically motivating for those who recognize them and objectively prescriptive for all of us. But if that means that lots of what we assert is false, then perhaps error-theorists should reconsider their interpretation of what ethical statements purport to be about.

Mackie has two avenues for responding to this worry. First, he (or at least a sympathetic interpreter[4]) might argue that in his view it's not ordinary ethical statements that come out false but the presupposition they commonly carry, viz. that ethical values are intrinsically motivating and objectively prescriptive. It's a vexed issue in the philosophy of language whether statements with a false presupposition should be counted as false, truth-value-less, or just odd. So if Mackie insisted on this, it would avoid him counting most of what people say when engaged in ethical discourse as false (though he'd still be committed to its manifesting some kind of pernicious ontological error). Second, in Mackie's book he argues that there's a very good reason that we tend to objectify our ethical values. Those values aren't whimsical preferences but rather commitments around which we try to coordinate our behavior in community with other people. As such, there is a strong practical motive for speaking and thinking as if there really are objective ethical facts: that's the best way to achieve coordination with one another around our ethical principles. Here, the idea behind his argument from relativity might be thought to help. Part of the reason we want there to be objectively right answers about matters of ethical controversy is precisely that there is disagreement and this disagreement matters for how we live with one another. Still, we may worry that this cuts both ways. Insofar as one recognizes the variability of ethical views across the world and the intractability of many disputes about those views, wouldn't one be inclined to reconsider whether those views are really about some objective realm of facts which (if we could only ascertain them) would settle the disputes once and for all?

A more specific way to challenge the error theory is to object to the idea that recognizing an action as good/bad would be intrinsically motivating. Recall that this is part of Mackie's positive conceptual/semantic claim about what ordinary ethical discourse presupposes. However, it is not obviously true. As we saw in Chapter 2, some philosophers deny motivational internalism, arguing that at least some ethical judgments are compatible with no particular motivational propensities. For instance, when we make ethical judgments about things that don't seem particularly connected to our actions, it is less intuitive to think that those judgments necessarily motivate us to act in particular ways. Assume, for example, that you know that it was wrong for Germany to invade the Soviet Union in 1941. Does that mean that you are motivated to act in any particular way? There isn't anything you can do about that now, and it's not like you are going to be in the position of Germany. Why do you think such ethical knowledge would have to be intrinsically motivating?

There are two responses available for error-theorists. First, they could argue that even if it's only the relatively small class of ethical judgments about our own potential future actions that are presumed to be intrinsically motivating by commonsense morality, that's still a commitment that has queer consequences for metaphysics. Second, they could argue that Mackie was wrong to include the assumption that ethical values would have to be intrinsically motivating as a presupposition of ethical discourse, but that still leaves objective prescriptivity, which is more plausibly construed as a presupposition of ordinary ethical discourse.

Recall that "objective prescriptivity" referred to the idea that ethical facts (if any actually obtain) would provide objective reasons for people to do things, i.e. that are independent of those people's particular desires, cares, and concerns. Mackie's idea that there couldn't be such things is related to the internalist view about reasons we discussed in Chapter 1. Indeed, although he doesn't give it a name, Mackie appears to accept this view. After all, part of his argument for saying that ethical facts would be queer, were they to exist, is that they would have to have the power to generate reasons to act which are not connected to our desires, cares, and concerns. But there's a different conclusion we might draw: that all of this just shows that morality is not objectively prescriptive. Maybe each of us has our own personal cares and concerns, but there are some very general principles that are such that, if we all aim to live by them, we will each do a better job promoting our own personal cares and concerns. If that were so, morality might be grounded in each of us having personal cares and concerns that are structured such that we all need to follow some moral principles to promote those cares and concerns. In this way, morality might still count as *universal* in the sense that it generates the same reasons for everyone. However, as long as the reason-giving power of ethical facts depended on people's desires, cares, and concerns, we wouldn't have to say that there was "to-be doneness" somehow contained in the facts themselves. These facts would generate reasons for each of us to do things because of how they connect with our personal desires, cares, and concerns.

> QU3: Which kind of "internalism" is related to "objective prescriptivity" and which is related to "intrinsically motivating"?

I want to mention one last way some have objected to the error theory. Recall that Mackie gives epistemological and metaphysical reasons for thinking that objective ethical values and facts, were they to exist, would be queer. There is a response to both of these sometimes called the **partners-in-crime response**. The idea is to point out that there are other kinds of things that we commonly take ourselves to know, and these raise exactly the same worries: if raising these worries is a philosophical "crime", they are partners in the crime. If this is right, it generates a dilemma for error-theorists. Either they have to extend the error theory to the other kinds of things too, or they have to abandon their error theory about ethical facts.

A common partner is mathematical facts. For example, Mackie argues that in order to know ethical values and facts, we'd have to have some special faculty for discovering them. But you might say the same thing about knowing facts of arithmetic, geometry, and calculus. These, it seems, aren't known through vision, hearing, smell, etc. It's unclear how they're known, but we ordinarily assume that there is some way to come to know these facts. Moreover, mathematical facts, if there are indeed such, have somewhat weird features. For example, they're abstract not concrete. And they would seem to hold of necessity. One might think these features are just as "queer" as to-be-doneness. Do error-theorists want to throw out mathematics with morality? Usually not, which means that they owe us an account of mathematical facts and knowledge that shows them not to be partners in the crime of which they charge morality.

Another way to pursue the partners-in-crime response would be by highlighting the distinction between *ethical* reasons and values, and other sorts of reasons and values. For example, we commonly assume that there can be objective reasons to *believe* something and that it's intellectually valuable to know and understand things. These are *epistemic* facts and values: does the error-theorist want to deny their existence as well? If so, it seems that he'd be paradoxically committed to denying the existence of objective reasons for believing his theory and denying the value of knowing and understanding things about the epistemology and ontology of ethics!

• VERSIONS OF FICTIONALISM

In metaethics, fictionalism emerged as a view inspired by error theory but with somewhat more sophisticated resources for avoiding some of the extreme consequences of error theory. To understand different versions of fictionalism it is helpful to distinguish declarative sentences (the words themselves) from their use to make assertions. Consider, for instance, the sentence:

(1)   Holmes lives on Baker Street.

Suppose first that you really know someone named Holmes, and I ask you where he lives; you might use (1) in order to assert that the person you know lives on Baker Street. And if we assume that you are being sincere, then that assertion expresses your belief that Holmes lives on Baker street. Next, however, suppose that we are in an English seminar discussing the works of Arthur Conan Doyle, and I ask you where his main character lives. In this case you might also use (1), but now it is less clear what you are doing. Here are two possibilities: (i) you are asserting that *in the fiction of Doyle's stories* the character called Holmes lives on Baker Street; and assuming that you are being sincere, that assertion expresses your belief that, in the fiction, this character lives on that street; (ii) your utterance shouldn't be interpreted as an assertion at all but rather as a different kind of speech-act of "talking within a fictional context" or engaging in "pretense" of some sort.[5] On the first possibility, the idea is that the sentence you have explicitly uttered is somehow incomplete or elliptical for what you're actually asserting. It's similar to when one says "it's raining" but means that it is raining in the place where they are located. On the second possibility, the idea is to take the sentence at face value but construe the speech-act of using the sentence as doing something other than asserting. It's similar to when someone says something like "I'm so hungry I could eat a horse." They're not really asserting that they could eat a horse; rather they're doing something else (exaggerating for effect).

These two possibilities correspond to two different fictionalist positions one could take up in metaethics. Some fictionalists argue that the relevant uses of ethical sentences are assertions about what's true *in a fiction*; others argue that these utterances shouldn't be interpreted as assertions at all but rather pieces of pretense. To appreciate the difference, consider the sentence:

(2)   Lying is wrong.

Imagine someone uses (2) in a ethical context, for example while explaining to a child why they shouldn't lie. The first kind of fictionalists, who we could refer to as **meaning fictionalists** hold that the meaning of this statement is more complex than the surface sentence would suggest. They think the person using it has asserted that, according to the fiction of morality, lying is wrong. So, while the sentence on the page is literally false, the asserted content is true; the beliefs expressed by typical utterances of that sentence are true (because they are implicitly about a fiction). The second kind of fictionalists, who we could refer to as **speech-act fictionalists** would hold that this statement is not appropriately interpreted as an assertion at all. Rather it is some other kind of speech-act, such as pretense or make-believe. On this view, someone who says (2) has said something literally false but they have not *asserted* a falsehood because they haven't asserted anything at all. Rather, they have engaged in a pretense.

> QU4: Consider the statement "The sun rises in the morning." What's the difference between meaning fictionalism and speech-act fictionalism about this statement?

Notice how both forms of fictionalism offer ways to respect the principle of charity that seemed to be violated by the error theory. Because fictionalists agree that there aren't really any ethical values or facts, they think basic ethical sentences such as (2) are literally false. However, rather than charging that most of what ordinary people assert about morality is false, fictionalists propose a more nuanced interpretation of ethical discourse. Meaning fictionalists suggest that the propositions we are asserting are more complicated (in being tacitly relativized to a fiction) than the surface sentences suggest. Speech-act fictionalists suggest that we aren't really asserting propositions, but rather pretending.

> ***Key Point***: Like error-theorists, fictionalists hold that basic ethical sentences are literally false (because there are no ethical facts to make them true). However, unlike error-theorists, fictionalists think that ordinary ethical discourse is in order: those sentences aren't used to assert false propositions but rather to do something else (assert more complex true propositions or engage in a form of pretense).

One serious challenge for meaning fictionalists is that it seems ad hoc and counter-intuitive to say that someone who uses (2) to make a statement in a moral context has asserted something about a fiction. This is because there doesn't seem to be any basis for thinking normal users of this sentence are talking about fictions (except, perhaps, for the theoretically self-serving reason of salvaging something like the error theory in light of the principle of charity). After all, unlike the statements about where Holmes lives, most people who make ethical statements don't take themselves to be asserting things about some fiction. Moreover, it is highly unclear which fiction we should say they are asserting things about—there are many possible moralities.

Because of this, speech-act fictionalism is perhaps better represented among meta-ethicsts today. Kalderon (2005) develops a version of this which promises also to be able to capture some of the intuitive attraction of the expressivist idea that ethical statements function to express positive and negative attitudes in the attempt to coordinate our emotional responses to the world with our community. In the characterization above, I said that speech-act fictionalists hold that ethical statements aren't assertions, and so they are not the expression of beliefs but rather pieces of pretense. So far that's mostly negative and vague. It doesn't yet tell us what ethical statements do express if they don't express beliefs. Kalderon argues that although ethical *sentences* are representational and so truth-apt in a perfectly robust sense, the standard use of them to perform a *speech-act* is expressive rather than representational. That is, much like the expressivists, he thinks ethical statements express positive and negative attitudes. If this is right, then he has just as good an explanation as the expressivist of the apparently tight connection between accepting an ethical statement and motivation to act (however tight this turns out to be, which may not be perfectly tight).

One thing to think about, however, is how plausible it is to claim that we express these attitudes by systematically uttering falsehoods. When it comes to other paradigmatically fictional discourses, we can imagine someone interrupting and saying, "Wait, the sentence you uttered is literally false. You don't mean that Holmes *really* lives on Baker Street, do you?" and this being followed by an impatient "No, I mean to be speaking from within the fiction; we're just pretending." But now imagine someone interrupted a piece of ethical discourse saying, "Wait, the sentence you just uttered is literally false. You don't mean that genocide is *really* wrong, do you?" Many people would be inclined to respond, "Yes, indeed, that's what I mean."

• CONCLUSION

Error theorists in metaethics defend two connected claims: (i) a positive conceptual/semantic claim about ethical discourse to the effect that its sentences represent facts with special features such as involving intrinsically motivating values and/or objectively prescriptive facts, (ii) a negative metaphysical claim to the effect that such things don't really exist. In this error-theorists agree with the semantics of nonnaturalism but the metaphysics of expressivism. The most prominent arguments for the error theory come in the various versions of what Mackie called the "argument from queerness." However, many philosophers have felt that something must be wrong about Mackie's error theory, because it so drastically violates the principle of charity.

A way to avoid violating the principle of charity while still endorsing (i) and (ii) is to take a fictionalist rather than eliminativist stance towards ethical discourse. Meaning fictionalists argue that, although ethical sentences are literally false, what people mean when using them to make assertions is something more complicated about the fiction of morality. Speech-act fictionalists, by contrast, argue that ordinary use of ethical sentences is not assertoric but rather a kind of pretense, perhaps one by which we express our moral attitudes. Even if some version of fictionalism can better respect the principle of charity than eliminativist forms of the error theory, we may still worry that they don't do a very good job respecting our ordinary self-conception of what we are up to when we engage in ethical discourse.

• CHAPTER SUMMARY

- Error-theorists and fictionalists defend two claims: a positive conceptual/semantic claim and a negative metaphysical claim.
- Mackie famously offered the "argument from relativity" and the "argument from queerness" for the error theory.
- There are epistemological and metaphysical versions of the argument from queerness.
- Mackie's error theory is based on the conceptual claim that ethical discourse is about intrinsically motivating values and objectively prescriptive facts, but both of these are controversial ideas that opponents of the error theory might argue against.
- Even if one endorses the two claims of an ethical error theory, one needn't take an eliminativist stance towards ethical discourse; this is because one can develop some form of fictionalism.

- Two forms of fictionalism are meaning fictionalism and speech-act fictionalism. The former says that ethical statements are assertions about what's true in the fiction of morality. The latter says that moral statements aren't assertions at all, but rather forms of pretense.

• STUDY QUESTIONS

1 Explain Mackie's argument from relativity. Why doesn't this fully support error theory?
2 What's the difference between the epistemological and metaphysical versions of Mackie's argument from queerness?
3 What is "objective to-be-doneness" and why would someone call it "queer"?
4 How is the argument from queerness related to the argument for expressivism from naturalism and Hume's Law?
5 What is the difference between eliminativism and fictionalism in the context of metaethical error theory?
6 Which better respects the principle of charity, meaning fictionalism or speech-act fictionalism?

• FURTHER RESOURCES

- Joyce, Richard. 2009. "Moral Anti-Realism," *The Stanford Encyclopedia of Philosophy* (Summer 2009 Edition), Edward N. Zalta, (ed.), http://plato.stanford.edu/archives/sum2009/entries/moral-anti-realism. [Contains a significant section on error theory, including a supplement discussing the particulars of Mackie's arguments for error theory.]
- Joyce, Richard. 2013. "Error Theory," in LaFollette, H. (ed.), *The International Encyclopedia of Ethics*. Blackwell: 1709–1716. [Concise explanation of moral error theory.]
- Kalderon, Mark. 2005. *Moral Fictionalism*. Oxford University Press. [Monograph-length development of speech-act fictionalism.]
- Mabrito, Robert. 2013. "Fictionalism, Moral," in LaFollette, H. (ed.), *The International Encyclopedia of Ethics*. Blackwell: 1972–1981. [Concise explanation of moral fictionalism, including a discussion of revolutionary fictionalism.]
- Olson, Jonas. 2011. "In Defense of Moral Error Theory," in Brady, M. (ed.), *New Waves in Metaethics*. Palgrave Macmillan: 62–84. [A careful study of several arguments in favor of moral error theory.]

• ANSWERS TO QUESTIONS OF UNDERSTANDING

QU1: (ii) is the conceptual/semantic claim as it's about mathematical thought and discourse rather than (directly) about what is real.

QU2: The first reason is about what it would take to *know* ethical facts, and epistemology is about knowledge. The second reason is about what ethical facts would have to be like, and metaphysics is about what various pieces of reality are like.

QU3: Internalism about justifying reasons is a thesis about what it takes for morality to generate reasons for people (it must connect to their cares and concerns), and so it is related to "objective prescriptivity." More specifically, if internalism about justifying reasons is true, it's difficult (though perhaps not impossible) to see how there could be objectively prescriptive facts. By contrast, motivational internalism is a thesis about the psychological role of ethical judgments. For ethical facts (assuming there are any) to be "intrinsically motivating," our belief in them would have to have the power to motivate action independently of any desires we have.

QU4: The meaning fictionalist thinks the actual sentence used is incomplete and so literally false, but the use of this sentence to make a statement should be seen as an assertion of some more complex proposition, such as that the sun rises in the morning *in the fiction*. This proposition is true. By contrast, the speech-act fictionalist denies that this statement is an assertion of any proposition; instead she thinks it is some other kind of speech-act, such as *pretending*.

• WORKS CITED

Joyce, Richard. 2001. *The Myth of Morality*. Cambridge: Cambridge University Press.
Kalderon, Mark. 2005. *Moral Fictionalism*. Oxford: Oxford University Press.
Mackie, J. L. 1977. *Ethics: Inventing Right and Wrong*. London: Penguin.
Stanley, Jason. 2001. "Hermenuetic Fictionalism." *Midwest Studies in Philosophy* 25 (1): 36–71.

• NOTES

1 This reference to *basic* ethical statements is meant to avoid a complication in talking about ethical statements quite generally, i.e. to include logically complex ethical statements. If "Murder is wrong" is a basic statement, then "Murder is *not* wrong" and "Murder is good *or* bad" are non-basic statements because of the presence of logical words such as 'not' and 'or.' Error-theorists and fictionalists typically don't claim that statements such as "Murder is not good" are false. This is not because they think murder *is* good but because they think *nothing* is good or bad. Similarly, they won't say that a statement such as "If murder is bad, then charity is good" is false, but that's again because they think nothing is good or bad.

2 A distinction is sometimes drawn between "hermeneutic" and "revolutionary" forms of fictionalism (Stanley, 2001), where the former is part of a descriptive project of explaining what some area of discourse is actually like and the latter is part of a normative project of explaining how we should alter or change our use of some area of discourse. So, you might think that ethical discourse isn't actually understood as convenient fiction but that it should be, in which case you'd be a revolutionary fictionalist. In this chapter, I ignore revolutionary fictionalism. This is because it does not directly compete with the other main metaethical views, which are all parts of the descriptive project of trying to explain what ethical discourse (and thought, and reality) are like. For a sustained defense of revolutionary fictionalism and discussion of related issues, see Joyce (2001).

3 Although Mackie thought both the intrinsic motivational character and the objectively prescriptive character of ethical discourse are features of the commonsensical conception of morality,

it's useful to distinguish them because we'll see below that it's controversial whether ethical discourse presupposes that ethical facts (if there are any) would be intrinsically motivating for those who recognize them. And it's also controversial whether ethical discourse presupposes that ethical values are objectively prescriptive for all of us. However, if just one of these characterizations of the presuppositions of ordinary ethical discourse is correct, then it puts an error-theorist in a position to argue for the negative metaphysical part of his error theory.

4 Selim Berker convinced me this is a possible interpretation of Mackie's text.

5 It's important to note that the idea in calling this "pretense" is not that you are *intentionally* pretending but rather that the language you are using isn't to be taken as literally asserting something. Compare an ordinary use of the sentence "The sun rose at 5am." Plausibly, for anyone who knows that the location of the sun in the sky is caused by the earth's rotation rather than the sun's levitation, a use of this sentence isn't appropriately treated as an assertion but rather as a kind of pretense or loose speak. However, we needn't think such people are intentionally pretending.

5
˙naturalism

All of the views we have discussed so far[1] accept the following claim:

(C)   If reality includes ethical facts, then they are not purely natural facts.

Nonnaturalists move from left to right: accepting that reality includes ethical facts, they try to figure out how to characterize them as nonnatural. By contrast, expressivists, error-theorists, and fictionalists move from right to left: being skeptical of facts that cannot be characterized in purely natural terms, they try to make sense of the idea that a full and complete metaphysical characterization of reality might in the end not mention ethical facts. But what if (C) is false? In Chapter 2, we canvassed arguments for thinking that ethical facts, were they to really obtain, would have to be nonnatural; and you'll recall that these arguments aren't airtight. So, perhaps we should consider the possibility that reality includes ethical facts *and they are natural*.

Ethical naturalism is the view that reality includes ethical facts and they are reducible to or otherwise can be made to fit within the facts we regard as natural. Different versions of ethical naturalism are distinguished by different strategies for explaining how ethical facts might in this sense be natural. Many philosophers think it would be nice if one of these strategies work, since we could then embrace a cognitivist conception of ethical thought in our philosophy of mind that makes it easy to understand why we commonly speak of ethical beliefs and ethical knowledge. We could also embrace a representationalist conception of ethical language, which coheres well with the way ethical sentences seem to work semantically more-or-less like ordinary descriptive sentences. Moreover, we wouldn't have to secure these views by recognizing nonnatural facts in our metaphysics. Indeed, ethical naturalism holds out the prospect of conceiving of ethical knowledge as just one more species of our knowledge of the natural world.

The key for any form of ethical naturalism is to develop a plausible explanation of why ethical facts are a species of *natural* facts. Unfortunately, as we discovered in Chapter 2, there is no uncontroversial characterization of what it takes for something to be *natural*. Nevertheless, nonnaturalists argued that ethical facts don't fit with other recognizably natural facts, such as physical, biological, psychological, etc.

facts in our conception of reality. So the main challenge for ethical naturalists is to convince us that this claim is false. In this chapter, we'll consider four strategies for doing so. The first challenges our previous assumptions about what counts as *natural*. The second challenges our previous assumptions about what it takes for there to be facts obtaining *objectively*. And the third and fourth argue for a new way of *reducing* ethical facts to facts discoverable by empirical science such as physics and chemistry.

Key Point: Metaethical naturalists are realists who think ethical facts are not "autonomous" from other natural facts but can be reduced to or otherwise made to fit with the sorts of facts we regard as making up the natural world.

• NEO-ARISTOTELIAN NATURALISM

Although we haven't been able to define what it is for a fact to count as natural, we have been working with the assumption that these are the sorts of facts discoverable by scientific methods as exemplified most clearly in modern physics and chemistry. However, there is a tradition stemming from Aristotle that places considerable weight on the idea that there is a further sort of natural fact, one which often requires significant metaphysical reflection to discover. This further sort is facts about things' **natures**. For example, we speak about "human nature." We also speak about "what's natural for x," where x picks out some species or natural grouping of beings; e.g. "Rough skin is natural for the common toad."[2]

The important idea in the present context is that these *natures* so-conceived are supposed to be *natural*, which means that facts about them are natural facts. If that's right and it's possible to derive significant ethical conclusions from facts about human nature, then ethical facts will begin to look like a species of natural fact. They won't be "natural" in the sense of discoverable by recognizably natural sciences such as physics and chemistry. But they'll still count as "natural" under a somewhat broader conception of the natural.

So, let's accept for the moment that facts about things' natures are natural facts. How do we get from there to locating ethical facts within the natural world? There are two related ideas that help to make this connection.

The first idea comes from Geach (1956), who famously distinguished between **attributive adjectives** and **predicative adjectives**. The distinction is best understood through the test he proposed. Geach asked us to consider phrases of the form "is an A B," where A is an adjective such as 'red' or 'big' and B is a noun like 'book' or 'flea.' When an instance of this formula can be split into "is A and is a B" without changing meaning, Geach refers to the use of A as *predicative*. The idea is that, in these cases, saying that something is an A B amounts to predicating A of it (and predicating B of it). By contrast, when you cannot split up the predicate in this way, Geach refers to the use of A as *attributive*. The idea is that, in these cases, saying that something is an A B amounts to qualifying one's use of B by A. In his example, "is a red book" predicates being red (and being a book) and so is predicative. However, "is a big flea" does not predicate being big (full stop) but only being big compared to other fleas.

QU1: Which of the following are attributive uses of an adjective: (i) a flat desk, (ii) a harmful comment, (iii) a laughing child, (iv) a costly meal?

Now, to see how this is relevant to metaethics, consider our previous question about the meaning of 'good.' Following Moore, we asked "What does 'good' mean?" and considered answers such as that it refers to a simple and irreducible nonnatural property. That means that, in seeking to answer that question, we were tacitly assuming that 'good' is a predicative adjective. We were, that is, asking what is meant when we say that something is *good*. But Geach wondered: what if it doesn't really make sense to ask if something is good (full stop); what if 'good' is an attributive adjective rather than a predicative adjective? More precisely, Geach argues that a lot of metaethics done in the wake of Moore made precisely this mistake. His idea was that a lot of the debate about what it is for something to be good (full stop) is misguided much like debate about what it is for something to be big (full stop) would be. We can of course sensibly ask what it is for something to be big or good *for an x* (e.g., flea, city, negative number, galaxy, philosophy department…). But Geach thought it was nonsense to ask what it is for something to be (simply) good.

His positive suggestion was that metaethicists should focus instead on what it is for someone to be a good *person*, and this will have something to do with what makes someone a good instance of the kind *human being*. But how do we go about identifying the attributes that make something a good instance of its kind, e.g., a good human being? Here is the second important idea: we can identify these by appealing to functions or (what is very similar) characteristic ways of living.

To see what this means, consider first the kinds of things we can easily define by appeal to their function (what are sometimes called **functional kinds**). For example, a knife is (more or less, by definition) something that's for cutting. Famously, Aristotle argued that, for things with a function, we can identify properties that make them a good instance of their kind by thinking about what would help them to perform their function well. Of course, not just anything that can be used to cut is a knife (random shards of glass can also cut); but with a knife, we can say that having the function of cutting is part of what it is to be a knife—part of its "nature." So a good knife will be one that cuts well. (Contrast: a shard of glass may cut well, but that doesn't seem to make it a good shard of glass.)

QU2: Which of the following are functional kinds: (i) car, (ii) moon, (iii) lamp, (iv) human being?

Given this, we can then ask which property of a knife would help it to cut well? (Ignoring the complication that different knives are for cutting different kinds of things in different circumstances), in general, it's something like *being sharp*. Hence, we might say that sharpness is a property that makes a knife a *good* knife. And voilà, from considerations about something's nature, we have reached a conclusion about what makes it a *good* instance of its kind.

> QU3: What are the features that make the following functional kinds good instances of their kinds: (i) shoes, (ii) power drill, (iii) textbook?

But there's a large gap between the nature of things like knives and *human* nature. Knives are pretty clearly for cutting, but what are humans for? It is not obvious how to answer this question. To see how we might close that gap, it's helpful to consider the natures of plants and animals first. It's controversial whether living things such as plants and animals have functions (things they are for), but we might view them as having something similar: **characteristic ways of living**, which can be more and less fully realized much like (though in a more complicated way than) knives can be more and less good for cutting.

It's controversial whether it makes complete sense that something's characteristic way of living generates standards for what counts as it living well. For it can be much harder to determine something's characteristic way of living. Aristotle's idea seems to have been inspired by the division of labor outlined in Plato's description of the ideal city, so another way to think about "characteristic ways of living" might be in terms of one's *job* or *role* in a group.

In any case, if we accept that living things have characteristic ways of living, then, following Aristotle, we seem to be in a position to identify the properties that make plants and animals good instances of their kind. These will be the properties that help them to realize the characteristic way of living for their kind of being. For example, oak trees characteristically grow to 65–130 feet. So the properties that make a particular plant a good oak tree are (among other things) the ones that help it to grow to 65–130 feet, e.g., a strong root system, leaves that are resistant to parasites, etc. (Note these properties are not identified as the properties that make a particular oak tree *good for* any particular human purpose, such as having a shaded yard, but rather as the properties that make it *good at* realizing the oak tree's characteristic way of living, or its "role" in the forest.)

Similarly for animals: the angelfish normally hides alongside a vertical rock face in order to avoid predators and ambush prey. So the properties that make a particular angelfish a good angelfish are (among other things) the ones that help it to hide alongside a vertical rock face, e.g., being thin and striped in colors like plants that grow up rocks. (Again, note these properties don't have anything specifically to do with human purposes for an angelfish, such as having beautiful fauna in one's aquarium; what matters are the properties that aid in achieving the organism's characteristic way of living.)

So we might say that the properties of being a good oak tree or being a good angelfish are constituted by a complex set of properties such as having a strong root system, having leaves that are resistant to parasites (in the first case) and being thin and striped in colors like plants that grow up rocks (in the second case). These, note, needn't be *statistically* common features in order to count as elements of the "characteristic" way of living. In some species, it may be only a select few who grow old enough to live in the characteristic way. Still, as long as we can reasonably identify a characteristic way of living for some living being, there will be properties that help it to realize this; and these will count as what makes something a good instance of the species.

The important point about these examples for metaethical naturalism is that it's plausible to think that these properties are *natural* properties; however, they might be thought to imply normative facts: how oak trees and angelfish *should* be. Going down this route promises a new way to show such 'should's to be about natural facts.

> QU4: How would a Neo-Aristotelian derive facts about how dairy cows should be?

Surely, however, the should-facts about oak trees and angelfish are not *ethical* facts. **Neo-Aristotelians** such as Hursthouse (1999) and Foot (1999) have argued that, whether or not we're inclined to count facts about how plants and animals should be as ethical facts, we can extend the basic framework to humans and then use reflection on *human* nature to determine how humans should be. This extension will give us purchase on a kind of *normative* facts, which are natural. Then from this we might derive facts about what actions are right and wrong. And these will begin to look much more like ethical facts.

Initially, though, that seems wrong. Humans are, of course, animals of a particular species, and we can grant this means that there are ways humans should be, so to speak, *biologically*. For example, humans should *biologically* have fully opposable thumbs; having these is a feature that helps us to realize the characteristically human way of living. Maybe this even implies that there is a right way for humans to do things like hold a hammer. But these facts, which we can grant to be natural because biological, are hardly *ethical* facts. So, if all we get are biological should-facts about humans, the Neo-Aristotelians haven't yet shown ethical facts to be natural facts (or how to derive ethical conclusions from facts about our natures).

Neo-Aristotelians are aware of this challenge, and they develop different ways of addressing it, deriving from considerations such as the positions of humans in complex social networks, our ability to engage in reflective thought, and the capacity we have to feel particular sorts of emotions. The details are somewhat complicated, and it is beyond the scope of this book to consider which of these routes is the most promising way to develop a Neo-Aristotelian view.

However, I do want to mention one important idea developed by Hursthouse and consider some of the challenges it faces, in order to give you a sense of how debate about a particular metaethical position might go. Hursthouse's idea is that *rationality* is an especially important feature of human nature. It gives us the ability to act from reasons rather than impulse. It also puts us in a position to reflectively endorse or disavow other features of our natures, in effect letting us choose the type of person we want to be. Accordingly, Hursthouse argues that some of the ways humans should be are special. She privileges those ways humans should be that derive from our capacity to be rational. While still belonging to the class of properties that help us to realize ways of living characteristic of human beings, these properties are not, in her view, merely biologically good-making features of a human being. They are *ethically* good-making features of a human being: what we might reasonably call **ethical virtues**. From the ethical virtues, Hursthouse proposes to derive facts about what actions are ethically right and wrong in various circumstances. To make a long story short, she does this by appeal to what the virtuous person would characteristically do in those circumstances.

Some will worry that the very specialness of rationality undermines any claim Hursthouse might have had to be an ethical *naturalist*. After all, we might grant that the ability to act from reasons distinguishes humans from other animals, but so do many other abilities and tendencies. From a biological, ethological, or even sociological point of view it is not clear why we should single out rationality as special in the characteristically human way of living. Indeed, some may even think that it's characteristically human (at least for our particular epoch) to be able to do something like embrace the absurdity and radical freedom that comes with a wholesale rejection of rationality. So, we might wonder: what makes our rationality so special?

There's one answer to this that Hursthouse cannot give without undermining her aspirations to defend a form of naturalism. She cannot say that ethics is *autonomous* in the way it is seated in our rationality and not in the other aspects of our natures. The problem with this answer is that it, in effect, assumes that one feature of our natures (and the should-facts that derive from it) is special, i.e. "sui generis" with respect to the other features that are recognizably natural. Hence, we'd be left without an answer to the question all naturalists have to answer: how is it that ethical facts reduce to or otherwise fit with recognizably natural facts? Hence, the nonnaturalist would see this manoeuver as a concession that ethics is sui generis. I should note that Hursthouse does respond to this objection by, in effect, challenging the conception of something's being natural implicit in the objection. She thinks it is too narrow. This is why I earlier characterized the position as one that attempts to undermine the previous conception of what it takes for a fact to be natural.

Another worry we might have, however, is whether Neo-Aristotelians end up with a plausible account of what the ethical facts are. After all, there are many characteristically human traits, even some that might depend crucially on our rationality, that can seem to encourage morally questionable behavior. For instance, waging tactical wars, rearing animals for food, lying about sexual infidelity, favoring others simply because of their religion, and finding and exhausting fossil fuels are all parts of what an ethologist might describe as characteristically human ways of life. But surely we can wonder whether those are ethically good ways for us to be. The problem here is one of methodology: if we're meant to give an account of ethical facts that makes them fit within the natural world, but the account we end up giving depicts ethical facts as radically different than we pretheoretically thought, we might begin to wonder whether the account is really an account of what we wanted to account for.

In response, a Neo-Aristotelian might try to focus on characteristically human ways of living that we pre-theoretically accept as ethically good, seeking to work towards reflective equilibrium between our pre theoretic intuitions and a systematic ethical theory. This methodology is characteristic of much ethical theorizing. When it comes to identifying ethically good ways of living that are characteristically human, we face a significant risk that there will be so much variability across different cultures and subcultures that nothing will emerge (as Hursthouse claims rationality does) that can be used to define the specifically ethical virtues.

> **Key Point**: Neo-Aristotelian naturalists seek to derive ethical conclusions from premises about human nature. If these premises can be reasonably treated as natural facts, the ethical facts that follow from them will have some claim to fit among other natural facts.

• RELATIVISM AS A FORM OF NATURALISM

Let's turn now to a different kind of metaethical naturalism. A common idea from anthropology is that right/wrong are *relative to* different "moralities."[3] In one sense, this may be a purely anthropological claim: different groups of people adhere to different norms, and the norms they adhere to determine what kinds of things they think are morally right and wrong. (We already saw echoes of this idea in Hare's missionary and cannibals example from Chapter 3.) Such **anthropological relativism**, however, doesn't yet amount to a view about the *nature* of ethical facts. To get the view called **metaethical relativism**, we need to think further that there's no such thing as an action being right/wrong full stop but only relative to this or that morality. Compare: there is no such thing as being on the left/right full stop but only relative to some perspective or point from which one is looking at something. Sometimes the basic idea is put by saying that morality isn't *objective*. Although suggestive, it's worth heeding two warnings about this way of framing metaethical relativism.

First, sometimes when we say that something isn't objective, we mean that it's subjective. And there is an extreme form of relativism known as **subjectivism**, which says that there's no such thing as an action being right/wrong full stop but only relative to this or that person's own personal values. However, subjectivism is not the only kind of metaethical relativism. The kind inspired by anthropological relativism is one which relativizes ethical facts to different *groups* of people. So we shouldn't think that metaethical relativists have to be subjectivists, though some are.

Second, the idea that morality isn't objective but rather relative problematizes the definition of ethical *realism* I gave in Chapter 2. There I defined realism in terms of a commitment to ethical facts obtaining objectively. But this raises the question: should we count the relativist as a realist or antirealist? Often metaethical relativists, and especially subjectivists, have been classified as antirealists, but depending on how we understand the term "objectively" there's a way to classify at least some of them as realists. In one sense, if some action is wrong only in the sense that it is forbidden by some person's or group of people's values, that means its ethical status is not *universal*. But the fact that some person's or group of people's values forbid the action would still seem to be a fact that is fully *out there* and not depending metaphysically on the "projection" or "construction" of human thought. To be sure, it may be a fact that is at least partly psychological in nature, but facts about a person's or group of people's psychologies might be reasonably thought to be perfectly natural facts.[4]

So, when some metaethicists deny that ethics is objective, it is not always clear what they mean (or what their critics mean when criticizing them for making such claims); and this interacts in a confusing way with the definition of realism. For the relativist's position to be a form of *naturalist* realism it must rest on the suggestion that ethical facts are "out there" but not *universal* in character. If we accept this, another kind of fact begins to look like a plausible candidate for being both ethical and natural: facts about the values or norms of different people or groups of people. Maybe, to pick up on the non-subjectivist forms, the facts about what is ethically right/wrong and good/bad are relative to different cultures very much like the facts about what is legal/illegal are relative to different jurisdictions or facts about what is polite/impolite are relative to different social groups. Is it wrong for couples to live together before they are married; is military valor good; should the dead be buried or burned? Maybe there are facts answering each question, but they depend tacitly on which moral community we are talking about.

There are many ways to develop this idea, and we won't be able to consider all of them here. But one characteristic relativist move is to argue that statements about what's morally right or wrong cannot be evaluated as true/false *simpliciter* very much like statements about what is large or small cannot be evaluated as true/false *simpliciter*. In both cases, relativists think we must fix some further **implicit parameter** in the statement before we can evaluate it as true or false. In the case of statements about size, pretty much everyone is a relativist in the sense that they agree that we need to determine a comparison class before we can evaluate the statement: When you say "Fluffy is small," do you mean small for a dog or small for a guinea pig? Before we know what you're comparing Fluffy to, we can't even begin to figure out whether what you say is true. Ethical relativists often argue something similar is true of statements about which actions are ethically right/wrong. The idea is that these depend crucially on the value of some further implicit parameter.

> QU5: What are the implicit parameters in the following sentences: (i) The table is flat, (ii) It's a long way to Houston, (iii) Sarah is very old?

In this vein, Harman (1975) argues that statements about what's ethically right/wrong make sense only relative to what he calls "agreements." By this he means explicit or implicit intentions among a group of people to adhere to some schedule, plan, or set of principles, under the understanding that others also intend to adhere to it as well, under a similar understanding. To see what he has in mind, imagine for instance two different communities of people: Community A "agrees" to bury their dead relatives; community B "agrees" to cremate their dead relatives. Now consider this statement: "It's ethically wrong not to bury a relative who dies." Is this statement true or false? Harman's answer is that there's no *objective* (in the sense of "universal") fact of the matter; rather it should be considered true relative to community A's agreement and false relative to community B's agreement.

In order to be more precise, we might say that this kind of ethical relativist is an antirealist about *universal* ethical facts, but they are realists about *relativized* ethical facts. Of course, everyone should agree that there are different things demanded by different cultural norms, but the relativist thinks these non-universalized norms are what properly ethical facts are about.

Explaining how the moralities of different cultures come about is a fascinating and difficult topic for ethologists, anthropologists, psychologists, sociologists, and historians. But if we assume that what they are explaining is as much of a feature of the natural world as the other sorts of culturally variable facts they attempt to explain (e.g., facts about what's legal/illegal or polite/impolite), then there will be a good case for thinking of ethical facts (understood as the relativist does) as a species of natural facts. So, in this way, ethical relativism can be seen to be a form of naturalism.

Before moving on to a different kind of metaethical naturalism I want to consider some objections and replies so you can see how debate over metaethical relativism might go. We might worry, first, that there's a crucial difference between one's view about what's polite/impolite and one's view about what's morally right/wrong. (The case of what's legal/illegal is complicated by the fact that some philosophers think legal duties are a species of moral duties, so it's controversial whether legal opinions are more like moral opinions or more like opinions about etiquette in the following regard.) The difference is that one's moral opinions seem to reveal at least partially how one is disposed to behave under various circumstances. If you tell me that giving to charity is morally required for people as well off as us, then it's reasonable for me to expect you to be at least somewhat motivated to give to charity. If it looks like you are completely cold to the prospect, I'll begin to wonder whether you were lying to me or didn't understand what you were saying. The same does not seem to be true for etiquette. If you tell me that it's impolite to eat with one's fingers, I could easily make sense of your total lack of motivation to follow this rule. You don't need to have lied or misunderstood what you were saying; maybe you just think the rules of etiquette in our culture (or at least this rule) are stupid. So, even if ethical statements are properly construed as representations of perfectly natural facts (roughly speaking, facts about what's right/wrong relative to different norms), they cannot be *mere* representations of these facts insofar as their connection to their author's motivations is markedly different from the connection born by statements about other culturally relative facts, such as etiquette.

This objection assumes motivational internalism, the doctrine we first encountered in Chapter 1, which says that an ethical judgment can motivate action without the help of any further desires, inclinations, or emotions. There is no temptation to think judgments of etiquette are like this, but there is some temptation to think ethical judgments are like this.

One response to this objection developed by Dreier (1990) is to argue that ethical statements are implicitly **indexical** in a characteristic first-personal way. Linguistically, indexicals are words such as 'here,' 'now,' and 'I,' which are used as indices referring in a systematic way to different things in different people's mouths. For example, if I say "I am happy," the word 'I' refers to me, whereas if you uttered the same sentence, the word 'I' in your mouth would refer to you. Generally speaking, 'I' is used to refer to the speaker him/herself. Some statements, it seems, may be *implicitly* indexical. For example, if I say "Tacos are yummy," the word 'yummy' means something like *generally tasty to me*, where this 'me' refers to *me*, the speaker of that sentence. In your mouth 'yummy' would mean something like *generally tasty for you*, where this 'you' refers to *you* the speaker of that sentence. I can of course make statements about what is yummy-for-you, but these won't connect to my culinary inclinations in the same way as my statements about what is yummy.

QU6: What are the implicit indexicals in each of the following sentences: (i) She's in front, (ii) Yesterday it was sunny?

Defending a subjectivist view, Dreier argues that statements about what is good are like this. One can makes statements about what is good-relative-to-Western-values or good-relative-to-capitalist-values without displaying any motivation to action. But when one makes a genuine *value* judgment about what is (simply) good, this should be understood as implicitly relative to one's own values. If part of what makes a statement about what's good a genuine value judgment is that it is implicitly indexed to the speaker's own values, then it would be unsurprising that we are generally though defeasibly motivated to act in accordance with our ethical statements.

A related objection to relativism is that ethical facts (if there are such things) seem capable of generating (justifying) reasons to act independent of our desires and concerns, whereas facts about etiquette don't seem to be like this. If it's morally wrong to steal money from the tip jar, that's a reason for you to refrain from doing this—no matter whether you don't care about what's morally wrong or anything related to it. By contrast, the intuition is that the fact that it's impolite in some cultures to talk on the phone while using the toilet can be a reason to refrain from doing this, but only if you care about being polite (or at least something related to it). On this score, the relativist's ethical facts appear not to be reason-generating in the right sort of way. The fact that it's wrong relative to some "agreement" not to bury one's dead relatives doesn't give me a reason to do anything, unless of course I care about that agreement.

> **Key Point**: Relativism is not always counted as a form of naturalist realism, but if relativists view ethical facts as non-objective because relative to something like different (people's or cultures') moralities, those facts can still be objective in the sense of "out there" for discovery by empirical science. In this case, it could be an attractive route for "locating" ethical facts among the natural facts.

Two further objections to relativism are worth mentioning. First, the standard objection to relativism is that it cannot make proper sense of moral disagreement. To be sure, Harman's relativism conceives of ethical facts as relativized to "agreements" we might have with the people with whom we live together in community. But what about the case where people from radically different cultures are discussing moral matters? Here, again, Hare's missionary and cannibal thought experiment from Chapter 3 is relevant. Part of the power of that example is that it really does seem like the missionary and the cannibals disagree about what is right/wrong. As far as relativism is concerned, however, unless they somehow share a morality, they are talking past one another. This suggests the second objection: relativism is based on the suggestion that there are different moral communities of people living by different moral rules and we're wrong to look for any universal rules. But what constitutes a moral community? The problem isn't that we don't have implicit agreements with many people about how to live together but rather that we have lots of these cross-cutting any plausible way of drawing the line between those who and those who do not share a moral community.

• A POSTERIORI NATURALISM

We turn now to some more complicated approaches to locating ethical facts among the natural facts. Although complicated, these turn on views about language and mind that have been worked out mostly independently of metaethics. So they might seem to be neutral tools that we can deploy from these other areas of philosophy to try to make progress in metaethics.

One prominent strategy for locating ethical facts among the natural facts depends on some ideas that gained currency in philosophy of language and philosophy of science in the 1980s. You'll recall from our discussion of the open-question argument that Moore thought we can say things of the form "I know x is N, but is x good?" (for many natural properties N). From this he concluded that the property of goodness is not plausibly thought to be the same as any of these natural properties (e.g., the property of causing pleasure, maximizing happiness, etc.). In response, however, many natural-ists have pointed out that most of the properties we think of as natural also wouldn't pass this test. The standard example is the property of being water. It is now quite widely known that water is H_2O, but before eighteenth-century chemists discovered this, someone could sensibly say "I know that x is H_2O, but is it water?" That is, they could ask this question without revealing confusion about the meaning of the relevant words or a less-than-adequate grasp of the relevant concepts. Indeed, someone could still sensibly ask a question like this today as long as they were simply ignorant of the chemical composition of water. This is because the chemical composition of water is something we discover **a posteriori**, i.e. via empirical investigation of the world rather than via **a priori** reflection on our concepts and the meanings of our words.

This means that the property F and the property G might be identical, even though our concept for F-ness is not identical to our concept for G-ness. Being water is identical to being H_2O, but one doesn't display conceptual or semantic confusion by wondering whether something that is H_2O is water; that just displays ignorance about a chemical fact. Similarly, some ethical naturalists have argued that ethical properties might be natural properties—just not in a way that would close Moore's open questions. Instead these naturalists propose to seek to fit ethical properties and facts within the natural world via a posteriori investigation of the world rather than via a priori analysis of our ethical concepts.

> QU7: Why is the fact that water is H_2O something that cannot be discovered a priori?

It's one thing to point out this lacuna in the open-question argument, it's another thing to propose a plausible form of a posteriori naturalism, one we might imagine confirming scientifically like chemists confirmed the molecular theory of water. It's not like we can collect a bunch of goodness in a test tube and analyze its molecular structure. Accordingly, most a posteriori naturalists concede that ethical properties are going to be somewhat complex and more difficult to analyze than the property of being water. However, one cause for optimism stems from the **causal theory of reference**. The basic idea of this theory is that some words refer to individuals or properties not because of anything we might find via analysis contained in the con-cepts these words express but rather because our use of these words is causally tied to those individuals or properties.

Kripke (1980) argued that this is true of *names*. He used an example of the name 'Gödel,' with which we might associate various ideas such as *being the mathematician who proved the incompleteness theorem.* Now imagine, however, that it turns out that we are mistaken, and someone else named 'Schmidt' was actually the person who proved the incompleteness theorem and Gödel stole his proof and became famous because of it. Kripke suggests (quite plausibly) that if this were the case we wouldn't say that the name 'Gödel' actually refers to Schmidt in virtue of his being the one who really proved the incompleteness theorem. Rather we'd say that we were mistaken about Gödel's mathematical accomplishments.

QU8: In Kripke's thought experiment, who does the name 'Gödel' refer to?

From this, Kripke concludes that the referent of a name is determined not by what ideas we associate with the name but rather by whatever individual happens to be causally linked to our use of the name. The important point for our purposes is that figuring out which particular person the name 'Gödel' refers to requires a posteriori investigation of the causal chain between our use of this name and the person originally baptized 'Gödel'—not a priori analysis of the ideas we associate with this name.

The reference of names is a controversial issue in the philosophy of language, but in a similar fashion, many philosophers of language following Putnam (1975a) have thought that natural kind terms, such as 'water' get their referents not from the ideas (e.g., wetness, clearness) we happen to associate with them but rather from causal chains between their regular use and the instantiation of some property (e.g., the connection between 'water' and instantiations of H_2O). The basic idea is that we need a posteriori investigation of the world rather than a priori analysis of concepts in order to determine what natural kind terms such as 'water' refer to.

If this is right, and we assume that 'good' is also a natural kind term, then figuring out the nature of goodness (just like figuring out the nature of water) would require a posteriori investigation of the causal chain between our use of this term and the property to which it refers. If this is right, then we shouldn't expect a priori conceptual analysis to be probative with respect to the nature of goodness any more than we expect it to be probative with respect to the nature of water or with respect to the prover of the incompleteness theorem.

That's a significant step towards a new a posteriori form of metaethical naturalism. However, even if we accept the causal theory of reference and apply it to 'good,' that still doesn't tell us what goodness is, such that this property can be seen to reduce to or otherwise fit with natural properties. In response, a posteriori naturalists tend to say that goodness is probably going to be quite complicated, but we should note that it's also quite complicated in other cases we regard as promising candidates for reduction. For example, it's not clear what exactly is involved in *being healthy* or *being alive*, but we have some ideas of the more basic natural (physical, chemical, etc.) properties involved in these things, and further scientific investigation will hopefully bring us closer to a full understanding of these properties and how they fit in the natural world. In a similar vein, Boyd (1988) suggested that goodness might be initially viewed as a cluster of natural properties: the ones conducive to the satisfaction of human needs, tending to occur together and with a tendency to promote each other (or to be promoted by the same sorts of things). It's not obvious what exactly is involved in this, but we surely have some idea of the sorts of things these could be. If this is right, then maybe we just need to do more scientific investigation to fully understand the nature of goodness. This would mean that the realist is as entitled to view goodness as a natural property as they are are to view being healthy or being alive as natural properties. This optimism about a posteriori reduction of the moral to the natural is characteristic of one prominent form of ethical naturalism: **a posteriori reductive naturalism**.

The main objection to a posteriori naturalism comes from the **Moral Twin Earth Thought Experiment** (Horgan and Timmons 1991, 1992), which is very similar to Hare's missionary and cannibals example. The idea is to imagine two worlds that are very similar: Earth and twin Earth. The only difference is that the properties that causally regulate the use of ethical terms in these two worlds are slightly different. For example, imagine that on Earth use of the term 'right action' is causally connected to whatever maximizes overall happiness, whereas on twin Earth use of the term 'right action' is causally connected to whatever is done for reasons that one could universalize. (Basically, they differ in whether they are implicitly utilitarian or Kantian about what's right action.) Nevertheless, the practical role of this term in each world is the same: thinking that an action is right tends to motivate people to do it, people are resented and punished when they knowingly don't do the right action, and so on. Now, if the causal theory of reference is correct, then the term 'right action' refers to a different property when used on Earth and twin Earth, since subtly different properties are causally linked to use of this term in the two worlds. Intuitively, however, it doesn't seem that Earthlings and twin-Earthlings are talking about different things when they talk about what actions are right. They're imagined to be in different possible worlds, so they can't talk *to* each other. But it seems that, if they were to talk to each other and disagree about whether a particular action is right, this would be a genuine disagreement rather than a case of talking past each other. After all, thinking that an action is right plays the same practical role for both of them.

This is called the *Moral* Twin Earth Thought Experiment because it's modeled on a similar Twin Earth Thought Experiment famously used by Putnam (1975b) to show that if twin Earthlings' use of the term 'water' were causally regulated by a different chemical compound from Earthlings' use of the term 'water,' we'd be inclined to think they're talking about different stuff, even if the stuff that flows in the rivers and streams is called water in both worlds. Horgan and Timmons suggest that our intuitions go the other way in the moral case, showing that the causal theory of reference cannot be used to support a posteriori reductionist forms of ethical naturalism. It's worth noting the structural similarities between this objection to naturalism and the previous objection from disagreement against relativism.

> **Key Point**: A posteriori naturalists think ethical facts can be reduced to natural facts, not by the sort of conceptual analysis that Moore criticized but by empirical identification of ethical properties with properties that are investigated by the natural sciences.

• A PRIORI NETWORK NATURALISM

Let's move on to a different strategy for explaining how ethical facts might be natural facts. As we saw before, traditional attempts at conceptual analysis of ethical terms in natural terms proved problematic in light of the open-question argument. However, some terms seem to hang together in a network of related concepts that likewise resists traditional analysis, but this doesn't lead us to say that they refer to nonnatural properties. For example, the words 'game,' 'rules,' 'play,' 'winning,' 'losing,' etc. seem to be closely related and to form some kind of package. We may be unable to reductively analyze any one of these in terms of the others, let alone wholly in terms not in the package. Nevertheless, some have thought it is still possible via a priori reflection to map out the network in a detailed enough way that we can identify the properties referred to by individual terms of the network with whatever property uniquely satisfies a particular role in the network.

The basic idea behind the last form of metaethical naturalism we will discuss here is that ethical terms hang together in a network like this, and mapping out the network is crucial for showing the properties they refer to to be natural. If that is right, then it shouldn't be surprising that we cannot provide an *atomistic* analysis of ethical terms in natural terms— as the open-question argument assumes the naturalist would have to do—but that won't impugn naturalism as long as a **network-style analysis** is available instead.

> QU9: Why does the open-question argument assume that the naturalist would have to give an *atomistic* analysis of ethical terms in natural terms?

(Warning: what follows gets considerably more complicated than most of the rest of this book, and I suspect it will be difficult for readers without a good understanding of formal logic. So it wouldn't be unreasonable to skip the rest of this section accepting only the very vague description of a priori network naturalism given above. Alternatively one might wish to skim this section and then read some of the literature on the so-called **Canberra Plan** before coming back to study this section more carefully.)

This network strategy traces back to Ramsey's discussion of how to understand degrees of beliefs and preferences in the prediction of people's behavior, but it has been more recently developed by Jackson (1998) for ethical terms. On his way of pursuing the idea, we seek to analyze a particular concept as expressing the unique property that satisfies a network of platitudes. Platitudes are usually thought of as claims that one's usage of a term must respect in order for it to count as revealing competence with the concept expressed.

Accordingly, a network analysis can be pursued in four steps:

1 List the platitudes in a standardized form ("property-name form").
2 Form a large conjunction of the platitudes.
3 Replace the concepts/properties being analyzed with free variables.
4 Bind the variables with existential quantifiers and add a uniqueness condition.

That's a bit jargony, but the best way to understand each of these steps is just to work through a non-ethical example (after Smith, 1994): color terms. First, we put platitudes about these into a standardized form which mentions the names of properties (this is what makes it in the "property-name form") e.g.:

Color platitudes

• Objects have the property of being red if they look to have the property of being red to normal perceivers under standard conditions.
• The property of being red is more similar to the property of being orange than to the property of being yellow.
• Objects have the property of being orange if they look to have the property of being orange to normal perceivers under standard conditions.
• The property of being orange is more similar to the property of being yellow than to the property of being green.
• Objects have the property of being yellow if they look to have the property of being yellow to normal perceivers under standard conditions.
• The property of being yellow is more similar to the property of being green than to the property of being blue.
• And so on.

Second, we form these into a large conjunction:

> Objects have the property of being red if they look to have the property of being red to normal perceivers under standard conditions **AND** the property of being red is more similar to the property of being orange than to the property of being yellow **AND** objects have the property of being orange if they look to have the property of being orange to normal perceivers under standard conditions **AND** the property of being orange is more similar to the property of being yellow than to the property of being green **AND** objects have the property of being yellow if they look to have the property of being yellow to normal perceivers under standard conditions **AND** the property of being yellow is more similar to the property of being green than to the property of being blue...

Third, we strip out mention of the "property-names" and replace them systematically with what logicians call free-variables (that is, variables floating freely in the formula and not linked up with any quantifier terms such as "for all x" or "there exists a y"):

> Objects have v if they look to have v to normal perceivers under standard conditions **AND** v is more similar to w than to x **AND** objects have w if they look to have w to normal perceivers under standard conditions **AND** w is more similar to x than to y **AND** objects have x if they look to have x to normal perceivers under standard conditions **AND** x is more similar to y than to z...

Since the variables aren't linked up with any quantifiers, that sentence doesn't really mean anything on its own. But we can make it meaningful again by doing what logicians call "binding" the free variables with existential quantifiers which look like this: $\exists$ (for "there exists"):

> $\exists v\exists w\exists x\exists y\exists z$... (Objects have v if they look to have v to normal perceivers under standard conditions **AND** v is more similar to w than to x **AND** objects have w if they look to have w to normal perceivers under standard conditions **AND** w is more similar to x than to y **AND** objects have x if they look to have x to normal perceivers under standard conditions **AND** x is more similar to y than to z...),

and we add a uniqueness condition to insure that there is not more than one of each property:

> **AND** if any v' satisfies this condition then $v'=v$, and if any w' satisfies this condition then $w'=w$, if any x' satisfies this condition then $x'=x$, and if any y' satisfies this condition then $y'=y$, and if any z' satisfies this condition then $z'=z$...

This big (and quite ugly) sentence claims that there are unique properties v, w, x, y, z... that are related in a network that would satisfy the color platitudes.

The preceding few paragraphs may seem totally complicated and arcane, but here's the payoff of these logical shenanigans: we now have a way of explaining what redness is which doesn't use any color terms whatsoever. We'll say that redness is the property x such that it satisfies this big conjunction (notice that the conjunction above doesn't have any color terms in it). Similarly, we can say that orangeness is the property w which satisfies this big conjunction. And so on, for each color, thereby providing a network analysis of color properties which doesn't itself use color concepts in the analysis. The key idea is that, although we might not be able to analyze 'red' by conceptually decomposing it into its atoms (on the model of 'bachelor' = 'unmarried man'), we're still in a position to use a priori reflection on our color concepts to explain in non-color terms what redness is: it's whatever unique property plays the relevant role in this network of concepts.

At this stage, you should be wondering how this is going to apply to the ethical case. Jackson's idea is that here too we might start by listing various platitudes, e.g., about what's right/wrong, good/bad, virtuous/vicious, and how they're related to each other.

Then we could pursue steps 1–4 as before. And if successful, we'd end up with an analysis of ethical properties such as goodness and rightness that explained their nature in wholly non-ethical (and hopefully appreciably naturalistic) terms, thereby providing an a priori network-style reduction of ethical properties to non-ethical properties.

In this case, however, there's a big challenge. Morality is a much more controversial topic than color, which means that it is hard to come up with very many platitudes. (Remember that "platitudes" are usually understood to be claims that one's usage of a term must respect in order for one to have revealed competence with the relevant terms.) To be sure, there are some very minimal things we might be able to say, e.g. (in the standardized property-name form):

Moral platitudes

- If an action has the property of being wrong, then doing it does not have the property of being right.
- Encouraging others to do actions with the property of being right itself has the property of being right.
- A person with the property of being virtuous does actions with the property of being good.
- And so on.

But as Zangwill (2000) argued, it's difficult to get much more substantive than that. But unless we do, there won't be enough platitudes to to have any hope of justifying the idea that some unique set of properties satisfies them.

Moreover, even if we do admit more ethical claims as platitudes, there's a risk that the a priori network analysis will still be unstructured enough to face what Smith (1994, 54–6) calls the **permutation problem**. This is the problem that, once we strip out all of the ethical terms from these platitudes and put in free variables, we could very well have a structure that can be inverted or systematically shifted (e.g., switching all positive terms such as 'good' with negative terms such as 'bad'). To see what he has in mind, imagine a "shifted" spectrum of color terms, where 'green' is used to refer to blueness, 'blue' is used to refer to redness, 'red' is used to refer to greenness, and so on. These color terms would equally well satisfy the network structure extracted from color platitudes above, but they'd seem to not provide the correct analysis of the meanings of 'red,' 'green,' and 'blue.' Similarly, we might imagine an inverted morality that satisfies the network structure extracted from the minimal list of moral platitudes above. Again this would mean that there needn't be a *unique* set of properties related in the way the network articulates. In technical terms, the "uniqueness condition" mentioned above would be unjustified.

Jackson himself tries to avoid these kinds of problems by suggesting that what should be fed into the network analysis as "platitudes" in the case of ethical properties is not merely the ethical claims that *everyone* could agree to but rather the fixed points of what he calls "mature folk morality." By this, he means something like the principles everyone would agree to if morality was perfected via critical reflection. His hope is that this will provide a more substantive list of "platitudes" on the back of which to pursue a network analysis. Indeed, we might even end up in a similar place to Boyd's brand of metaethical naturalism via a much different route: saying, e.g., that goodness is a cluster of natural properties conducive to the satisfaction of human needs, tending to occur together and with a tendency to promote each other (or to be promoted by the same sorts of things). If that is indeed the unique property satisfying the goodness-node in a network of concepts extracted from the fixed points of mature folk morality, then perhaps we should recognize goodness as that (complex) property.

However, one might reasonably worry that analyzing goodness in this way undermines the aspirations of a priori analysis to provide an exposition of the contents of our ordinary ethical concepts. For the platitudes were supposed to capture the commitments, the denial of which would reveal some kind of conceptual/semantic incompetence with the relevant terms. The problem is that failing at the critical reflection needed to arrive at "mature folk morality" doesn't reveal that one is incompetent with the terms one uses in our everyday moral discourse. Moreover, as Yablo (2000) points out, appealing to *mature* folk morality may smuggle in an ethical concept into an analysis that was supposed to be entirely reductive in the sense that it explains the nature of ethical properties without appealing to ethical concepts. If "mature folk morality" is just a way of saying the morally right morality for us to appeal to, then obviously we haven't reductively analyzed ethical concepts via the network analysis.

> *Key Point*: A "network analysis" promises to provide an a priori reduction of ethical properties to natural properties by analyzing each ethical property as qualities that play a particular role in a network of related qualities that can be understood a priori.

• CONCLUSION

In this chapter we have explored four versions of ethical naturalism, the doctrine that there are ethical facts and they are natural. One of the complicating factors in this debate is that no one has an uncontroversial definition of what it takes for a fact to count as natural. But assuming the facts in principle discoverable by science or figuring in the law-like explanations characteristic of scientific explanation are natural facts, the challenge for the naturalist is to show how ethical facts might reduce to or fit among such facts.

The attractions in attempting to do this and the main general arguments in favor of naturalism can be put in terms of (i) metaphysics and epistemology, and (ii) philosophies of language and mind. Metaphysically, naturalism is a form of *realism*: ethical facts really obtain. But unlike the nonnaturalist, the naturalist thinks these facts fit within the natural world. If the view can otherwise be made to work, this means that it doesn't require adding a stock of sui generis and poorly understood "nonnatural" facts to our overall ontology. Moreover, this holds out some promise of explaining how we come to know ethical facts without appealing to some special faculty by which we glom onto to sui generis facts. In the philosophy of language, naturalism is a form of *representationalism*: ethical statements are like other statements of fact in that they represent a way reality could be, and they are true or false depending on whether reality is the way they represent it as being. This is because they express beliefs about how reality is, which is why the naturalist is, in the philosophy of mind, a *cognitivist* about ethical thought. Here too, if the view can otherwise be made to work, this is attractive theoretical territory to occupy. For linguistically the sentences with which we make ethical statements seem to behave like other statements commonly regarded as representations of reality (e.g., they're truth-apt, embeddable under 'if' and 'might'). Moreover, it's quite unremarkable for us to talk about ethical beliefs and knowledge, which inclines many metaethicists towards some form of noncognitivism.

As we have seen, there are several strategies for locating ethical facts among the natural facts, and each strategy faces its own specific objections. But we might say that the main liability of naturalism lies in the philosophy of language and the philosophy of mind. Each form of naturalism here trades on controversial assumptions in the philosophy of language. Moreover, for most natural facts, such as facts discovered by chemistry or physics, stating that one of them obtains does not (all by itself) reveal in the speaker any particular motivations to act, and the obtaining of one of these facts does not (all by itself) generate reasons for someone to act. So when it comes to the nature of ethical facts, on any particular naturalist view, it's worth asking: if ethical facts were like that, would belief in them plausibly generate (defeasible) motivations? And: would a fact like that be able to generate reasons to act all by itself?

• CHAPTER SUMMARY

- Neo-Aristotelian naturalists expand the conception of the natural standardly assumed in the metaethical debate and attempt to derive ethical facts from human nature.
- It is challenging for the neo-Aristotelian naturalist to distinguish how humans biologically should be from how humans ethically should be without smuggling in ethical considerations into the determination of what counts as human nature.
- Ethical relativists challenge the aspirations of other forms of ethical realism to secure universal ethical facts. If we instead accept that ethical facts are relativized to cultures or individual value systems, it is much easier to locate such facts among the facts we already regard as natural.
- Traditional arguments for nonnaturalism assume that for ethical fact to be shown to be natural, we would have to be able to decompose ethical concepts in purely naturalistic concepts. By appealing to the difference between metaphysical identity and conceptual analyzability (e.g., water = H_2O), a posteriori naturalists point

out that this is a bad assumption and argue that there is reason for optimism that ethical properties are identical to natural properties.
- A posteriori naturalists are threatened by the moral twin Earth objection.
- Network analyses offer an alternative model for a priori conceptual analysis of ethical terms than that assumed by Moore and his critics.

• STUDY QUESTIONS

1 What does it take for a fact to count as "natural"?
2 What would count as a "virtue" of a car, a cactus, and a tiger on the neo-Aristotelian approach? Explain your answer.
3 Are there unethical aspects of human nature?
4 Are ethical relativists realists or antirealists about ethics?
5 Explain the causal theory of reference.
6 Why is the possibility of a "moral twin Earth" a threat to a posteriori naturalists?
7 What is an example of a moral platitude; would platitudes like this support a network analysis of ethical terms?

• FURTHER RESOURCES

- Gowans, Chris. 2015. "Moral Relativism," *The Stanford Encyclopedia of Philosophy* (Summer 2015 Edition), Edward N. Zalta (ed.), http://plato.stanford.edu/archives/sum2015/entries/moral-relativism. [A detailed general introduction to various forms of relativism in ethics.]
- Harman, Gilbert and Thomson, J. J. 1996. *Moral Relativism and Moral Objectivity*. Blackwell. [Book-length debate between a relativist and an objectivist about morality.]
- Hursthouse, Roslind. 1999. *On Virtue Ethics*. Oxford University Press. [A book-length development of the neo-Aristotelian approach to ethical naturalism.]
- Lenman, James. 2014. "Moral Naturalism," *The Stanford Encyclopedia of Philosophy* (Spring 2014 Edition), Edward N. Zalta (ed.), http://plato.stanford.edu/archives/spr2014/entries/naturalism-moral. [A detailed general overview of naturalist positions in metaethics outside of relativism.]
- Papineau, David. 2015. "Naturalism," *The Stanford Encyclopedia of Philosophy* (Fall 2015 Edition), Edward N. Zalta (ed.), http://plato.stanford.edu/archives/fall2015/entries/naturalism/. [Section 2.3 contains further discussion of the "Canberra Plan."]

• ANSWERS TO QUESTIONS OF UNDERSTANDING

QU1: (i) and (iv) are attributive.
QU2: Cars and lamps are functional kinds, moons are not (because it's not part of being a moon that it has any particular function). The case of human beings

is the interesting one—do we have a particular function (or purpose?) which is essential to being human? Some have argued yes and others have argued no. Crucially for what follows, you don't have to think humans have a particular function to pursue neo-Aristotelian naturalism, but you do have to think that humans have something from which we can derive what it is to be a good human.

QU3: Your answers to this question may differ, as there are often many different features that make something which is a functional kind a good instance of its kind. For example, shoes are good shoes when they're comfortable, durable, fashionable, etc. Power drills are good power drills when they have sufficient torque, are easily gripped, have variable speeds, etc. And, perhaps, textbooks are good textbooks when they have questions of understanding such as this one.

QU4: First, try to come up with an account of the characteristic way of living for a dairy cow. Next, figure out which features of a dairy cow facilitate its excelling at this characteristic way of living. These are the features a dairy cow (in light of it being a dairy cow) should have.

QU5: There may be more than one in each sentence, but at least the following: (i) is relative to something like a degree of precision or a practical purpose, (ii) is relative to a kind of trip, and (iii) is relative to what type of person we're comparing Sarah to.

QU6: To understand an utterance of sentence (i) we need to know *which direction* determines front and back. To understand an utterance of sentence (ii) we need to know when counts as "today" relative to which "yesterday" is the previous day; we also need to know where is "here" for the utterance.

QU7: However carefully we examine our concepts, we won't discover that what it is to be water is to be H_2O; for that we need to do empirical investigation of samples of water, applying the tools of modern chemistry.

QU8: The name 'Gödel' still refers to the man named Gödel. It's just that he turned out not to have been the mathematician who proved what we now call "Gödel's incompleteness theorem."

QU9: Because the open-question argument demands an analysis of a term such as 'good' that breaks it down into other terms which are natural. This is why Moore is sometimes accused of confusing the nonnaturalness of goodness with the simplicity of goodness.

• WORKS CITED

Boyd, Richard. 1988. "How to Be a Moral Realist." In *Essays on Moral Realism*, edited by G. Sayre-McCord. Ithaca, NY: Cornell University Press.

Dreier, James. 1990. "Internalism and Speaker Relativism." *Ethics* 101 (1): 6–26.

Foot, Philippa. 1999. *Natural Goodness*. Oxford: Clarendon Press.

Geach, P. T. 1956. "Good and Evil." *Analysis* 17 (2): 33–42.

Harman, Gilbert. 1975. "Moral Relativism Defended." *The Philosophical Review* 84 (1): 3–22.

Horgan, Terence, and Mark Timmons. 1991. "New Wave Moral Realism Meets Moral Twin Earth." *Journal of Philosophical Research* 16: 447–65.

———. 1992. "Troubles on Moral Twin Earth: Moral Queerness Revived." *Synthese* 92: 221–60.

Hursthouse, Roslind. 1999. *On Virtue Ethics*. Oxford: Clarendon Press.

Jackson, Frank. 1998. *From Metaphysics to Ethics*. Oxford: Oxford University Press.

Kripke, Saul A. 1980. *Naming and Necessity*. Cambridge, MA: Harvard University Press.

Putnam, Hilary. 1975a. *Mind, Language, and Reality*. Cambridge; New York: Cambridge University Press.

———. 1975b. "The Meaning of 'Meaning'." In *Philosophical Papers, Vol. II: Mind, Language, and Reality*. Cambridge: Cambridge University Press.

Smith, Michael. 1994. "Internal Reasons." *Philosophy and Phenomenological Research* 55 (1): 109–31.

Yablo, Stephen. 2000. "Red, Bitter, Best." *Philosophical Books* 41: 13–23.

Zangwill, Nick. 2000. "Against Analytic Moral Functionalism." *Ratio* 13 (3): 275–86.

• NOTES

1 With the possible exception of some forms of quasi-realist expressivism. When this view was first developed by Blackburn in the 1980s and early 90s, it appealed to minimalism about 'true' and 'believes' to earn the right to use some of the realist sounding language about ethics that is part of ordinary everyday ethical discourse. One way the view has been developed, however, lets this minimalism extend to any metaphysical terminology, whether or not it is part of ordinary everyday ethical discourse. If this also includes the idea of "reality including facts" of some type, then strictly speaking, the quasi-realist needn't accept (C) as it is stated above. I'll ignore this complication in what follows.

2 It's a controversial issue in metaphysics how exactly to understand such "natures." The concept is related to but more narrow than the idea of an essence.

3 Sometimes philosophers distinguish between a *descriptive* claim about morality (roughly, its demands vary across cultures) and a *normative* ethical claim (we should respect cultural differences and not expect that all people live by the same basic moral rules). It's important to note that the form of relativism discussed above is the descriptive sort. The normative claim is ostensibly a *universal* ethical claim—so if it is true, then it undermines the descriptive relativist's claim that there is no universal moral truth.

4 In Chapter 7, we'll encounter response-dependence and constructivist theories that hold that there are ethical facts but insist that they are not fully "out there" because their ontological status depends somehow on the responses or constructions, actual or hypothetical, of some kind of mind. It's a controversial issue in metaethics whether to view these as a sophisticated form of realism, not quite conforming to the standard definitions, or to view these as sophisticated forms of antirealism. I'll treat them as antirealist proposals in Chapter 7, but I do so in the context of a discussion about whether some of the standard categories begin to break down in various ways in more recent metaethical debate.

6

summary & chart

In Chapter 1, I said that one way we might think of metaethics is as the subdiscipline of philosophical study of ethics that seeks to answer questions in other areas of philosophy, such as metaphysics, epistemology, philosophy of language, and philosophy of mind *as they apply to ethics*. We have now explored the four main theoretical traditions. Throughout this book, we have understood the four main theories both in terms of their commitments along various dimensions of metaethics and in terms of choice points that are represented in Figure 6.1 (which is a slight enhancement of Figure 1.1).

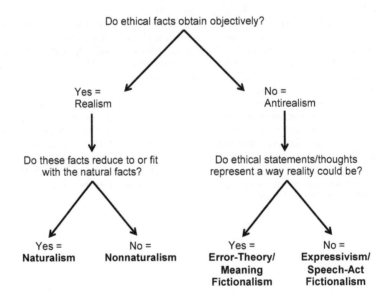

Figure 6.1 Traditional metaethical theories

We are now in a position to generate a chart, separating these theories along four dimensions. The goal of this chapter is to develop this chart in order to put you in a position to think carefully about which of these views you find most attractive, by weighing the various costs and benefits of each theory.

> **Key Point**: The main methodology of metaethics is *theoretical cost–benefit analysis*. This means that deciding which metaethical theory you find most attractive will often be a matter of weighing the theoretical benefits of a theory in metaphysics, epistemology, philosophy of language, and philosophy of mind against its theoretical costs in these areas, and then comparing the result to competing theories.

• THE FOUR MAIN AREAS

To develop the chart, I will go back over some of the same ground we've covered before but in a different order and with a more general perspective.

Metaphysics

Recall that the metaphysical issues that come up in metaethics are about whether ethical facts really do objectively obtain and if, any do, what they are like. In Chapter 1, I suggested the main theoretical traditions can be first categorized into realist and antirealist theories, based on their views about the reality of objective ethical facts. Assuming, for example, that murder is wrong, a realist will say that this is a fact that objectively obtains: the wrongness of murder is just as real as the solidity of stones. Antirealists, on the other hand, deny that reality really contains objective ethical facts. They might still *say* that murder is wrong, for example, but they'll go on to argue that this statement is either literally false or the expression of some noncognitive attitude such as condemnation.

So there's a sense in which it's only the realists that have further metaphysical questions to answer. Since they believe that ethical facts objectively obtain, we can ask them what these facts are like. Regarding this question, we've observed an initial two-way split among theories. First, convinced of the "autonomy" of ethics compared to empirical observation of the world, nonnaturalists argue that ethical facts are sui generis—of their own kind, not classifiable as a kind of natural fact (nor as a kind of supernatural fact). This raises important questions about the apparent supervenience of the ethical on the natural. In contrast, naturalists argue that ethical facts reduce to or can otherwise be recognized to fit among recognizably natural facts. This raises important questions about how to make that fit work.

We might start the chart with Table 6.1.

Table 6.1 Four metaethical traditions with metaphysics

	Metaphysics
Nonnaturalism	Realist Nonnatural
Expressivism	Antirealist
ET/Fictionalism	Antirealist
Naturalism	Realist Natural

Epistemology

I have placed less focus on epistemology than metaphysics in the preceding chapters, but it raises important issues that often go hand-in-hand with metaphysical issues. For if you claim that facts of a particular kind obtain, it's reasonable to ask you how someone (like yourself) might come to know one of these facts to obtain. How, for example, do we know whether Manning's leaking classified documents was morally wrong? This epistemological issue poses one of the biggest challenges for nonnaturalists, since they think ethical facts are sui generis, i.e. a special kind of fact that is unlike other facts with which we are familiar. Because of this, nonnaturalists generally posit a special faculty by which we come to know ethical facts—this is usually called "intuition," but its relation to what we would ordinarily call intuition is debatable. Some nonnaturalists try to assimilate our knowledge of ethical facts to other things we know through the faculty of understanding or through reflection on how things seem to us pre-theoretically. However, it is unclear whether these projects can be carried off plausibly, which would leave ethical knowledge as sui generis as ethical facts. In any case, although there may be exceptions to this rule, nonnaturalists usually endorse an intuitionist moral epistemology.

> QU1: Is it a cost or a benefit of nonnaturalism that it requires something like
> an intuitionist moral epistemology?

By contrast, while naturalists could in principle endorse an intuitionist epistemology, they don't have to and they tend not to. This is because naturalists maintain that ethical facts fit among natural facts, i.e. the sorts of facts we ordinarily come to know by some combination of empirical observation, scientific testing and theorizing, and reflection. Different naturalists place more and less stress on each of these various ways of coming to know a fact, depending on their specific account of what the ethical facts are like. For example, a posteriori naturalists might lean on an analogy with our knowledge of complicated facts about biology or chemistry, which would lead them to stress observation and scientific testing and theorizing. By contrast, network-style a priori naturalists leaning on our ability to keep track of the different nodes of a network of related concepts might stress reflection, especially reflection on how our various ethical concepts fit together and what kinds of things could satisfy them. Either way, most naturalists work with some combination of an empiricist and coherentist picture of moral knowledge, whereby the justification for our moral beliefs derives from their overall coherence in a web of observations and reflections.

Antirealists such as expressivists and error-theorists/fictionalists deny that there are ethical facts, so initially they are off the hook when it comes to telling us how one could come to know such facts. In most cases, philosophers adopt this position because they are skeptical of our ability to know ethical facts as they are construed by realists. That is, if ethical facts are thought to be sui generis nonnatural facts, an antirealist might be skeptical that we could ever know them (maybe because she is skeptical that there is such a thing as the faculty of moral intuition). Or, similarly, if ethical facts are complicated natural facts that involve something like the instantiation of a homeostatic cluster of properties, or the unique fulfillment of the node in a complex network of interconnected concepts, the antirealist might be skeptical that we could ever know them.

Nonetheless, that doesn't change the fact that ordinary people commonly *talk about* ethical knowledge. So even if antirealists are off the hook for explaining how it is that we track ethical facts, considered as somehow out there in reality, they still owe us some account of what's going on when ordinary folk talk about knowing, e.g., that murder is wrong. Unless the antirealist wants to say that claims to know something like this are mistaken or nonsensical, she needs to come up with some non-tracking account of ethical knowledge. It's unclear whether this should be counted as an "epistemology" for antirealists; and there is no unified thing that antirealists say. Sophisticated expressivists tend to develop a quasi-realist story about this issue. Fictionalists tend to stress the analogy with knowledge of other fictions.

In any case, we can use the above reflections to extend the chart with Table 6.2.

Table 6.2 Four metaethical traditions with metaphysics and epistemology

	Metaphysics	Epistemology
Nonnaturalism	Realist Nonnatural	Intuitionist
Expressivism	Antirealist	Skeptical or Quasi-realist
ET/Fictionalism	Antirealist	Skeptical or Fictionalist
Naturalism	Realist Natural	Empiricist/ Coherentist

Philosophy of language

The main issue for metaethics from the philosophy of language is whether ethical sentences are representations of a way reality could be. This question forces a different grouping: Error-theorists/fictionalists agree with nonnaturalists and naturalists that ethical sentences, when literally construed, represent a way reality could be. It's just that error-theorists/fictionalists typically deny that basic ethical sentences, construed literally, ever *successfully* represent reality.

QU2: Why do error-theorists and fictionalists restrict their core claim in the philosophy of language to *basic* ethical statements rather than *all* ethical statements?

The primary contrast here is expressivism, which holds that ethical statements function not to represent reality but to express noncognitive attitudes of some sort. For example, different expressivists have tried to work out the suggestions that ethical judgments are emotively laden evaluations, complex interlocking preferences and intentions, plans, or desires of some sort. Because of this view, early expressivists denied that ethical statements are truth-apt. This means that they argued that it's strictly speaking wrong to say that an ethical statement is true or false, because such utterances are really in the business of expressing noncognitive attitudes rather than representing reality. However, later expressivists have developed subtle ways of combining expressivism with a minimalist theory of truth, according to which, saying a sentence is true is basically to say the same thing as the sentence itself. If this is right, then ethical statements might be truth-apt but still expressive of noncognitive attitudes rather than representational of reality.

Key Point: Expressivists are antirepresentationalists about ethical language; the other theories are representationalist.

This means we can further extend our chart with Table 6.3.

Table 6.3 Four metaethical traditions with metaphysics, epistemology, and philosophy of language

	Metaphysics	Epistemology	Language
Nonnaturalism	Realist Nonnatural	Intuitionist	Representationalist Truth-apt
Expressivism	Antirealist	Skeptical or Quasi-realist	Antirepresentationalist Not truth-apt (or Minimalist)
ET/ Fictionalism	Antirealist	Skeptical or Fictionalist	Representationalist Truth-apt
Naturalism	Realist Natural	Empiricist/Coherentist	Representationalist Truth-apt

Philosophy of mind

The final main area of metaethics we have been discussing is the philosophy of mind (especially as it connects to action theory and moral psychology). Here, the initial division is the same as in the philosophy of language. Realists (of both nonnaturalist and naturalist stripes) accept that the mental state expressed by an ethical judgment is cognitive or, as we called it before, "belief-like." This means that these thoughts are about a way reality could be; and as realists, these philosophers accept that some such beliefs are *true*. Error-theorists and fictionalists tend to accept the first part of this: moral thought is cognitive. But they deny the second part: atomic moral thoughts are never literally true but rather based on some sort of ontological error or covertly fictional in some way. The contrast, again, is expressivism. On this view, the mental state expressed by an ethical judgment is noncognitive or, as we put it before, "desire-like."

This division between cognitivist and noncognitivist views of ethical thought is important for understanding where various metaethical views stand with respect to the question of motivational internalism. As we saw in Chapter 1, some philosophers have been persuaded that ethical judgments are much more tightly connected to action than ordinary beliefs about reality; hence, they endorse the idea that an ethical judgment guarantees at least some (conditional and defeasible) motivation to act. For example, if I sincerely judge that giving to charity is the right thing for me to do, the motivational *internalist* says that I will be at least somewhat motivated to give to charity (if the condition for doing so arises, though this motivation might be outweighed or undercut by my other inclinations). Motivational *externalists* deny this, arguing that although ethical judgments might often connect with our desires, intentions, and plans, there is nothing incoherent about someone sincerely making an ethical judgment and being entirely unmoved to act in its accord. Hence, metaethical theories can be divided based on where they stand on the question of motivational internalism/externalism.

> QU3: Is it a cost or a benefit for a theory to be consistent with motivational internalism?

Most of the views we have considered so far are consistent with some version of the belief–desire psychology of motivation (which is often called "Humean"), which says that the mental states involved in motivation to action divide neatly into those which aim to fit the world (uncharged "representations" of how things are) and those which aim to change the world to fit them (charged "directions" of how to make things become). If we accept this and motivational internalism, there is pressure to embrace a form of expressivism. The idea is that ethical judgments are more tightly connected to motivation than beliefs about reality because they are at base desire-like rather than belief-like in their motivational potentials.

One can, however, resist this pressure. One way to do so is to argue that, because of what they are about, ethical judgments are tightly connected to having the desires needed to be motivated to act in their accord. For example, a nonnaturalist might suggest that one of the reasons for thinking ethical facts are nonnatural is precisely that they are a special kind of fact, recognition of which tends to make one desire to act in its accord. Indeed, this way of thinking about what ethical facts would have to be like on the nonnaturalist theory is part of the reason error-theorists and fictionalists argue that there really aren't any such facts, though we speak and act as if there are (either erroneously or as part of a convenient fiction). So, error-theorists and fictionalists might agree with nonnaturalists' philosophy of mind (while disagreeing with their metaphysics).

Regarding this issue, naturalists traditionally took up one of two stances. First, as we saw, some naturalists think ethical facts are ultimately facts about our own moral viewpoints or intentions considered parts of agreements for how to live together. If this is right, then the naturalist can embrace a form of internalism in a similar way to the nonnaturalist: claim that the distinctive internal connection between ethical judgments and motivation is guaranteed by what the judgment is about. Since they are partially about one's own motivational states, it is not surprising that ethical judgments are more closely associated with motivation than ordinary beliefs about reality. Second, other naturalists reject motivational internalism, arguing instead that, although there may be a normal connection between one's making ethical judgments and being at least somewhat motivated, this isn't guaranteed or distinctive of ethical judgments.

Once rejecting motivational internalism is on the table, it seems to also be available to the nonnaturalist as well. Perhaps the best response to the error-theorist's critique of nonnatural facts as "queer" (because they are intrinsically motivating) would be to argue that they are not intrinsically motivating after all. One might argue, e.g., that they are the sorts of facts that merely normally motivate (good) people who recognize them.

In light of these considerations, we come to Table 6.4 as the full version of our chart.

Table 6.4 Four metaethical traditions with metaphysics, epistemology, philosophy of language, and philosophy of mind (with optional alternative commitments in parentheses)

	Metaphysics	Epistemology	Language	Mind
Nonnaturalism	Realist Nonnatural	Intuitionist	Representationalist Truth-apt	Cognitivist Internalist (or Externalist)
Expressivism	Antirealist	Skeptical or Quasi-realist	Antirepresentationalist Not truth-apt (or Minimalist)	Noncognitivist Internalist
ET/ Fictionalism	Antirealist	Skeptical or Fictionalist	Representationalist Truth-apt	(Cognitivist) (Internalist)
Naturalism	Realist Natural	Empiricist/ Coherentist	Representationalist Truth-apt	Cognitivist Internalist or Externalist

• COSTS AND BENEFITS

As I explained in Chapter 1, we shouldn't expect for there to be conclusive arguments for or against any of these views. Rather, the methodology of metaethics is largely one of theoretical cost–benefit analysis. When we explored each family of theories in Chapters 2–5, I explained the sorts of considerations that its proponents cite as points in its favor—these are the purported theoretical benefits—but I also explained the sorts of considerations that its opponents cite as points against it—these are the purported theoretical costs. By developing a chart of these theories' answers to some of the main questions of metaethics, I hope to put us in a position to begin to weigh such theoretical costs and benefits. Ultimately, however, weighing these costs and benefits against one another is a difficult task that students of metaethics must do for themselves, as one's views about how much each cost and benefit "counts" can reasonably vary.

Given the chart above, there are two ways we might try to proceed. First, we might try to find some independent way of assigning "plausibility points" at each cell of the chart and then try to add them up for each theory, assessing in the end which theory is most plausible. In practice, however, it tends to be very near to impossible to get working metaethicists to agree on relative plausibility points for, e.g., an intuitionist ethical epistemology or a naturalist metaphysics. So, second, we might instead trace out various "dialectical paths," beginning with one of the views about metaphysics, epistemology, language, or mind that we find plausible. In doing so, we'll come to see how easy or hard it is to develop a full metaethical view in light of various objections and alternatives at each sector of the chart. This is the more usual methodology of metaethics.

For example, if one is strongly committed to the representationalist view of moral language, then the expressivist proposal will seem to carry heavy costs that could be outweighed only by very significant benefits on the other side. Maybe strong commitments to motivational internalism plus Humeanism about the psychology of motivation would incline someone in this position to seriously consider one of the relativist versions of naturalism that promises to make sense of these things within a representationalist conception of language. However, if one finds the relativist/subjectivist implications of such positions unpalatable, one might be forced to reopen the question about whether representationalism is correct about moral language.

Instead, one might start out strongly skeptical of the reality of anything but the natural facts. If so, then the nonnaturalist proposal will seem to carry heavy costs that could be outweighed only by significant benefits on the other side. Maybe in this case a commitment to a non-skeptical stance on ethical facts will lead one also to rule out error theory and fictionalism. This will leave expressivism and naturalism. The former requires some special story about what we're up to when we talk about moral knowledge, assuming that ethical judgments aren't beliefs about the way reality is but rather noncognitive attitudes. If one doubts such a story can be made to work, that will incline one to try to articulate and defend a version of naturalism. Here, which version one favors will then depend on whether one finds the arguments for motivational internalism compelling and what one thinks the best moral epistemology is.

Those are just a couple of examples of how we can use the chart above to trace a variety of dialectical paths, starting with one's commitments in one of the columns through one's views about other issues to the type of view one finds most plausible. Fully understanding metaethics requires not just understanding each sector on this chart, but also understanding how one traces these various paths.

It's worth mentioning one further complication regarding costs and benefits. It's controversial among metaethicists and philosophers more generally whether there can be *practical* costs and benefits for a metaethical theory. For example, some think that the error theory carries the cost of disenchanting ethics and thereby making people who believe in it less likely to behave well, which would have obvious practical costs. Could this kind of consideration be a reason to abandon the error theory? Insofar as we think of metaethical theories as descriptive theories of how things are with respect to the metaphysics, epistemology, philosophy of language, and philosophy of mind as they apply to ethics, then such practical considerations would seem to be the wrong sorts of reasons for embracing or rejecting a metaethical theory. However, if we think these theories are not themselves *descriptive*, but rather *normative*, then the role of such practical costs and benefits becomes much less clear.

• CONCLUSION

In this chapter, we have reaped the benefits of the hard work in previous chapters of coming to understand the four major theoretical traditions in metaethics and how they answer questions about metaphysics, epistemology, philosophy of language, and philosophy of mind. By taking a birds-eye view of the debate, we have developed a chart of the four main theories and their characteristic stances on questions in the four main areas of metaethics. This is intended to help you to understand these theories better by helping you to distinguish one from the other with respect to various key questions. But it is also groundwork for pursuing your own evaluation of the theoretical costs and benefits of various theories and understanding how others might come to competing evaluations by taking different dialectical paths through the positions represented on the chart.

• CHAPTER SUMMARY

- Metaphysically, metaethical theories can be divided between the realist and antirealist, where the former allows for further distinction between the naturalist and nonnaturalist.
- Epistemologically, metaethical theories can be divided between the skeptical and the antiskeptical, where the latter allows for further distinction between intuitionist and empiricist/coherentist. Those who are skeptical about knowing genuine ethical facts are usually antirealists of some sort, but even they need to develop a story of what ordinary people are up to when talking about ethical knowledge.

- In the philosophy of language, metaethical theories can be divided between representationalist and antirepresentationalist, which usually maps directly onto a distinction in the philosophy of mind between cognitivist and noncognitivist theories.
- The philosophy of mind, or more specifically action theory and moral psychology, is where things get messier. We can, however, discern general theoretical inclinations based on how well each metaethical theory coheres with motivational internalism and the Humean psychology of motivation.
- The primary methodology of metaethics is theoretical cost–benefit analysis, taking one's intuitions in each of these four areas of philosophy and applying it to ethics in order to determine which theory carries the best balance of benefits over costs.

● STUDY QUESTIONS

1 Assuming one's strongest commitment in this area is to the reality of ethical facts, what are some of the routes one might take towards settling on a complete metaethical theory?
2 Assuming one's strongest commitment in this area is to a representationalist/cognitivist conception of moral language and thought, what are some of the routes one might take towards settling on a complete metaethical theory?
3 Assuming one's strongest commitment in this area is to a naturalist worldview, what are some of the routes one might take towards settling on a complete metaethical theory?
4 Assuming one's strongest commitment in this area is to motivational internalism, what are some of the routes one might take towards settling on a complete metaethical theory?

● ANSWERS TO QUESTIONS OF UNDERSTANDING

QU1: It's generally seen as a cost because there is no independent reason to think we have a special faculty of intuition, so the existence and nature of this (putative) faculty is controversial. No one denies, however, that we have intuitions about things, and recently epistemologists have paid a lot of attention to the epistemology of intuitions. So, if the nonnaturalist can explain how the faculty of moral intuition fits with this broader and less controversial notion of intuition, there may be a way to turn this cost into a benefit.

QU2: Consider an atomic ethical statement, such as "Aggressive war is morally wrong." This can be negated as follows: "Aggressive war is not morally wrong." Error-theorists and fictionalists will typically think the negated sentence is *true*—not because they believe aggressive war is morally right, but because they think nothing really has ethical properties such as rightness and wrongness.

QU3:   A theory's merely being consistent with motivational internalism couldn't
        be a cost, as the theory could also be consistent with motivational external-
        ism. Many metaethicists are, however, persuaded by that it would be utterly
        weird if someone claims that an action is the morally right thing to do but
        has absolutely no motivation to perform the action. And this leads them to
        endorse some form of motivational internalism. So, if you're persuaded by
        that, a theory's being *inconsistent* with motivational internalism would be a
        cost.

7

theories that are hard to classify in traditional terms

In this chapter, we'll consider other metaethical theories that, in one way or another, reject some of the basic distinctions that we previously used to classify the four main theoretical traditions in metaethics. I will group these remaining theories into three main categories. First, there are several theories offering a more nuanced answer to the question: are ethical thoughts cognitive states ("belief-like") or conative states ("desire-like")? There are a few different ways to respond to this question by arguing that it is a false dichotomy. Perhaps ethical thoughts have belief-like *and* desire-like aspects or components. Second, there's a theoretical tradition tracing back to Hobbes' political philosophy whereby facts about political legitimacy are said to be "constructed" rather than, so to speak, already out there to be discovered. This is related to a tradition in moral philosophy that construes ethical properties as defined in part by the way people would react to situations under certain specified circumstances. Recently, some metaethicists have tried to extend and combine these ideas to defend the view that there are, in a sense, ethical facts but they are, quite generally, constructed out of the reactions of people in particular situations rather than already out there to be discovered. Third, quite independently of metaethics, some philosophers have expressed skepticism about the common model of language that assumes, as the default view, that statements are attempted representations of reality. As we've seen, expressivists argue that ethical statements are not attempted representations of reality, but they tend to assume that's an exception to the general rule about assertoric language. However, rather than see the burden of proof on anti-representationalists about ethical statements, a more general antirepresentationalism in the philosophy of language might shift the burden of proof to representationalists. One of the main traditions in the philosophy of language is a view that explains meanings in terms of conceptual roles rather than representation. Here, we'll explore how it might provide some means for this burden-shifting move and its consequences for metaethics.

All of these ideas have knock-on effects for the way we think of the chart of metaethical theories and the dialectical situation one faces as one moves through that chart in search of the theory with the best ratio of theoretical benefits to costs.

• BELIEFS OR DESIRES—WHY NOT A BIT OF BOTH?

McDowell

In a set of papers far too rich to do full justice here, McDowell (1998, pt. 2) defends a metaethical view that doesn't fit neatly into our previous categories. This is mainly for two reasons.

First, McDowell defends a form of realism which he construes as naturalistic; however, he denies that ethical facts reduce to or otherwise "fit" among the scientifically discoverable facts. Rather than embrace nonnaturalism, however, he accuses other philosophers of a pernicious **scientism** in their conception of nature. That is, he suggests we have been wrong to think that the ultimate standard for determining whether a putative fact counts as a natural fact is whether it reduces to the kinds of fact that figure in the law-like explanations of empirical sciences. He argues instead for an expansion of our conception of nature "beyond what is countenanced in a naturalism of the realm of law"(McDowell, 1994, 88). This is a conception of nature as including a set of facts about reasons for action that are not discoverable by science but only by developing our wisdom through a process of socialization in community and practical education. He writes, "the picture is that ethics involves requirements of reason that are there whether we know it or not, and our eyes are opened to them by the acquisition of 'practical wisdom'"(1994, 79).

It's worth noting that, like Foot and Hursthouse, McDowell is inspired by Aristotle, but his claim to be a naturalist about ethical facts is importantly different from theirs. They propose to expand a previously narrow conception of scientifically discoverable facts (consisting mainly of physical and chemical facts) to also include facts about human nature (discoverable through sciences like biology, ethology, anthropology, sociology, etc.); and from this they try to derive ethical facts from facts about how humans should be in light of our characteristic way of living. So they would seem to accept that science is our route to knowledge of the natural world; they just accept a more capacious understanding of what counts as science than is typically presupposed by metaethical discussion of naturalism. By contrast, McDowell's suggestion is that it's simply wrong to think that science is the arbiter of what facts really obtain as part of nature. This means that, although he adopts the mantel of "naturalism," he doesn't show how ethical facts reduce to or otherwise fit among facts uncontroversially regarded as natural.

Second, McDowell rejects the Humean psychology of motivation that was a background assumption in much of our previous discussion of various metaethical views. That is, he denies that the mental states contributing to the motivation to act can always be neatly divided into those which aim to fit the way the world is and those that aim to change the world to fit them. Instead, he thinks that ethical knowledge involves intertwined descriptive and directive aspects of our thought that make it impossible to factor neatly into "belief-like" and "desire-like" components. This rejection of the Humean psychology of motivation makes room for the suggestion that there is some knowledge that one simply cannot have without also being (at least partially) motivated in certain ways. His thought is that ethical knowledge is like that—it has both cognitive and conative aspects, but these cannot be factored into separable components.

To appreciate what McDowell has in mind, let's consider an example. Assume that a good person knows, and so believes, that spreading damaging gossip is a nasty thing to do. McDowell's suggestion is that a belief like this one is a fully cognitive state of mind: it represents the action of spreading damaging gossip as being a nasty thing to do. However, he'd also say that one doesn't count as having that belief unless one is motivated to avoid spreading damaging gossip. This is the case not because the content of the belief implicates desires, rather it's because the belief itself guarantees (partial) motivation to avoid spreading damaging gossip. The idea is that to count as applying the concept "a nasty thing to do" in the full-fledged way characteristic of ethical knowledge, one must have enough practical wisdom to be motivated not to do things to which one applies this concept.[1]

If this is right, McDowell can endorse a form of motivational internalism without having to follow the expressivist in saying that ethical judgments express desire-like attitudes rather than beliefs. That means that by giving up on the Humean psychology of motivation, he aspires to the advantage expressivists claimed over rival theories to capture motivational internalism about ethical judgments. But he does so without succumbing to the disadvantages expressivism seems to suffer in making sense of the semantics of ethical language and the possibility of genuine ethical knowledge.

> QU1: What would a Humean about motivation say about the example of someone's believing that spreading gossip is a nasty thing to do?

To assess this view for yourself, you'll want to consider whether you find McDowell's soft naturalism too soft to fit with your prior views about naturalism about what's real. You'll also want to consider whether it's acceptable to reject the Humean psychology of motivation.

Ecumenical expressivism

A different way to try to get some of the advantages of expressivism while avoiding some of the disadvantages is to be "ecumenical" about what mental states are expressed by ethical judgments. That is, when asked whether ethical judgments express cognitive or noncognitive states, some philosophers respond with: why not both?

We can divide metaethical views pursuing this strategy into two groups. The first group is *expressivist* in the sense that, like other expressivists, they think it is crucial to understanding the meaning of ethical sentences that we view them as conventional vehicles for expressing conative states. However, they are **ecumenical expressivists** because they also think part of the story about the meaning of ethical sentences will also advert to their being conventional vehicles for expressing cognitive states linked to the conative states in the right way.[2]

There are several different ways to work out this idea. But the basic form is to start with the thought that all sentences mean what they do partially in virtue of the states of mind conventionally linked to them. Then the ecumenical expressivist argues that the state of mind linked in this way to an ethical sentence is a kind of hybrid consisting of both conative and cognitive elements. For example, a traditional expressivist might claim that the sentence "Stealing is wrong" means what it does partially in virtue of expressing disapproval. However, there's room to argue that this is not disapproval of some specific action, person, state of affairs, etc. but rather disapproval of things in general, insofar as they have a particular property—what might be thought of as the naturalistic basis of the disapproval (e.g., the property of causing a lot of pain). And making that move would allow one also to claim that this sentence means what it does partially in virtue of expressing a belief that stealing has that property (e.g., the property of causing a lot of pain). That is, a simple version of ecumenical expressivsm says that the meaning of the sentence is a matter of its expressing both disapproval of things insofar as they have some natural property, call it F, and a belief that stealing is F. In short, ethical sentences mean what they do because they express both a belief and a desire-like state.

In a quasi-realist spirit, ecumenical expressivists usually go on to insist that there's nothing wrong with claiming that ethical sentences simply express ethical "beliefs," as long as we recognize that the nature of these beliefs is hybrid in the sense that they contain both cognitive representations of reality as being a certain way (e.g., stealing causes a lot of pain) and noncognitive attitudes linked to this belief in the right way (e.g., disapproval of things insofar as they cause a lot of pain). The view intended as a form of expressivism because the mental state expressed by ethical sentences is, as part of why these sentences have the meanings that they do, partially noncognitive. This means that, although ethical thought represents ways reality could be on this view, the ecumenical expressivist isn't committed to the reality of genuinely ethical properties. It's only the cognitive element of an ethical thought that represents reality.

Ecumenical expressivists characteristically claim to get the "best of both worlds" when it comes to the cognitivism vs. noncognitivism debate. Like cognitivists, they can explain why ethical thought often behaves in ways characteristic of belief (e.g., its content can be embedded in various ways related to the Frege–Geach Problem); but like noncognitivists they can explain why ethical thought behaves in ways characteristic of desires (e.g., it has the potential to motivate action without the help of further desires).

> **Key Point**: Ecumenical expressivists think that ethical thoughts (i.e. the mental states expressed by ethical statements) are hybrid in that they have separable cognitive and conative elements.

To assess this view for yourself, you'll want to consider whether there is a *principled* motivation for pasting cognitive and conative elements together in our view of ethical thought. If not, ecumenical expressivism begins to look to be an ad hoc amalgamation of two competing ideas motivated only by the fact that neither is completely defensible. You'll also want to consider whether the view really does get the best of both worlds, and whether the price it pays for this (mainly in theoretical complexity when it comes to the philosophy of language and philosophy of mind) is worth that, given other options.

Hybrid cognitivism

The second group of philosophers pursuing the "why not both?" strategy are ethical naturalists who find room for the expression of desire-like states somewhere else in their overall philosophy of language as it applies to ethical discourse. Recall that ethical naturalists are realists, but unlike nonnaturalists they hold that ethical facts are a species of natural fact. In Chapter 5, we discussed various strategies naturalists have pursued for explaining which natural facts are the ethical facts. On some of these, the ethical claims turn out to be (perhaps surprisingly) about our own motivations, in which case it is explicable how the beliefs expressed by these claims might be tightly connected to motivation. However, those views have subjectivist or relativist implications (leading to difficulty explaining moral disagreement, and the problem of delimiting the relevant community) that many find unpalatable. But all of the other alternatives seem committed to denying that ethical beliefs are *internally* connected to motivation; and being driven to motivational externalism seems to many to be a theoretical cost. But it wouldn't be such a cost if ethical statements were thought to express not only beliefs about some natural fact but also some desire-like state of mind. Unlike the ecumenical expressivist, however, **hybrid cognitivists** argue that this isn't due to the literal meaning of the relevant sentences but rather some aspect of their pragmatic function or characteristic use.

To understand what this might mean, it's helpful to understand the phenomenon of **implicature**. Grice (1989) pointed out that what someone says and what they mean in saying it are not always the same; indeed often we say one thing but mean another. Grice called this phenomenon "implicature"; the idea being that there's often a difference between the literal content of one's assertion and what one implicates by this assertion. There is a rich literature on the various kinds of implicature, but we can restrict our focus to two kinds.

First, contextual elements of an ongoing conversation are often tacitly employed by speakers to implicate something and tracked by hearers to make sense of what the speaker means. For example, if we meet on the street during a week of rainy weather, you might say, "It's another nice day." Although your assertion literally means *that it is another nice day*, you don't mean that and I know you don't mean that. You implicate something like, "The weather this week has been horrible." This phenomenon is called **conversational implicature** because the implicature is achieved through variable features of the context in which the statement is made (i.e. the weather conditions of which speaker and hearer are both fully aware) rather than anything having to do with the conventions with which we use words. Because of this, it doesn't seem to be part of our specifically linguistic abilities that we can understand how what someone means differs from the literal content of the sentences they use to express themselves; rather it's part of our general purpose ability to keep track of sundry features of our environment and understand why other people do what they do.

Second, some words and phrases seem to have been conventionalized as mechanisms for implicating something. For example, on some views of the conjunctions 'and' and 'but' they carry the same literal semantic content (conjunction), but the latter also implicates that there is some tension between the two things conjoined. Consider the difference between someone saying, "He's from the hills of eastern Kentucky and wicked smart," and "He's from the hills of eastern Kentucky but wicked smart." Unlike the former, the latter suggests somehow that it is surprising that someone from the hills of eastern Kentucky might be wicked smart. Some philosophers of language attribute this to a convention attaching to 'but' which means that it implicates some tension between the elements it coordinates in a sentence. This phenomenon is called **conventional implicature**.

QU2: Imagine someone said "Even Joe passed the test," what would this implicate?

It is controversial in linguistics and the philosophy of language how best to understand implicature and whether this division between conversational and conventional implicature is the right way to make sense of the linguistic phenomena. But using that distinction as a rough tool, we can now begin to see how an ethical naturalist might defend the claim that an ethical judgment expresses a belief about some natural fact but also expresses a desire-like attitude relevant for the psychology of motivation. The basic idea would be to argue that although ethical sentences are literally about natural facts, their use to make a statement implicates that the speaker has some desire-like attitude.

There are different versions of this idea. Using the model of conversational implicature, a hybrid cognitivist might argue that the expression of a desire-like attitude is a possible (or even common) feature of the context in which ethical sentences are ordinarily used, but not something that attaches to those sentences in virtue of the linguistic conventions surrounding the words they contain. For instance, Finlay (2005) argues that ethical statements can conversationally implicate that the speaker desires some end or goal. On the other hand, using the model of conventional implicature, a hybrid cognitivst might instead argue that ethical words carry a conventionalized role of conveying that the speaker desires something. For instance, Copp (2001) argues that ethical statements conventionally implicate that the speaker desires (at least somewhat) to act in their accord.

There's another way for a hybrid cognitivist to go here (Tresan, 2006). Rather than relying on pragmatic notions about what ethical statements implicate (either conversationally or conventionally), they might argue that what makes a statement an *ethical* statement is that the speaker has a profile of desires, preferences, plans, etc. that is characteristic of people engaged in ethical discourse. More specifically, in order to count as participating in the practice of genuine ethical discourse, we might think someone must have whatever desire-like states are needed to explain the tight connection between ethical judgment and motivation. So, on this kind of view, it's not an implicature of a particular speech-act which ensures the presence of a desire-like state, rather this is part of what makes one's speech part of the language-game of ethics: one doesn't count as making an *ethical* statement unless one has the relevant desire-like state.

I've just put the point in terms of ethical *language*, but we can make the same point at the level of *thought*. That is, one might suggest that what makes a belief an *ethical* belief is that the believer has a profile of desires, preferences, plans, etc. that is characteristic of people engaged in ethical thought: more specifically, whatever desire-like states are needed to explain the tight connection between ethical judgment and motivation.

Like ecumenical expressivism, hybrid cognitivism also attempts to claim the best of both worlds. To assess them for yourself, you'll want to consider whether they integrate the desire-like element connected to ethical discourse in a plausible way. As naturalist views, these theories are also committed to making good on the challenge to explain which natural facts are the ethical facts. So, we'll still need to assess their ability to make ethical facts reduce to or otherwise fit with uncontroversially natural facts.

• ETHICAL FACTS—WHY DO THEY HAVE TO BE "OUT THERE"?

One might hold—as we've seen that error-theorists and fictionalists do—that representationalism is true but that no ethical facts objectively obtain, somehow "out there" in reality for us to discover. This seems to commit one to the radical view that atomic ethical beliefs and the statements that express them (such as your belief that murder is wrong or my statement that charity is good) are literally false. To avoid such radical commitments, many cognitivists are "success theorists," in the sense that they think at least some ethical facts obtain objectively, rendering some (possible atomic) ethical beliefs and statements true. As we've witnessed, however, this seems to commit realists to developing a metaphysical account of what objective ethical facts are like, and herein lay the challenges for metaethical nonnaturalism and non-naturalism that we discussed in previous chapters.

All of that might lead one into the expressivist's arms. But an alternative response to these challenges to representationalism is to suggest that we've got the wrong picture of what ethical facts would have to be like in order for our ethical claims to be true. By assuming they would have to be "objective" in the sense of antecedently there to be discovered by ethical inquiry, we occlude the possibility that ethical facts obtain, but are in some way significantly ontologically dependent in some way on our sentiments, reasoning, or points of view. On this kind of view, there are ethical facts but they aren't completely "out there" in the sense of characteristic of more robust forms of realism. There are several different ways to develop this line of thought, but here we'll focus on two core ideas: the idea that ethical facts are ontologically dependent on the hypothetical responses of some appropriately placed observer and the idea that ethical facts are "constructions" of human thought.

Response-dependence

Response-dependent views hold that an action's having an ethical property is ontologically dependent on how observers of some yet-to-be-specified kind under some yet-to-be-specified conditions would respond to the action.[3] On some ways of developing that idea, it simply becomes the subjectivist form of the relativist view we considered in Chapter 5. You'll recall that the subjectivist claims that ethical facts are identical facts about the subjective values of different people. For example, the statement "It was wrong for Bush to start the war in Iraq" would be treated by the subjectivist as the expression of a belief about what follows from the speaker's own subjective ethical commitments or values.

Although views like these are sometimes considered antirealist, I suggested before that we might understand them as forms of naturalistic realism, albeit ones maintaining that at least some core ethical facts are not universal. As long as the ethical facts (construed as facts about the subjective values of different people) are in principle discoverable by empirical methods, we might maintain that they are as "out there" as any other empirically discoverable fact. At least they're as "objective" as facts about human psychology. For example, when Hume wrote, "[W]hen you pronounce any action or character to be vicious, you mean nothing, but that from the constitution of your nature you have a feeling or sentiment of blame from the contemplation of it" (2000, 469), it could mean that moral judgments are simply factual judgments about our own feelings.

However, that's probably not exactly Hume's fully considered view. And, in any case, there are related views that pursue more subtle strategies for fleshing out the idea that an action's having an ethical property is ontologically dependent on how observers of some yet-to-be-specified kind under some yet-to-be-specified conditions would respond to the action. These are more difficult to place within the realism/

antirealism dichotomy. They are also in a better position than subjectivism to respect many of our pretheoretic intuitions about ethics.

To see what kinds of view I have in mind, it can be helpful to make two cross-cutting distinctions regarding these views. First, metaethicists often distinguish between **sentimentalism** and **rationalism** as ways to develop versions of response-dependent views depending on the kinds of responses that are thought to be relevant to constituting ethical facts. Sentimentalists hold that it is the ideal observer's conative responses such as approval and disapproval that constitute morality; by contrast, rationalists hold that it is the ideal observer's beliefs (i.e. cognitive reactions) that something is good/bad that constitute morality. Second, metaethicists often distinguish between universalistic and relativistic versions of response-dependent views depending on whether one thinks that there is some one response that determines morality for everyone or the possibility of multiple incompatible responses determining morality for different groups of people.

If Hume wasn't a subjectivist, then it is likely that he accepted some sort of sentimentalist response-dependent view. Adam Smith also developed a view in this general direction. However, it is Firth (1952) who did the most to reintroduce response-dependent views into twentieth-century discussions of metaethics. He argued for a universalistic version of the view and at least suggests sentimentalism (though leaves open the precise psychological nature of the ethically relevant responses). His view was universalistic because he characterized an ideal observer whose dispositions to have an ethically significant reaction to something x were claimed to be determinative of whether x had the relevant ethical property. Firth argued that we could characterize the ideal observer by examining the abstract features of ethical decision making that we regard as rational to deploy. Doing this, he thought of the ideal observer as a kind of theoretical construct of what it would take to be the perfect ethical judge: someone who is omniscient with regard to the non-ethical facts, omnipercipient with regard to the types of things that one might experience, impartial concerning competing interests of any parties involved, dispassionate, consistent, but otherwise normal. Given this, then, a judgment such as "It was wrong for Bush to start the war in Iraq" would—on Firth's view—be true just in case Bush's starting the war would elicit negative ethical reaction from an omniscient, omnipercipient, impartial, dispassionate, consistent, but an otherwise normal judge.

This counts as sentimentalist insofar as we think of the ethical reaction as a sentimental and so "conative" response. For example, if we think of it as a negative emotion towards the object of ethical evaluation, then it's the ideal observer's disposition to have certain *sentiments* that ultimately grounds the wrongness of the action. On the other hand, one could use the same basic framework to develop a rationalist version of the response-dependent view by thinking of the relevant ethical reaction as a belief and so "cognitive" response to the object of ethical evaluation.

Another way to understand response-dependent views is by comparing ethical concepts to color concepts. It's not obvious that colors are response-dependent, but they're a pretty good candidate for something whose reality is in some sense in the eye of the (possible) beholder. The rough idea is that the best handle we have on what it means to think of something as red, for example, is to think about what it would look like under ideal conditions for viewing something's color. It is relatively straightforward to characterize ideal conditions for seeing something's color: it has to be daylight; the observer cannot be wearing tinted glasses; drugs affecting color vision must be avoided, etc. Then, one might say that what it is for something to be red is just for it to be such that an ideal observer would think that it was red. Notice that this doesn't make something's color depend on the actual existence of an observer. Objects in a dark room where no one is observing would still count as red on this view. It's just that they would have to be such that *were* they observed by an ideal observer, that person would judge that they are red.

Metaethicists such as Johnston (1989), Lewis (1989), Smith (1994), and Prinz (2007) have sought to adapt this model to ethical values. I won't get into the (often complex) details of their views, except to say that the comparison can be used to develop all four possible combinations of sentimentalist/rationalist and universalistic/relativistic versions of the view. For example, Lewis develops a sentimentalist universalistic version of the view, while Smith develops a rationalist universalistic version of the view, and Prinz uses response-dependence to work out relativistic sentimentalism. Whatever the exact combination, the important point, for our present purposes, about the comparison to colors is that there seem to be facts about what colors things are, but these facts have seemed to many to be not as "out there" in the fabric of reality as other facts (such as facts about the chemical constitution of various substances). If that's right, and ethical facts are similarly response dependent, then we might have a view of ethical facts that treats them as perfectly real but not completely "out there" in the sense characteristically claimed by more robust forms of realism.

> *Key Point*: Response-dependent views treat ethical facts as ontologically and/ or conceptually dependent on the dispositions of some kind of observer to respond to things in certain ways. Because of this, ethical facts are less "out there" than facts ordinarily subject to empirical discovery.

It's worth noting in this context that one prominent way to develop the **divine command theory**, which we encountered briefly in the Introduction, is along the lines of a response-dependent view. The idea would be to appeal to *God* as the ideal agent, whose (perhaps merely hypothetical) responses to an action constitute its ethical rightness/wrongness.

Constructivism

A related but subtly different constellation of ideas proposes to treat ethical facts as "constructions" of practical reasoning rather than something obtaining independently that practical reasoning aims to discover. Working out this possibility is the heart of a contemporary view in metaethics known as **constructivism**.

Although the term comes from a view in the philosophy of mathematics (which construes mathematical truths as constructions of human thought rather than obtaining independently of our abilities to think abstractly), constructivists in metaethics are often inspired by the tradition of social-contract theory in political philosophy tracing through Hobbes, Rousseau, Kant, and Rawls. In the political context, the issue isn't ethical facts in general, but a species of ethical facts, such as facts about our rights.

One way to understand the basic idea is by thinking that facts about justice (e.g., what rights we have as members of a political community) are not something we could *discover* by some kind of empirical investigation, but rather something that is *constructed* out of the contours of a particular sort of practical challenge we face in living together. Rawls for example asked us to imagine an **original position** where people are designing the basic principles of society but behind a **veil of ignorance** about which particular people they will be in society they are legislating for. Participants in the original position are assumed to be applying various principles about how to choose principles to live by, and they are assumed to agree broadly on what sorts of things it takes to make a life go well (though they may have different conceptions of the good life). Rawls' thought then, is to construe facts about justice as having no independent status but rather as being constructions of this hypothetical choice situation: in sum, facts about justice (e.g., that free speech is a right) are constituted as what would be agreed to in the original position.

The key point for metaethics is the suggestion that the procedure for determining outcomes within a particular standpoint is fundamental in our understanding of what those facts are like. Accordingly, a constructivist about justice holds that there are facts about justice, but these facts aren't "objective" in the sense of standing free from the procedures of something like the original position that are used to determine them. Rather those facts are constituted by their emerging from certain procedures deployed from a particular standpoint (e.g., participants in the original position agreeing on what rights to confer to everyone).

As far as that goes, however, the constructivist position applies only to a species of ethical facts (facts about justice). However, a proponent of the view uses other apparently ethical concepts (principles about how to choose and agreement about what it takes for a life to go well) in their characterization of the procedure, emergence from which would constitute the relevant facts. As such, the constructivist position in political philosophy seems to just push the relevant metaethical questions back a stage: do claims about what choice principles participants of the original position use count as "representations" of some objective facts, do any such facts really obtain, and if so are they natural or nonnatural? How should we conceive of views about what it generally takes to make a life go well—are these cognitive representations of reality or noncognitive attitudes towards things or some kind of pretense? Because of this, constructivism about justice seems to be a complication we could add to any of our main metaethical views rather than a freestanding alternative to those views.

Hence, to have a constructivist view in *metaethics*, one needs to claim that *all* ethical facts are "constructions" rather than apt for discovery. However, this immediately raises a challenge. If we understand "constructions" as what emerges from some procedure, then constructivists face a dilemma (Hussain and Shah, 2006; Enoch, 2009). On the one hand, if the procedures are procedures we can characterize in completely naturalistic terms, then the view looks to be a fancy form of naturalistic realism rather than an alternative to it. On the other hand, if the procedures a constructivist appeals to are ones we must use irreducibly ethical (or at least normative) concepts to characterize, then the view looks to be a fancy form of nonnaturalistic realism.

QU3: Consider the view that something's being valuable is constituted by its being such that an average person would value it at least a little bit. Why might one think that's just a fancy form of naturalist realism?

In light of this challenge, recent metaethical constructivists such as Korsgaard (2003) and Street (2010) have tended to characterize their constructivism in terms of what follows from the "practical standpoint" rather than in terms of what would emerge from some hypothetical procedure. Their idea is to distinguish a disengaged point of view from which we might represent the value-free way things are in reality from an engaged point of view from which we take some things to be more and less valuable, thus generating reasons for us to act in various ways. This should remind you of the move expressivists make encouraging us to ask not about value (whose metaphysical status is controversial) but about valuing (which is conceived as a perfectly natural attitude humans and others might have towards something). However, unlike expressivists, constructivists then make claims about what the practical standpoint *as such* entails. The import of "as such" is to force us to think abstractly about practical reasoning in general rather than about one among several possible practical outlooks. The original position, as Rawls characterized it, imports substantive assumptions about what are better and worse ways to choose basic principles to live by, whereas a thoroughgoing form of constructivism would need to operate with a thinner or merely "formal" characterization of practical reasoning and the standpoint it comprises. In this way, constructivists hope to argue that one doesn't count as taking some things to be more and less valuable unless one is committed to certain ethical facts.

Hence, according to metaethical constructivists, if there were no beings who could take some things to be valuable, then nothing would be valuable. For there to be reasons to act, there must be agents taking up the practical standpoint, trying to decide how to act. So, although constructivists conceive of ethical judgments as beliefs, and indeed beliefs which can be true because of the obtaining of the corresponding facts, these beliefs are not conceived as being about some piece of reality obtaining independently of the (at least possible) existence of agents taking up the practical standpoint. In this way, they're importantly different from the way we standardly conceive of beliefs about the natural world.

Does that mean that ethical facts aren't *objective?* In a sense, yes. Constructivists hold that there are ethical facts but these are a construction of the practical standpoint rather than facts obtaining objectively in the sense of being "out there" independent of human modes of thought. However, in another sense, constructivism leaves the question about objectivity open. Korsgaard defends a "Kantian" version of constructivism, according to which certain *universal* ethical truths are entailed by the practical standpoint considered as such (or characterized merely formally). This means that there are some reasons every agent has, no matter what their particular desires or ends happen to be. If such universal norms of conduct are indeed entailed by the practical standpoint, considered as such, there would be another sense in which those ethical facts are objective, even though constructed. However, Street defends a "Humean" version of constructivism, according to which no substantive universal ethical truths are entailed by the practical standpoint considered as such. Instead, she thinks practical reasons emerge for an agent only once we add to the practical standpoint his or her particular and contingent cares and concerns. So, for her, there are no objective values, but only the values that follow from one's evaluative starting point when focussed through the practical standpoint.

> **Key Point**: Metaethical constructivists hold that there are ethical facts but they are "constructed" rather than apt for discovery, in the sense that whatever reality they have depends on the standpoint of reasoning practically.

• PRAGMATISM

The main antirepresentationalist option among traditional metaethical theories is expressivism. Metaethical expressivists typically accept as a kind of default rule that declarative sentences are about the way reality is, and their distinctive claim is that ethical sentences are different: They are not best understood as representations of reality but rather expressions of something like emotion, preference, norm-acceptance, or plan. This is what makes expressivists antirepresentationalists *about ethical discourse.* As we have seen, this position promises advantages in metaphysics and the philosophy of mind, but it carries costs in epistemology and the philosophy of language.

Somewhat independently of metaethical debate, there is a tradition in the philosophy of language and mind that might be applied to ethical discourse and thought. And when it is, it would seem to carry some of the same advantages as expressivism, but it might avoid some of these costs. This is called **pragmatism**.

There are many different theses and theoretical persuasions going under the label "pragmatism" (which I won't attempt to survey here). The key claim that is relevant here is that there is a rich plurality of kinds of words and concepts, and that the best way to understand a particular word or the concept it expresses is not by asking what it stands for but by asking what it does for us in the various conceptually infused practices in which we humans engage. For example, consider the logical word 'not,' as in "Ian is *not* at home." In the pragmatist's view, to understand the meaning of this word (and the concept it expresses) we should focus on what it does for us rather than on what it stands for. In this case, the beginning of a plausible account is that the word 'not' provides us a way to *reject* or *deny* something. We might end up saying that 'not' denotes *negation*. But according to the pragmatist this isn't because there is some element of reality (not-ness?, negativity?) which a sentence (like the one about Ian) somehow represents, but rather because of the distinctive role this term has in the practice of rejecting and denying.

Here's another example: consider the **epistemic modal** 'might,' as in "Ian *might* be at home." Is there something this word refers to, such as the "might-ness" of Ian's being at home that this sentence represents as part of reality, and whose nature we could investigate? The pragmatist thinks this is the wrong question to ask. Instead the pragmatist encourages us to ask about the function of the word 'might' in our practices. The beginning of a plausible account is that this word provides a means for qualifying an outright assertion relative to our evidence. For instance, rather than saying that Ian *is* at home, one says he *might* be at home when one cannot rule it out but also cannot assert it outright. By switching our focus from what terms refer to or what sentences represent to what function they play in our diverse practices, pragmatists hope to paint a more varied picture of language use (and conceptually infused thought).

This should sound familiar. When we discussed expressivism in Chapter 3, I said that expressivists typically encourage us to begin our metaethical enquiry by asking not about (i) the nature of some kind of supposedly real thing: ethical value, but about (ii) the nature of one of our practices: making ethical evaluations. Then, their answer to question (ii) typically claims some interesting disanalogy between ethical evaluations and representations of reality. We might now view this as an instance of the core pragmatist approach. But pragmatists typically go on to argue that the same approach should be applied outside of ethics—e.g., to logical terms such as 'not,' and to epistemic modals such as 'might.' This isn't because statements containing these terms express desire-like attitudes rather than beliefs, but because their role in our practices is something other than representing pieces of reality (Chrisman, 2014). Indeed, pragmatists needn't be committed to the characteristic expressivist answer to this question about ethical language. If there is a diverse plurality of kinds of words and concepts, each with different functions in our practices, then as long as we can find some function plausibly attributed to ethical words that isn't one of representing ethical properties, and this function can be sustained without thinking of ethical words as also representational, we will have secured an antirepresentationalist account of ethical language. This means that pragmatists in metaethics gain whatever advantages are accorded to expressivism in virtue of their antirepresentationalism in the philosophy of language. Moreover, pragmatists have more flexibility to develop a nuanced account of the non-representational function of ethical thought (since expressing desire-like states doesn't *have* to be part of the story as long as doing something other than representing reality is part of the story). This means that pragmatists in metaethics potentially improve on the advantages accorded to expressivism in virtue of its philosophy of mind.

What about the potential costs of expressivism in epistemology and the philosophy of language? Here, a lot is going to depend on the specific story about ethical discourse developed by pragmatists, but we can say something general. If ethical discourse isn't special in being nonrepresentational because there are other sorts of discourse that are nonrepresentational, then there cannot be a special problem about ethical knowledge and the semantics of ethical sentences stemming from the pragmatist claim that ethical discourse is not for representing reality. After all, something one might *know* is that Ian is not at home or that Ian might be at home. So, if these sentences aren't construed as representations of reality, we're going to need some more general pragmatist-friendly account of knowledge which is not of the way reality is.

Similarly, sentences containing 'might' and 'not' are clearly embeddable in semantically complex contexts such as in "if-then" conditionals. So if these sentences aren't construed as representations of reality, we're going to need some more general pragmatist-friendly account of the composition of semantically complex sentences containing these sentences as parts. (Notice that this is a kind of "partners-in-crime" response on the part of the metaethical pragmatist to the problems facing expressivism in epistemology and the philosophy of language.)

> QU4: What might a metaethical pragmatist say to the objection that ethical sentences are clearly truth-apt and so must be seen as representations of reality?

Some philosophers have suggested that the pragmatist maneuver (of switching our focus from questions about the referents of words to their function in our diverse practices) will—insofar as it is successful—undermine the very idea of some bits of language representing pieces of reality. Indeed, some pragmatists have embraced this consequence, casting their view in the philosophy of language as a sort of **global expressivism**: where the expressivist thought only ethical language expresses rather than represents, the pragmatist says that all language expresses rather than represents (Price, 2011). One thing you'll want to consider as you evaluate metaethical pragmatism for yourself is whether this is indeed a consequence of the view, and, if so, whether it is a bad consequence.

• CONCLUSION

The main metaethical positions considered in the previous chapters broke into four categories based on three questions:

1 Do ethical facts obtain objectively? (Realism vs. Antirealism)
2 If so, do these facts reduce to or otherwise fit with the natural facts? (Naturalism vs. Nonnaturalism)
3 If not, do ethical statements/thoughts represent a way reality could be? (Error theory/Fictionalism vs. Expressivism)

In this chapter, however, we have seen how these categories can be challenged. In different ways, McDowellians, ecumenical expressivists, and hybrid cognitivists all argue that it's a false dichotomy to wonder whether ethical thoughts are representations of reality *or* motivational pressures on action, since they could possibly involve both. Response-dependent views and constructivist views hold that the question of whether ethical facts obtain objectively doesn't admit of a straightforward answer. Their view is that ethical facts are not "out there" waiting to be discovered, since they are ontologically dependent on the hypothetical responses of an ideal agent or obtain as "constructions" of the practical standpoint. Finally, pragmatists argue that there are other avenues for arguing that ethical statements/thoughts do not represent a way reality could be besides the expressivist claim that ethical statements are distinctive in expressing desire-like attitudes rather than beliefs.

In a much more tentative vein, we might try to capture the more complicated theoretical landscape with Figure 7.1.

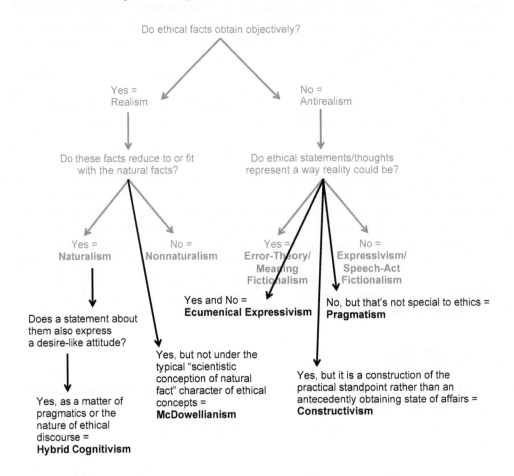

Figure 7.1 Some hard to classify metaethical theories

Metaethics is an exciting subdiscipline of philosophy in part because of the possibility of bringing to bear the methodology of theoretical cost–benefit analysis on these new positions in order to evaluate whether any of them are more attractive overall than the traditional positions. It is outside the scope of this book to explore these positions that break some of the traditional categories in any more detail. However, current debate in metaethics often addresses these (and some more) nuanced positions.

● CHAPTER SUMMARY

- McDowell argues that ethical judgments can both represent reality and motivate action because the conditions of possessing particular ethical concepts carry a requirement of having the practical wisdom to exercise these concepts correctly in action.
- Ecumenical expressivists argue that ethical statements express an amalgam state consisting of both a belief about reality and an interlocking desire-like pressure on action.
- Hybrid cognitivism is a form of metaethical naturalism that attempts to steal the motivation for expressivism by finding other ways to view ethical statements as expressing desire-like attitudes (in additions to beliefs about reality).
- Response-dependent views treat ethical facts as ontologically dependent on the hypothetical responses (either sentimental or rational) of idealized observers, and so in that sense not fully "out there" like other sorts of empirically discoverable facts.
- Constructivism in metaethics argues that ethical facts do not obtain objectively, in the sense of being "out there" to be discovered, but are rather constructions of the practical standpoint.
- Metaethical pragmatists argue that pragmatism as a general philosophy of language and mind provides different resources for an antirepresentationalist account of ethical language than traditional expressivism.

● STUDY QUESTIONS

1 How does McDowell's Aristotle-inspired "naturalism" contrast with Hursthouse's Aristotle-inspired "naturalism"?
2 Ecumenical expressivists are typically seen as antirealists drawing on the tradition of expressivism, whereas hybrid cognitivists are typically seen as realists drawing on the tradition of naturalism. What is the difference in their ontological commitments, and which side is better for this?
3 What's the difference between constructivists in metaethics and quasi-realist expressivists?
4 What's the difference between pragmatists in metaethics and quasi-realist expressivists?

• FURTHER RESOURCES

- Chrisman, Matthew. 2011. "Ethical Expressivism," in *The Continuum Companion to Ethics*. Continuum. [Covers ecumenical expressivism in more detail.]
- Chrisman, Matthew. 2014. "Attitudinal Expressivism and Logical Pragmatism," in Hubbs, G. and Lind, D. (eds.), *Pragmatism, Law, and Language*. Routledge: 117–35. [Introduces pragmatism in metaethics.]
- Finlay, Stephen. 2007. "Four Faces of Moral Realism," *Philosophy Compass* 2 (6): 820–49. [Discusses constructivism in more detail.]
- Fletcher, Guy and Ridge, Michael (eds.) 2014. *Having It Both Ways: Hybrid Theories and Modern Metaethics*. Oxford University Press. [A volume of collected essays on the "why not both" option.]
- Ridge, Michael. 2006. "Ecumenical Expressivism: Finessing Frege," *Ethics* 116 (2): 302–36. [Seminal essay introducing ecumenical expressivism.]
- Schroeder, Mark. 2009. "Hybrid Expressivism: Virtues and Vices," *Ethics* 119 (2): 257–309. [Influential essay comparing and contrasting various ways of working out the "why not both" option.]
- Street, Sharon. 2010. "What is Constructivism in Ethics and Metaethics?" *Philosophy Compass* 5: 363–84. [Introductory essay on constructivism.]

• ANSWERS TO QUESTIONS OF UNDERSTANDING

QU1: The Humean will insist that we can separate belief in a particular fact from desire-setting goals that move us in light of our beliefs. So even if people happen to be motivated not to do things they think are nasty, this will be because (a) they also have a desire to avoid doing nasty things, or (b) the thought that something is nasty is more like a preference not to do it rather than a representation of it as having a particular property. If this is right, for whatever interlocking pairs of cognitive representations of reality and goal-setting motivational state one has, we could always imagine some possible person having one of them but not the other. McDowell argues in contrast that some cognitive representations necessarily also carry goal-setting motivations.

QU2: This statement implicates that Joe was one of the least likely to pass the test, and so the test was probably very easy. This is a *conventional* implicature because it is part of the conventionalized linguistic role of 'even' in this sentence. (Notice how we don't require any particular set up of the conversational context to tell what implicature this statement carries.)

QU3: It's plausible that valuing something is a completely natural attitude (something like the attitude of preferring or taking pleasure in). And if that's right, then, according to the view sketched above, something's being valuable would in the end be a matter of whether the average person prefers it or takes pleasure in it. Since this is a natural fact, facts about what's valuable are natural facts.

QU4:   Pragmatists will deny that truth is in general a matter of correct representation of reality. Indeed the minimalist theory of truth we encountered in Chapter 3 can be viewed as another instance of the general pragmatist approach: ask not about what 'true' refers to but rather about what this word does for us in our diverse practices.

• WORKS CITED

Chrisman, Matthew (2014) "Attitudinal Expressivism and Logical Pragmatism," in G. Hubbs and D. Lind (eds.), Pragmatism, Law, and Language, Routledge: 117–35.

Copp, David. 2001. "Realist-Expressivism: A Neglected Option for Moral Realism." *Social Philosophy and Policy* 18: 1–43.

Enoch, David. 2009. "Can There Be a Global, Interesting, Coherent Constructivism About Practical Reason?" *Philosophical Explorations* 12 (3): 319–39.

Finlay, Stephen. 2005. "Value and Implicature." *Philosophers' Imprint* 5 (4): 1–20.

Firth, Roderick. 1952. "Ethical Absolutism and the Ideal Observer." *Philosophy and Phenomenological Research* 12: 317–45.

Grice, H. P. 1989. "Logic and Conversation." In *Studies in the Way of Words*, edited by H. P. Grice, 41–57. Cambridge, MA: Harvard University Press.

Hume, David. 2000. *A Treatise of Human Nature*. Edited by D. and M. Norton. Oxford Philosophical Texts. Oxford; New York: Oxford University Press.

Hussain, Nadeem, and Nishiten Shah. 2006. "Misunderstanding Metaethics: Korsgaard's Rejection of Realism." In *Oxford Studies in Metaethics, Vol. 1*, edited by R. Shafer-Landau, 1:265–94. Oxford; New York: Clarendon Press.

Johnston, Mark. 1989. "Dispositional Theories of Value." *Proceedings of the Aristotelian Society (Supplementary Volume)* 62: 139–74.

Korsgaard, Christine. 2003. "Realism and Constructivism in Moral Philosophy." *Journal of Philosophical Research, APA Centennial Supplement*, 99–122.

Lewis, David. 1989. "Dispositional Theories of Value." *Proceedings of the Aristotelian Society (Supplementary Volume)* 63: 89–174.

McDowell, John. 1985. "Values and Secondary Qualities." In *Morality and Objectivity*, edited by T. Honderich, 110–29. London: Routledge; Kegan Paul.

———. 1994. *Mind and World*. Cambridge, MA: Harvard University Press.

———. 1998. *Mind, Value, and Reality*. Cambridge, MA: Harvard University Press.

McNaughton, David. 1988. *Moral Vision*. Oxford: Basil Blackwell.

Price, Huw. 2011. "Expressivism for Two Voices." In *Pragmatism, Science and Naturalism*, edited by J. Knowles and H. Rydenfelt, 87–113. Frankfurt am Main: Peter Lang.

Prinz, Jesse J. 2007. *The Emotional Construction of Morals*. New York: Oxford University Press.

Ridge, Michael. 2006. "Ecumenical Expressivism: Finessing Frege." *Ethics* 116 (2): 302–36.

———. 2014. *Impassioned Belief*. Oxford: Oxford University Press.

Schroeder, Mark. 2009. "Hybrid Expressivism: Virtues and Vices." *Ethics* 119: 257–309.

Smith, Michael. 1994. *The Moral Problem*. Philosophical Theory. Oxford: Blackwell.

Street, Sharon. 2010. "What Is Constructivism in Ethics and Metaethics?" *Philosophy Compass* 5 (5): 363–84.

Toppinen, Teemu. 2013. "Believing in Expressivism." In *Oxford Studies in Metaethics, Vol. 8*, edited by R. Shafer-Landau, 252–82. New York: Oxford University Press.

Tresan, Jon. 2006. "De Dicto Internalist Cognitivism." *Noûs* 40 (1): 143–65.

Wiggins, David. 1987. "A Sensible Subjectivism?" In *Needs, Values and Truth*, 185–214. Oxford: Oxford University Press.

• NOTES

1 Some of McDowell's critics use the term **besire** (as an amalgamation of 'belief' and 'desire') to refer to McDowell's proposal that ethical beliefs necessarily carry motivational effect. This is not McDowell's term, and it is not clear that McDowell thinks every application of an ethical concept in a belief requires the attendant desire. But it's worth knowing the term as it is sometimes used in metaethical discussions as a term of mild derision for views that propose to expand our standard stock of psychological concepts, which includes beliefs and desires, to include one more which is the supposedly unseparable amalgam of both of the other two.

2 The term "ecumenical expressivism" is due to Ridge (2006). For similar views, see Schroeder (2009), Toppinen (2013), and Ridge (2014).

3 Some (e.g. McDowell, 1985, Wiggins, 1987, and McNaughton, 1988) argue that it's not how some agent *would* respond that constitutes the ethical properties of an action, but how they *should* respond. More specifically, they speak of an action's "meriting" or "warranting" various responses. While these are important and interesting views that can be difficult to place within the standard map of metaethical theories, I wouldn't classify these as response-dependent views in the sense relevant here unless they are explaining the notion of meriting or warranting a response that requires ineliminable reference to an observer. Otherwise, ethical properties are not ontologically dependent on the observer's responses; rather the correctness of the observer's responses is determined by independently obtaining ethical facts.

8

˙outstanding issues

At the beginning of this book, we considered ethical judgments such as the one made with the statement "Bush's invading Iraq was wrong." We haven't ventured any opinion here on whether such judgments are correct. Instead we've investigated the status of these judgments. This has involved exploring issues in metaphysics, epistemology, philosophy of language, and philosophy of mind as they apply to ethical thought and discourse. That is, we've focussed on metaethics.

One of the exciting recent developments around metaethics is the extension of the discussion of metaphysical, epistemological, linguistic, and psychological issues to other domains. For example, much like one can say that Bush shouldn't have started the war in Iraq, one might say that he shouldn't have believed that there were caches of weapons of mass destruction. However, evaluating beliefs in this way is not (normally) ethical; rather it's "epistemological." That is, it's about whether the belief meets *epistemic* standards for good belief, where these are usually based on evidence and truth rather than morality.

In a similar vein, we might ask whether someone's belief is epistemically right/wrong or good/bad, and also about whether a believer is epistemically virtuous/vicious. This is not the same as, but it is analogous to, how we ask about whether actions are ethically right/wrong or good/bad, and also about whether agents are ethically virtuous/vicious.

Thought and discourse about such matters is epistemological thought and discourse. And it would seem that all of the same metaphysical, epistemological, linguistic, and psychological questions we have been exploring about ethical thought and discourse could also be raised about such *epistemological* thought and discourse. In doing so, we are no longer doing metaethics; we're doing **metaepistemology**.

> **Key Point**: Metaepistemology is to epistemology and epistemological thought and discourse as metaethics is to ethics and ethical thought and discourse.

Broadening our focus in this fashion suggests a further interesting question. What do ethics and epistemology have in common such that they're species of some genus; and are there any other species of this genus? The short answer we've already encountered in previous chapters is that the genus is *normativity*. Just like we might try to distinguish normative ethics (first-order) from metaethics (second-order), we might try to distinguish "normative epistemology" from metaepistemology. But there seem to be other normative domains. For example, focussing only on what would best promote a particular person's well-being, we can ask about what actions that person *prudentially* ought to perform. Prudential normativity is arguably different from (though connected to) ethical and epistemological normativity.

We can also ask about what actions would be rational to pursue given some stipulated end given the agent's background beliefs. That is, we can ask about what is **instrumentally** right/wrong, good/bad, etc. for achieving a stipulated end (which needn't be ethical or prudential). So, instrumentality (perhaps as a kind of rationality) might be viewed as another domain of normativity beside ethics, epistemology, and prudence. Moving away from actions and beliefs, we can also ask about what emotions or feelings are reasonable, rational, or justified to have in various circumstances. Sometimes this is an ethical question, but it's not always a matter for ethics. Should I feel elated if my team wins the championship? Probably so, but that's not really an ethical matter, yet it is an issue about a "should" and so the "fittingness" of attitudes might be conceived as another species of normativity. In a somewhat similar vein, focussing only on considerations about beauty and style, we might consider what is aesthetically right/wrong, good/bad, etc. So aesthetics too might be viewed as another domain of normativity.

With each of these domains of normativity, we can imagine a meta-level investigation into their status, i.e. an analog to metaethical investigation but into the metaphysics, epistemology, philosophy of language, and philosophy of mind for these other normative domains. Moreover, this suggests a further development in recent metaethical discussions: what happens to the debate when we broaden the focus to normativity *in general*? As before, rather than asking first-order normative questions, this is conceived as a second-order investigation into questions about metaphysics, epistemology, philosophy of language, and philosophy of mind as they apply to our first-order normative thought and discourse, in its full generality. It is controversial how exactly to use the technical term "normativity," but whatever the various domains of normativity are, this represents an expansion of metaethics into what is sometimes called **metanormative theory**.

> QU1: What are some terms or concepts that apply to multiple normative domains?

In this chapter, we shall start with metanormative theory and consider the question of how those favoring one of the four traditional metaethical theories might react to the expanded focus on normativity in general. What we'll see is that many (though not all) of the arguments for and against those traditional theories can be refashioned as arguments for and against similar theories about so-called **all-things-considered normativity**. This will provide a review of many of the arguments of Chapters 2–5. Then we'll consider one specific domain of normativity that is not ethics: epistemology. We'll explore some of the theoretical options and associated costs and benefits in order to give you a sense of how a similar debate might take place with respect to a specific non-ethical but still normative domain.

As these are areas of philosophical inquiry that are only now beginning to receive much attention, this chapter is intended as a very open-ended conclusion that will hopefully put you in a position to see how many of the issues we've covered in previous chapters might be extended and and adapted to other domains in exciting and novel ways. Just as metaethics largely involves a fruitful application of other areas of philosophy to the ethical domain, we'll begin to see here how metaethics can be extended and morphed in ways that benefit our understanding in other areas of philosophy.

• FROM METAETHICS TO METANORMATIVE THEORY

Consider again the statement "Manning shouldn't have released classified documents to Wikileaks." We've investigated various metaethical positions one might take about the status of this statement considered as the expression of an *ethical* judgment. Nonnaturalism, expressivism, error theory/fictionalism, naturalism all constitute families of views about the status of judgments like this one. There is, however, a way to hear this statement where it isn't specifically ethical. For instance, if someone points out how bad it has turned out for Manning (e.g., how she will now spend many years in prison), this person may be neutral on the *ethics* of releasing the classified documents but still insist that it was a *prudentially* very bad thing to do. That is, someone might think that, whether or not it was ethically right, releasing the documents was the wrong way for Manning to promote her own well-being.

This distinction raises an interesting and difficult issue. Granting that ethics and prudence aren't the same thing, one might now wonder what Manning should have done *all things considered*. That is, considering every relevant factor from ethics to prudence to anything else that might be relevant, what should she have done?

More generally, this question is sometimes put by asking what someone *just plain* ought to do. Ethics and prudence concern norms (paradigmatically) for action, but it is far from clear how they interact with each other and with other norms for action. Some philosophers think ethics trumps other norms. So, on this view, a prudential reason could add to an ethical reason to give someone even more reason to do something, but if ethics and prudence point in opposite directions ethics always wins. Other philosophers, however, hold the opposite view: prudence trumps ethics.

A third possible position is that there is no trumping normative domain: ethics and prudence (and perhaps other kinds of normativity) contribute reasons bearing on action, and it requires careful practical reason to figure out what we "just plain" ought to do. Determining the right view here is an interesting and difficult question at the interface of normative and metanormative theorizing.

Given our focus earlier in this book on issues in metaphysics, epistemology, philosophy of language, and philosophy of mind, metanormative theorists will also want to ask how these meta-level issues extend to all-things-considered normativity. As this is such a new area of philosophy, there are not that many positions to consider. But one thing we can do is to ask how each of our traditional metaethical theories would extend to all-things-considered normativity.

Nonnaturalism

Let's begin as we did before with nonnaturalism. One of the central reasons some philosophers find this position attractive in metaethics is that they think our ethical thought and discourse seems to be fact stating and answerable to something objective but its role in our deliberations seems to be fundamentally different from the role of thought and discourse about the natural (or supernatural) world. So these philosophers draw the conclusion that ethical facts must be sui generis.

As I pointed out in Chapter 2, by "sui generis" nonnaturalists should not be interpreted as meaning that ethical facts are fundamentally different from other *normative* facts. Now we're in a position to see why. The same motivation one might have for thinking that *ethical* facts are nonnatural can lead one to think that *normative* facts are nonnatural. When deliberating about what to do, we reach conclusions that can seem to be answerable to something objective but not reducible to the facts of the natural (or supernatural) world. If a nonnaturalist endorses the view that ethical norms are trumping, then nonnaturalism about all-things-considered normativity is almost automatic. But even if one endorses one of the other views about the relation between ethical normativity and all-things-considered normativity, the basic motivation towards nonnaturalism remains the same. And most contemporary meta*ethical* nonnaturalists are also meta*normative* nonnaturalists.

> QU2: When nonnaturalists say that ethical and normative facts are sui generis, with what other kinds of facts are they contrasting ethical and normative facts?

Notice, moreover, that the three more specific arguments we considered for nonnaturalism about ethical facts seem not to trade on anything specifically ethical but rather work equally well when refashioned to be about all-things-considered normativity. The first argument came from Hume's Law, which recall is the idea that you cannot derive an 'ought' from an 'is.' If this is true, it would seem to apply just as much to the all-things-considered 'ought' as it does to the ethical 'ought.'

The second argument was Moore's open-question argument, which traded on the apparent semantic gap between ethical words such as 'good' and 'right' and any proposed analysis in purely naturalistic terms. Interestingly, if we restrict consideration to what is good for promoting some particular end, or what action is the instrumentally right action given one's evidence, then it's easier to imagine that facts about this are natural facts. They're just facts about probabilities, arguably discoverable by empirical science. However, when applied to all-things-considered normativity, the open-question argument would seem to work as well or even better as it does in ethics. After all, one of the tricky issues about all-things-considered normativity is how exactly each different species of normativity ought to be balanced. So there is even more scope for a semantic gap between naturalistic terms and normative terms.

Finally, the last argument we considered was the deliberative indispensability argument. Roughly, this was the idea that we have to assume the existence of facts about what we ought to do in order to make sense of the way we deliberate practically. In Chapter 2, we saw how this argument actually doesn't directly establish nonnaturalism about *ethical* facts, as it is not obvious that we have to assume the existence of specifically ethical norms to make sense of practical deliberation. If anything, it establishes nonnaturalism about all-things-considered normative facts (and extends to ethical facts because of their centrality to general normativity).

Just as much as the motivations towards a nonnaturalist view in metaethics extend to metanormative theorizing, the arguments against it remain powerful. We considered four main objections: the objection from a naturalistic worldview, epistemological objections, challenges from the practicality of ethics, and an argument from supervenience.

Surely, if one is inclined to reject nonnaturalism about ethics because of one's commitment to a naturalistic worldview, expanding our focus to all-things-considered normativity is unlikely to make one any less skeptical of adding new sui generis kinds of facts to our ontology. As I explained in Chapter 2, a more specific form of this objection to nonnaturalism derives from considerations in epistemology about how we could come to know nonnatural facts; and this applies to all-things-considered normative facts as much as it does to specifically ethical facts. If these are not knowable via a posteriori observation and a priori reflection, we will have to posit some new faculty by which we know them. This imposes a heavy explanatory burden on the nonnaturalist to work out a plausible view of where this faculty comes from and how it works. Moreover, many philosophers will think that judgments about what I "just plain" ought to do are surely as action-guiding if not more than judgments about what I *ethically* ought to do. That's not to say that any of these three objections provide "knockdown arguments," but they do seem to extend from ethics to all-things-considered normativity.

The supervenience objection to nonnaturalism is more delicate to extend from meta-ethics to metanormative theory. Recall that the term supervenience refers to the idea that issues in one domain (e.g., how much punishment some kind of criminal deserves) cannot vary without some underlying variation in another domain (e.g., the facts about what they did). Most philosophers think ethical normativity supervenes on natural fact, because otherwise the ethics of a situation would seem arbitrary. For similar reasons, many philosophers will also think what one just plain ought to do also supervenes on natural fact. There may, however, be a kind of existentialist viewpoint according to which at least some question of what one ought all-things-considered to do are systematically thwarted by a kind of radical freedom, forcing unreasoned choice rather than norm following. The very intelligibility of this viewpoint makes the supervenience argument a bit more difficult to apply to all-things-considered normativity. However, notice that most nonnaturalists wouldn't want to grant that sometimes what one just plain ought to do is a matter of radical choice rather than belief tracking some external fact—for then they lose some of the motivation for thinking that there are such facts. Moreover, this move would seem to concede something important to the expressivist who thinks such judgments are more like intentions or plans than like beliefs about some piece of reality. Anyway, it is not obvious that the existentialist viewpoint mentioned here is intelligible in the end, so these issues remained vexed.

Expressivism

Expressivism, you'll recall, began its life in the form of emotivism, which said that ethical statements are the expression of emotive reactions to reality rather than representations of reality. This may seem more plausible for ethical normativity than for normativity in general. After all, it often does seem that our ethical opinions are laden with emotive affect, but it is less obvious that one's opinion about what to do all things considered is similarly emotive.

It's important to remember, however, that emotivism was only one early version of expressivism, and the expressivist position became much more sophisticated as it developed over the twentieth century. And contemporary expressivists tend to see their view as one about all-things-considered normativity which has applications in domains such as ethics and epistemology. Keeping that in mind, let's now consider whether the main arguments given for expressivism in the ethical case extend to the case of normativity in general.

The first argument we explored before was basically a twist on the argument from Hume's Law for nonnaturalism. The idea was that if one thinks Hume's Law provides a reason to doubt that ethical facts can be reduced to natural facts, but one is deeply committed to a naturalistic worldview, then one won't want to endorse nonnaturalism, and expressivism seems like the main alternative. For expressivists can respect a fundamental difference between "ought" and "is." They chalk it up not to two different kinds of facts but rather to two different roles statements can play in our language: descriptive statements about how reality is and emotive/prescriptive statements about what people ought to do. This argument has nothing specifically to do with ethics and so works equally well when applied to all-things-considered normativity.

The second argument for expressivism we considered in Chapter 3 was the argument from motivational internalism and the Humean theory of motivation. The idea was that there is a specially tight or "internal" connection between ethical judgments and motivation to action. And assuming motivation to action always requires the cooperation of two kinds of mental states, one representational and the other directive, the most plausible explanation of the internal connection between ethical judgment and motivation is that these judgments are more desire-like (directive) than belief-like (representational). As we discussed in Chapter 3, the internalist thesis about ethical judgments is very controversial. Some have argued that there could be psychopaths or amoralists who make ethical judgments in full awareness of what they mean but who lack all motivation to act in their accord. If anything, this objection is less forceful when we turn to all-things-considered normativity. For it is more difficult to imagine the analog of a psychopath or an amoralist about what one "just plain" ought to do. However, another worry that we raised for this argument was that we often make ethical judgments about things very different from us or far removed from us, and it is far less clear that these bear the same "internal" connection to motivation as ethical judgments about our own prospective courses of action. This worry applies to a similar argument from internalism plus the Humean theory of motivation for expressivism about all-things-considered normativity.

The final main argument we considered for expressivism in the ethical case was the argument from supervenience. The basic idea was that ethical right/wrong, good/bad, virtuous/vicious appear to supervene on non-ethical facts, and expressivism provides a strong explanation of this appearance. Insofar as supervenience counts as a theoretical cost for the metaethical nonnaturalist, it is a theoretical benefit for the metaethical expressivist. Many philosophers will think the situation is exactly the same as regards all-things-considered normativity. However, as I mentioned above, some may think that the intelligibility of a radical existentialist viewpoint about what one all-things-considered ought to do reveals a difference for this issue when extended to all-things-considered normativity. If that's right (and this is a big "if"), then the supervenience argument for expressivism wouldn't be as powerful in the case of all-things-considered normativity. On the other hand, as I also mentioned above, if this viewpoint is intelligible, that might play into the expressivists' hands, since it would provide some support for the idea that at least some normative judgments are more decision-like than belief-like.

QU3: What would it be for all-things-considered "ought" to supervene on the nonnormative?

The arguments against expressivism in the ethical case extend to the case of all-things-considered normativity. In Chapter 2, I presented these and explained how they have motivated adaptations (improvements?) in the expressivist position since its early emotivist form. For example, emotivism seems to many philosophers to face difficulties making sense of ethical disagreement and the way we take ethics seriously. But prescriptivist, projectivist, and norm-expressivist versions of the view do better on this accord. These seem to be just as powerful worries in the case of all-things-considered normativity as they are in the ethical case. So expressivists wanting to extend their view will want to use one of these more sophisticated forms of the view. Same too regarding the truth-aptness (and associated features) of normative language and the possibility of embedding normative sentences in conditionals, interrogatives, etc. Here, the quasi-realist program instigated by Blackburn has been to explain how an expressivist can make sense of these features of normative discourse. Blackburn and those who have followed him in developing this program have always been concerned with more than just ethical normativity, seeking to extend their view to all forms of normativity. Whether they can successfully do so remains one of the key challenges to expressivism about all-things-considered normativity.

Error theory/fictionalism

Let's turn then to error theory and fictionalism. Mackie's error theory, which we discussed in Chapter 4, was the view that ethical thought and discourse is based on an error and should therefore be eliminated. Ethics presupposes the existence of intrinsically motivating and objectively prescriptive values, but there are no such things—or so Mackie thought, which is why he argued that all basic ethical statements are false. As we discovered, part of his reason for thinking this seems to have been based on the assumption that reasons for people to do things must be connected to those people's particular desires, cares, and concerns. But Mackie thought that ethical facts would have to be facts that generated reasons for action independently of people's particular desires, cares, and concerns.

This may suggest that there is little prospect for extending the error theory to all-things-considered normativity. For part of Mackie's argument for the error theory about ethics is based on an assumption about what reasons for action are like. So, even if he denies the existence of *ethical* reasons, he must think that there are *some* kind reasons; and so he must think that some all-things-considered normative ought-claims are true. Moreover, Mackie drew an eliminativist lesson about what we should do in light of his view that ethics is based on an ontological mistake: we *should* stop talking about ethical right/wrong, good/bad, etc. and shift our practice to talk about the sorts of reasons that there actually are for acting in various ways (i.e. the considerations attaching to people's particular desires, cares, and concerns). But surely he must think this should-claim is true, and plausibly it is intended as an all-things-considered normative claim. So even if the error theory is correct in the ethical domain, it doesn't appear to be extendable to the more general normative domain.

That may ultimately be right, but the line of thought just rehearsed can be resisted. For one thing, although Mackie's argument for the error theory drew on a view about the nature of practical reasons, not all arguments need to do this. One might think, for example, that any claim about there being reasons for someone to do something presuppose free will and then deny the existence of free will. This would imply that no claim about there being reasons for someone to do something could be true. That wasn't Mackie's argument, but it is an argument for error theory which would allow the view to be extended to all-things-considered normativity.

Moreover, the practical lesson Mackie recommends in light of his error theory about ethics is not the only lesson one could draw from the idea that all basic ethical statements are false. As we saw in Chapter 4, some philosophers embrace a form of fictionalism (speech-act fictionalism) which agrees with Mackie that all basic ethical sentences, if they were used literally to make assertions, would be false; but these philosophers argue for a more generous interpretation of ordinary ethical discourse than the interpretation Mackie embraced. These fictionalists interpret normal use of an ethical sentence as performing some other speech-act than assertion: e.g., pretense, moralizing, speaking-relative-to-a-fiction. Alternatively, some error-theorists have recently argued that even though basic ethical sentences are used to make assertions and these are literally false, there is good reason to retain the practice of making ethical assertions (Olson, 2010, Chapter 9). After all, we often have good reason to say false things. So we should conserve ethical thought and discourse in spite of its systematic basis in ontological error. Either way, if we adopt a fictionalist or **conservationalist** stance to the putative error in ethical thought and discourse, then we might extend this stance to all-things-considered normativity. For we might think that even the non-ethical "should" involved in claims about what we should do if the error theory is correct could be interpreted without contradiction along fictionalist or conservationalist lines.

> QU4: What would speech-act fictionalists say about the claim that we ought (all-things-considered) to continue using all-things-considered norma-tive discourse?

So it does seem possible to embrace the error theory not only about ethics but about normativity more generally. Of course, for anyone who objected to the error theory about ethics, this may simply amplify their worries. The main worry we discussed in Chapter 4 was based on the principle of charity. This was the idea that, when interpreting other people, we should assume that most of what they say is true; and when our interpretation violates this assumption, the burden of proof is on us to show that they really mean what we say they mean by what they say. So if it's not just lots of ordinary ethical statements that are claimed to be false but rather lots of more general normative statements, then there will be an even stronger burden to reconsider our interpreta-tion of ordinary discourse. As far as that goes, however, it may just push us more in the direction of some kind of fictionalism about all-things-considered normativity.

We discussed two different forms of fictionalism in Chapter 4: meaning fictionalism and speech-act fictionalism. The meaning fictionalist thinks that moral statements are genuine assertions but their content is implicitly relativized to some fiction. The speech-act fictionalist, as we've just seen, thinks that moral statements aren't really assertions, but rather some other kind of speech-act. These are both positions that someone initially inclined towards error theory might take about all-things-considered normativity.

It's worth noting, however, that the main worries we considered about each theory seem to get stronger when the theories are extended. Meaning fictionalism requires thinking that ordinary users of the target discourse are "semantically blind," which means that they don't really understand the content of what they are saying. It's not that they could not articulate it explicitly (we don't expect ordinary speakers to be linguists in their ability to do semantics), but rather that they wouldn't even recognize the sort of implicit relativity to a fiction in their linguistic behavior that the fictionalist posits. So any attempt to extend meaning fictionalism from the ethical domain would require positing even more semantic blindness.

The objection about semantic blindness is part of the reason, I suggested in Chapter 4, that speech-act fictionalism is more prominent in contemporary meta-ethics. Moreover, even if we don't ordinarily talk about ethical statements as pretense or speaking-within-the-fiction, it is not uncommon to think that ethical thought and discourse is serving a "moralizing" rather than descriptive purpose. However, the challenge to identify the precise speech-act becomes all the more important and difficult as soon as the fictionalist claims that all-things-considered normative discourse involves a different kind of speech-act from assertion.

Naturalism

We discussed several different kinds of naturalism in Chapter 5. I won't review all of them here or discuss how they might be extended to all-things-considered normativity. Suffice it to say that each kind of naturalist about ethical normativity will probably want to extend their view to all-things-considered normativity, but the prospects for doing so depend on the particulars of each argument for and against each of the versions of naturalism. To give you an initial impression of this terrain, it may prove useful to consider just two prominent ways one might get to a naturalist view about all-things-considered normativity.

The first is often described as Humean because of how Hume thought reason is the slave of the passions, and the way this has been interpreted along the lines of internalism about justifying reasons as meaning that there are no reasons for action independent of agents' particular desires, cares, and concerns. (You should note, however, that this interpretation of Hume is controversial, and other metanormative views might also claim Hume as an inspiration.) If you think this, and you think that having a desire, care, or concern is a perfectly natural phenomenon of human psychology, then you might argue that reasons to do things are simply the consequence of perfectly natural facts about human psychology.

For example, if I want to eat some ice-cream, and my freezer contains a carton of ice-cream, then plausibly I have a reason to open my freezer. A naturalist might say that this reason simply is the fact about my desire combined with the fact about where the ice-cream is. Those are perfectly natural facts, and so facts about reasons of this kind can be perfectly natural. So far, of course, that is not *all-things-considered* normativity, since I might have other reasons against opening my freezer. For example, if I want to stick to my diet and opening my freezer will tempt me to break my diet, then plausibly I have a reason *not* to open my freezer. Of course, a naturalist will insist that the fact that I have this reason is also a perfectly natural fact. To get to a Humean naturalist view about all-things-considered normativity, however, we also need a story about how reasons such as these (and *any* others that there may be) combine to determine what one just plain ought to do. We can get there with two controversial claims. First, these kinds of reasons—those made out of facts about what someone wants and facts about what has to happen in the world to satisfy this desire—are the only kinds of reasons there are for doing something. So, if these "Humean" kinds of reasons are natural, then all reasons are natural. Second, there is a plausible naturalistic account of the weighting of various reasons to determine what someone ought all-things-considered to do. Since desires come in different strengths and there are different degrees of probability that some action will satisfy some desire, perhaps a naturalist can combine these into an account of how reasons for and against any action weigh together to determine for each situation what someone just plain ought to do.

Like I said, these claims are controversial and developing the Humean naturalist view about all-things-considered normativity will require theoretical work. However, in some ways, the ethical case provides the biggest challenge to this project, as ethical norms are precisely the ones that are most often thought to provide reasons extending beyond people's particular desires, cares, and concerns. For this reason, the subjectivist form of metaethical relativism that we discussed in Chapter 5 might seem like a good starting point for developing a Humean naturalist view about all-things-considered normativity. If ethical facts are ultimately construed as facts about what one's own ethical values dictate, and these values count as a special class of one's desires, cares, and concerns, then the Humean naturalist would have overcome one of the major hurdles to her view. Of course, the main worry about metaethical subjectivism was that it couldn't make sense of moral disagreement. And this worry may seem to suggest a less radical form of relativism: one which allows for overlapping or shared values to make sense of disagreement. Still, if a naturalist can develop an account of how people's particular desires, cares, and concerns can interact to form an overlapping or shared set of communal values, then perhaps these could still be seen as perfectly natural. Indeed, one needn't reject the possibility of universal norms to be a Humean naturalist. For as long as one could make sense of the possibility of there being reasons to do some things that any particular set of desires, cares, and concerns would support, one might argue that these are still perfectly natural facts about humans and the way they are situated in a world which has to cooperate for them to satisfy their desires, cares, and concerns.

The other kind of naturalist view about all-things-considered normativity I want to mention is one based not in facts about people's particular desires, cares, and concerns, but rather facts about human nature. As you'll recall, neo-Aristotelians argue that humans like many other natural systems have functions or "characteristic ways of living," which are central elements of our natures. And these philosophers seek to ground ethical facts about how we ought to act in facts about how it is good (or virtuous) for us to be, which in turn they want to ground in human nature. In Chapter 5, I presented this view as one about ethical normativity, but proponents of this view often suggest that it is a mistake to expect any sharp distinction between ethical normativity and prudential normativity. If that's right, then we might begin to think of this as a view about all-things-considered normativity. That is, we might think that what one "just plain" ought to do is grounded in one's nature. Concern for one's self, family, community, humanity, other living beings, nature, etc. might all be part of this. And the precise weighting of the reasons deriving from each of these sources might itself be something to be settled by an appeal to our natures.

That would constitute a neo-Aristotelian view about normativity in general (from which neo-Aristotelianism about ethical normativity would be an upshot). As I mentioned in Chapter 5, one of the main challenges to the neo-Aristotelian view is finding a conception of human nature meeting two constraints apparently in tension. First, this has to be a conception of human nature supporting norms that look to be genuinely ethical norms and not just biological or anthropological regularities. However, second, it must also be a conception of human nature plausibly thought to be an element of the natural world, discoverable in principle by empirical observation and scientific theorizing rather than via some sui generis faculty of intuition. In some ways, rejecting the sharp distinction between ethical normativity and prudential normativity might seem to help the neo-Aristotelian to address this worry. However, it remains to be seen whether their account of human nature can support intuitive claims about what we just plain ought to do. This is both because we can easily imagine situations where these point in different directions from what is biologically or anthropologically normal and because it's not obvious that there is any unified core to all of human nature.

> *Key Point*: For each of the four main metaethical traditions, we can easily imagine parallel views in metanormative theory. The arguments for and against often look similar, but the theoretical terrain isn't exactly the same.

• FROM METAETHICS TO METAEPISTEMOLOGY

Hopefully the discussion above of normativity in general and how our four main metaethical traditions might be developed into views about what one ought, all-things-considered to do, will help you to see how metaethics is evolving and extending its reach in the recent literature. Another exciting development is the way metaethics is being used as an analogy to investigate meta-level questions about other specific normative domains. Above I mentioned epistemology, prudence, instrumentality, emotions, and aesthetics as possible further normative domains. We won't explore all of these, but I hope it will aid understanding of some of the possibilities to delve a bit deeper into metaepistemology.

Traditionally, epistemologists sought to provide an analysis of knowledge, where this was assumed to be an analysis of the *concept* of knowledge that would tell us something about the nature of the *relation* someone stands in when they know a proposition. The classic "JTB" analysis of knowledge can be viewed in this light. It breaks down the concept of knowledge into the concepts of justified, true, belief. So, for instance, if someone says that Bush knows that there are weapons of mass destruction in Iraq, then on the JTB analysis this epistemic claim is analyzed into three parts: (i) Bush believes this, (ii) it is true, and (iii) Bush's belief that it is true is justified.

But what is it for a belief to be *justified?* With this question, we begin to see an entry to metaepistemological issues. For the concept of being justified is a normative concept. And a first-order epistemological theory of justified belief is like a first order ethical theory of right action—it's a *normative* theory. This means that it's a theory about when some normative concept applies.

So, although they have rarely been viewed in this way, we can view many traditional epistemological theories as providing accounts in **normative epistemology**, viewed as a partial analog to normative ethics. For example, a rationalist theory of justification that says that one's belief must be based on good reasons in order to count as justified could be viewed as similar to a Kantian theory of right action that says that one's action must be based on good reasons in order to count as the right thing to do (though, of course, these theories may differ about when reasons are "good").

The parallel between normative ethics and normative epistemology is not perfect. But what's relevant for our purposes here is not the detail about any specific epistemological theories of justification and knowledge, but rather the fact that one can ask similar meta-level questions about the claims of these theories to the meta-level questions we asked about the claims of normative ethical theories. Not only that; even outside of the theoretical discussions of philosophy, it's a commonplace to talk about whether a belief is reasonable, justified, or rational. This is clearly similar to the way we talk about actions as reasonable, justified, or rational. Because of this, we can also ask questions about the status of ordinary epistemic thought and discourse that are analogous to the questions we have been exploring earlier in this book about the status of ordinary ethical thought and discourse.

So, whether it is the theoretical claims of normative epistemology or the ordinary claims of everyday epistemic discourse, philosophers may wonder what we're up to when we make epistemic judgments. That is, we may wonder about the status of claims about beliefs being justified and about people knowing things. And this is the beginning of metaepistemology, much like similar questions served as the beginning of metaethics.

This is only the beginning though. As before, we can make questions about the status of some normative domain more precise by dividing them into questions of metaphysics, epistemology, philosophy of language, and philosophy of mind. In this case, that is, we can ask about the metaphysics of knowledge and justification: are these objective properties "out there" in reality; and if so, what is their nature? We can ask about the epistemology of epistemology: when we know that someone knows something, how do we know this? We can ask about the meaning of epistemic statements: are these representations of reality or expressions of attitude, or something else? Finally, we can ask about what's going on in the mind of someone who makes an epistemic judgment: does judging that I ought to believe p automatically motivate me to believe p?

Metaepistemological realism

In large part, philosophers have only recently begun to address these meta-level questions about epistemic thought and discourse. So it's much harder to outline a set of canonical metaepistemological viewpoints comprised of interlocking commitments in these four domains. However, I think it is fair to say that the traditional project of analyzing knowledge, e.g., as justified true belief, was based on an assumption that knowledge and justification are real relations somehow "out there" comprising a part of objective reality. So this is a kind of metaepistemological realism, which would go hand-in-hand with an assumption that epistemic statements are representational and epistemic judgments are belief-like rather than desire-like.

Once in the domain of realism, the immediate next question we should ask ourselves is metaphysical: do the relevant pieces of reality fit within the naturalistic worldview? In the epistemological case, this amounts to asking whether relations such as knowing and being justified are natural relations. Many versions of reliabilism about justification and knowledge might be seen as congenial to the naturalistic worldview? The basic idea behind these theories is that justification for a belief is a matter of being formed by a process or method that tends to get at the truth. And as long as this statistical notion of "tending to get at the truth" is viewed as naturalistic, these theories seem to construe justification as a naturalistic relation.

QU5: If one is a naturalist about epistemic justification, what will one's view be in the philosophy of language and mind about epistemic statements and the judgments they express?

On the other hand, other epistemologists insist that justification is an inextricably normative notion (perhaps intimately tied up with other paradigmatically normative notions such as believing for *reasons* or believing as one *ought* to do). Someone with this view may grant that reliability has something to do with justification but maintain that there is no specific degree of reliability that adds up to justification. This in turn leads some metaepistemologists to embrace a form of nonnaturalism with respect to justification. This is a view, just like the nonnaturalist view in metaethics, that holds that epistemic judgments purport to represent reality and some of them succeed, but the facts represented don't fit within the naturalistic worldview (see Cuneo, 2007).

Another way to motivate a kind of nonnaturalism in metaepistemology is to use Moore's open-question argument as a lens through which to view the literature responding to the **Gettier problem**. Gettier famously challenged the traditional JTB analysis of knowledge by providing clear cases of someone with a justified true belief that we wouldn't typically call knowledge. And for each tweak or complication proposed to avoid such cases, ingenious epistemologists have come up with new cases of someone meeting all of the proposed criteria but failing to have knowledge. As we discussed in Chapter 2, the most plausible way to view Moore's argument is in inductive terms: (roughly) all attempts to analyze X can be seen to fail to close what should be a closed question, so X is simple and unanalyzable. Moore applied this to the concept of goodness and considered only a few proposed analyses to confirm his semantic intuition that 'good' simply cannot mean the same as 'N' for any proposed naturalistic N. In epistemology, our semantic intuitions are probably less strong. Is it an open question to ask, "She has a justified true belief that p, but does she *know* that p?" Perhaps our semantic intuitions don't settle the matter, hence the need for clear counter-examples to undermine a proposed analysis. So the post-Gettier literature could be seen as considering many proposed analyses of knowledge and showing them to fail via counter-examples meant to shore up semantic intuitions. Maybe this supports the view that knowledge is simple and unanalyzable. Indeed, some recent **knowledge-first epistemology** inspired by Williamson (2000) can be seen as diagnosing the failure of epistemologists to come up with an analysis of knowledge by the simple and unanalyzable nature of knowledge.

Metaepistemological antirealism

You'll recall, however, that Moore's open-question argument has provided as much motivation for expressivist views in metaethics as it has for nonnaturalist views. The idea we discussed in Chapter 3 is that Moore's open questions might indicate not that ethical facts are nonnatural, but rather that proposed naturalistic analyses of ethical concepts leave out the prescriptive or endorsing element of the relevant ethical concept. A similar idea could be applied in the epistemic domain. For instance, one might think that there are various naturalistic relations between believers and propositions that are relevant to whether their beliefs count as justified or knowledge, but one might still deny any of these relations fully analyze the concepts of justification and knowledge. For one might think that those concepts have an endorsing or prescriptive element that cannot be carried by the naturalistic relations alone.

This leads us away from metaepistemological realism to an expressivist form of metaepistemological antirealism. You'll recall that meta*ethical* expressivists think that ethical statements are not (solely) representations of how reality is, but rather serve primarily to express some attitude with a directive rather than descriptive direction of fit with the world. Meta*epistemological* expressivists think something similar about epistemic judgments. There are various ways to develop this thesis. One might think, with Austin (1979, 99), that claims to knowledge involve the expression of some kind of guarantee, or with Rorty (1979, 175), that claims that a belief is justified or constitutes knowledge are more comments on its status among one's peers as descriptions of the relation between mind and world.

However, the most sober and systematic forms of epistemic expressivism are developed in analogy to more contemporary forms of ethical expressivism. Indeed, one of the first places where epistemic expressivism was developed was by *ethical* expressivists. For example, Blackburn argues that, "the primary function of talking of 'knowledge' is to indicate that a judgment is beyond revision" (1998, 318). In his view, it is marked out as "beyond revision" in the sense that "no further useful investigation or thought ought to undermine the [judgment]" (1996, 87). Similarly, Gibbard argues that attributions of knowledge, such as "Joe knows there are cows on the hill," means "very roughly…that judgments like his are to be relied on" (2003, 227). This means that these judgments count as what he would call "plan-laden" rather than descriptive of reality.

So the core idea in metaepistemological expressivism is that judgments about someone's belief being justified and/or someone knowing something are not purely descriptive but in part the expression of a desire-like attitude. The reasons ethical expressivists such as Blackburn and Gibbard sought to develop this kind of view alongside their versions of expressivism about ethics are interesting for the example of how meta-level theories of different domains of normativity can seem to hang together in one big package.

Here's one reason: if you think that part of what's crucial to a concept being "normative" is that it expresses prescriptive or endorsing attitudes, and you think that evaluating actions as ethically *justified* involves the application of a normative concept, then evaluating beliefs as epistemically *justified* should also seem to involve the application of a normative concept and so the expression of an endorsing or prescriptive attitude. Hence, the convinced expressivist about ethical normativity might quickly become a convinced expressivist about epistemic normativity, simply by recognizing the concept of *justification* as normative.

Here's another reason for ethical expressivists to be epistemic expressivists: recall that early expressivists denied the possibility of *ethical* knowledge. But this commitment flies in the face of ordinary ethical discourse, where it is a commonplace to claim to know something to be right/wrong, good/bad, etc. This is part of the reason philosophers such as Blackburn and Gibbard began to develop the "quasi-realist" program of explaining how, from within an expressivist viewpoint, we could still make sense of ordinary talk of ethical truth, belief, and knowledge. Now, if we assume, as the metaepistemological realist seems to, that knowledge is basically some kind of relation between mind and reality, but we deny that ethical facts are really "out there" in reality, then it will be mysterious how it could make sense to speak of knowing some ethical truth. If, on the other hand, one thought that talk about knowledge was itself, at least in part, a form of prescription or endorsement rather than representation, then the path is opened to an easier quasi-realist explanation of what is going on when we claim ethical knowledge.

Those are not, however, the only reasons philosophers have given for epistemic expressivism. Leaving aside metaethics for a moment, from strictly within epistemology, some philosophers have argued that the term 'knows' is somehow context-sensitive. That means, in some contexts a lot of evidence is required to claim truly to know something (e.g., as a witness in a murder trial), whereas in other contexts not much evidence is required to claim truly to know something (e.g., in recounting one's day while sharing a drink at the pub). In the past few decades, this has led to the development of various forms of epistemic **contextualism**, the view that what it takes to truly be said to know something varies with context. (This might be the context in which the putative knower finds herself or the context from which the knowledge is attributed, representing two different forms of contextualism.)

One big challenge for contextualists, however, is to make sense of intuitions of disagreement and changing one's mind when it comes to knowledge attributions made in different contexts. For example, if in the bar I say:

(1)   I know that James was at the office on Christmas day.

But then in a court of law I say:

(2)   I don't know that James was at the office on Christmas day.

Someone who heard me say both (1) and (2) might ask me why I changed my mind. But on the contextualist view, I might insist that I haven't changed my mind: when I said (1) it was true, and when I said (2) it was true too; I'm just speaking in different contexts. Similarly, you might say in a low-standards context:

(3)   Sara knows that the post office is open on Saturday.

While I might say in a high-standards context that, no, (3) is wrong:

(4)   Sara doesn't know that the post office is open on Saturday.

In this kind of case, it can seem to a third-party that, in saying (3) and (4), you and I are disagreeing about whether Sara has a particular piece of knowledge. But as far as contextualism is concerned, both you and I could be speaking truly. So it is unclear where the disagreement lies.

The careful reader will have noticed that this is an analogous problem to the problem from disagreement faced by metaethical relativists. The contextualist in epistemology is a kind of relativist about knowledge attributions. She claims (roughly) that "S knows that p" means that S's belief that p is legitimate given evidential norms N; and she allows that N can vary from context to context like the ethical relativist allows that ethical norms can vary from place to place. An norm-expressivist following Gibbard (1990), however, might argue that ethical and epistemic claims are not the *representation* of what is legitimate relative to norms but rather the expression of a commitment to those norms. That is, an epistemic expressivist might reject contextualism in favor of the view that "S knows that p" is a vehicle for expressing commitment to some set of evidential norms. Then, the apparent variation of standards for knowledge can be explained by different evidential norms being endorsed in different contexts in which 'knows' is used. But the intuitions about changing one's mind and disagreement can be explained in terms of the sort of "disagreement in attitude" that comes along with endorsing different norms. Anyway, that's the sort of argument for epistemic expressivism pursued in more detail in Chrisman (2007, 2012). It doesn't depend on a commitment to ethical expressivism.

We've quickly surveyed some arguments for expressivism about epistemic normativity as a form of metaepistemological antirealism. It's worth asking whether the other main antirealist tradition in metaethics—error theory/fictionalism—offers an alternative form of metaepistemological antirealism. Traditionally, there has been a kind of **radical skepticism** which might be interpreted as a form of metaepistemological error theory. It is not enough to argue that we don't know much of what we think we know, for as long as one holds that there is knowledge, one will think some possible knowledge attributions are true. But if one thought that the very idea of knowledge (and/or justified belief) contained some kind of error, such that there couldn't be knowledge (and/or justified belief), then one would be a metaepistemological error-theorist. Some classical stoical arguments for skepticism have this character. And more recently, error-theorists about normativity in general have argued against the reality of reasons, both practical and epistemic (see Olson, 2011). This too would generate a form of metaepistemological error theory.

We have by no means exhausted the possibilities for metaepistemological theorizing, or even gotten a good lie of the land in this brief survey. But I hope the discussion has helped you to see some of the issues that are parts of the debate actively underway in the contemporary literature.

• CONCLUSION

This final chapter has opened up the discussion turning from metaethics to other cognate areas.

First we considered normativity in general, conceiving of ethics as a species of this larger genus. This relatively new area of philosophical inquiry is called metanormative theory. As a partial review of the theoretical traditions considered earlier in the book and as part of surveying some of the initial theoretical possibilities in metanormative theory, we considered what each of nonnaturalism, expressivism, error theory/fictionalism, and naturalism would look like when transposed to all-things-considered normativity. What we found is that many but not all of the arguments for and against these views would apply to the more general normativity.

Then we drilled down to the epistemic domain, as this is one of the species of normativity that has received the most attention in recent literature. This provides a good example of how the sorts of meta-level metaphysical, epistemological, linguistic, and psychological issues that frame metaethical theorizing can arise in other normative domains.

• CHAPTER SUMMARY

- Metanormative theory concerns questions about the status of *normative* judgments, much like metaethics concerns questions about the status of *ethical* judgments.
- It is possible to develop forms of nonnaturalism, expressivism, error theory/ fictionalism, and naturalism about all-things-considered normativity.
- Proponents of these views about ethics will often think they are also the correct views to take about normativity in general, as many of the positive arguments in favor of those theories carry over to metanormative theory.
- However, many of the counter-arguments also carry over.
- Metaepistemology is the analog of metaethics, where ethics and epistemology are conceived as two separate normative domains.
- Much traditional epistemic theorizing in the attempt to analyze knowledge can be interpreted as a form of metaepistemological realism. However, it is unclear whether it should be interpreted as a form of nonnaturalism or naturalism.
- There are forms of metaepistemological antirealism, especially in the form of expressivist views about justification and knowledge.

• STUDY QUESTIONS

1 What are two arguments for a metaethical view that don't seem as plausible when transposed into arguments for a metanormative view? Explain your answer.
2 What is an objection to a metaethical view that loses some of its force if applied to the analogous metanormative view?

3 Is the "existential viewpoint" mentioned a kind of error theory about all-things-considered normativity?
4 In what sense is *justification* a normative concept? Is this the same sense of "normative" as involved in the assumption that ethical right/wrong are normative concepts?
5 What are some of the factual conditions that must apply for someone to know something? Why might someone think this doesn't exhaust the concept of knowledge?
6 What are some of the potential problems with metaepistemological expressivism?

• FURTHER RESOURCES

- Chrisman, Matthew. 2012. "Epistemic Expressivism," *Philosophy Compass* 7 (2): 118–26. [Survey of many of the arguments for and against epistemic expressivism.]
- Cuneo, Terence. 2007. *The Normative Web*. Oxford University Press. [Research monograph arguing that epistemic and ethical normativity hang together, deserving a nonnaturalist treatment.]

• ANSWERS TO QUESTIONS OF UNDERSTANDING

QU1: Some general normative terms are *reason, should, ought, rational, right/wrong, permissible/impermissible*. Sometimes we also include *better/worse* and *virtue/vice*.
QU2: Natural and supernatural facts.
QU3: If there are two situations identical in all nonnormative respects, then the supervenience intuition is that what one ought all-things-considered to do in the first situation must be the same as what one ought all-things-considered to do in the second situation.
QU4: They would say that this claim too is not an assertion but rather some other speech-act, and as such it can be perfectly in order even if the sentence used to make it is literally false.
QU5: Naturalists are typically representationalist success-theorists in the philosophy of language, which means that they hold that epistemic statements purport and succeed in representing reality. This goes hand-in-hand with cognitivist views about the type of mental states expressed by epistemic statements. That is, naturalists will usually think that such statements express beliefs.

• WORKS CITED

Austin, J. L. 1979. *Philosophical Papers*. Oxford: Oxford University Press.
Blackburn, Simon. 1996. "Securing the Nots: Moral Epistemology for the Quasi-Realist." In *Moral Knowledge: New Readings in Moral Epistemology*, edited by W. and M. Timmons Sinnott-Armstrong. Oxford; New York: Oxford University Press.

————. 1998. *Ruling Passions: A Theory of Practical Reasoning*. New York: Oxford University Press.

Chrisman, Matthew. 2007. "From Epistemic Contextualism to Epistemic Expressivism." *Philosophical Studies* 135: 225–54.

Chrisman, Matthew. 2012. "Epistemic Expressivism," Philosophy Compass 7 (2): 118–26.

Cuneo, Terence. 2007. *The Normative Web*. New York: Oxford University Press.

Gibbard, Allan. 1990. *Wise Choices, Apt Feelings: A Theory of Normative Judgment*. Cambridge, MA: Harvard University Press.

————. 2003. *Thinking How to Live*. Cambridge, MA: Harvard University Press.

Olson, Jonas. 2010. "In Defence of Moral Error Theory." In *New Waves in Metaethics*, edited by M. Brady. New York: Palgrave Macmillan.

————. 2011. "Error Theory and Reasons for Belief." In *Reasons for Belief*, edited by A. Steglich-Petersen and A. Reisner, 75–93. Cambridge: Cambridge University Press.

Rorty, Richard. 1979. *Philosophy and the Mirror of Nature*. Princeton, NJ: Princeton University Press.

Williamson, Timothy. 2000. *Knowledge and its Limits*. Oxford; New York: Oxford University Press.

glossary

a posteriori
Knowledge is a posteriori if it requires experience of particular features of the world.

a posteriori reductive naturalism
The view that ethical facts can be reduced to natural facts by empirical discovery (rather than conceptual analysis).

a priori
Knowledge is a priori if it does not require experience of particular features of the world.

action theory
This is the area of philosophy (part metaphysics and part philosophy of mind) that investigates the nature of action, especially how mental states and reasons figure in action.

akrasia
Thinking that one ought to ϕ (or that ϕ-ing would be overall best), but lacking sufficient (or, in the extreme, all) motivation to ϕ.

all-things-considered normativity
The reasons or 'ought's that result from not just ethical, prudential, epistemological, etc. considerations but from all relevant considerations.

anthropological relativism
The anthropological claim that different groups of people adhere to different norms or ways of living together. (Contrast metaethical relativism.)

antirealism
This is the denial of realism.

antirepresentationalism
This is the denial of representationalism.

argument from queerness, the
A family of arguments due to Mackie for the error theory based on the idea that ethical facts can't really obtain because they would have to be too weird to fit into our standard pictures of reality and human knowledge.

argument from relativity
Mackie's argument for the error theory that is based on the idea that ethical beliefs vary across the world.

attributive adjective
Geach's label for a term such as 'big' that gets its meaning in particular sentences from the way it modifies a subsequent term (e.g. "big flea") in forming a predicate rather than providing freestanding content. (Contrast predicative adjective.)

belief–desire psychology of motivation
This is another name for the Humean theory of motivation.

besire
The name given to the supposed inseparable amalgam of a belief and a desire.

Canberra Plan
A term for using a priori network analyses to understand key philosophical concepts.

causal theory of reference
The view that the referent of a word is determined by causal (and so historical) connections to things in reality (rather than by the descriptions associated with the word).

characteristic ways of living
Something like a function which might determine what traits are virtues for a particular kind of living thing.

cognitivism
This is the view that ethical judgment culminates in belief.

coherentist conception of knowledge
The view in epistemology that knowledge is based on the coherence of our beliefs in a wide network or system of mutually supporting beliefs.

compositionality assumption
The assumption at the heart of theories of meaning which says that the meaning of wholes (e.g., sentences) is a function of the meaning of its parts (e.g., words) and how these parts are put together.

conservationalist
A form of error theory that says that we should continue to use ethical or normative concepts even though their application is in error, contrasting with Mackie's eliminativist stance towards ethical concepts.

constructivism
The view that some realm of facts isn't "out there" for discovery but rather "constructed" by some procedure or standpoint.

contextualism
A familiy of views in epistemology that hold that what it takes to truly attribute knowledge varies from context to context, allowing for a spectrum of contexts from high standards to low standards.

convenient fiction
Something we don't believe to be precisely true but pretend to be true because it is convenient for various purposes.

conventional implicature
What is conveyed by the use of a sentence in virtue of linguistic conventions, though not part of its literal content.

conversational implicature
What is conveyed by the use of a sentence given contextual clues, though not part of its literal content.

correspondence theory of truth
The view that a sentence S is true in virtue of corresponding to some piece of reality, the fact that S.

directions of fit
This is Anscombe's metaphor now commonly used to divide between representational mental states such as belief and goal-setting mental states such as desires and intentions.

divine command theory
The view that moral facts are constituted by the commands of some supreme being.

ecumenical expressivist
Someone defending the view that ethical sentences express, as a function of their meaning, both belief-like and desire-like mental states.

emotive meaning
The emotional connotations of a term or statement, contrasted with factual meaning.

empirical investigation
This is the way we come to know things about reality through observing the world around us. We do this in a mundane way all the time; but science is also built on more precise empirical observation, involving forming and testing hypotheses.

epistemic modal
A word such as 'might' used to qualify the modal status of the content it embeds with respect to evidence.

epistemology
This is the area of philosophy concerned with knowledge and justification for our beliefs.

error theory
This is the metaethical view that holds that ethical judgments (at least the simple ones) attempt to represent reality but fail because there are no ethical facts.

ethical judgments
These are first-order claims about what is right/wrong, good/bad, virtuous/vicious, etc. Metaethics doesn't consist in making and defending ethical judgments, but rather asking about the practice of making them.

ethical virtues
Character traits that make one an ethically good person.

expressivism
This is the metaethical view that holds that ethical statements are not straightforward expressions of beliefs about reality but instead get their meaning from being the expression of nonbelief attitudes.

externalism about justifying reasons
This is the view that a consideration (or fact) can be a reason for someone to act even if it doesn't bear that person's desires, preferences, or plans, or even on those they would have were they suitably well-informed and logically consistent in their mental states.

fallacy of equivocation
The fallacy of inferring in a way that trades on assigning two different meanings to terms of the argument.

fictionalism
This is the metaethical view that ethical sentences are used as a kind of convenient fiction, not literally true but usefully treated as true.

foundationalist conception of knowledge
The view in epistemology that knowledge is based on our beliefs being supported, ultimately, by some foundational beliefs or experiences.

Frege–Geach problem
The multifaceted challenge to expressivists stemming from Frege's observation that a sentence's content can occur in asserted contexts (such as statements) as well as unasserted contexts (such as the antecedent of a conditional or in an interrogative).

functional kinds
Something that can be classified in terms of its function, e.g., doorstop.

Gettier problem
A famous challenge to the JTB analysis of knowledge, illustrating cases where someone could have a justified true belief but doesn't seem to have knowledge.

global expressivism
The idea that all language—not just ethical language—expresses noncognitive attitudes rather than beliefs about reality.

Hume's Law
The idea that one cannot derive an 'ought' from an 'is.'

Humean theory of motivation
This is the view that motivation to act always involves the cooperation of two kinds of mental states, one with a goal-setting direction of fit and the other with a reality-representing direction of fit.

hybrid cognitivist
Someone defending the view that ethical statements express both a belief about some ethical fact and also a desire-like attitude.

implicature
The phenomenon whereby meaning is conveyed by the use of a sentence even though it is not part of the literal content of the sentence. (See conversational implicature and conventional implicature.)

implicit parameter
A logical parameter in the meaning of a sentence taking different values in different contexts of use, but not showing up explicitly as an indexical word in the sentence.

indexical
A word that refers to different things in different contexts of use in a systematic way; e.g., 'now,' 'here.'

inference to the best explanation
When we infer something because it provides the best explanation of something else. Sometimes called "abductive" reasoning to contrast it with deductive and inductive reasoning.

instrumentally
The relation between means and ends.

internalism about justifying reasons
This is the view that a consideration (or fact) cannot be a reason for someone to act unless it bears on one of their desires, preferences, or plans, or would do were they suitably well-informed and logically consistent in their mental states.

intrinsically motivating
The idea that something could be such that just recognizing it would move our wills.

intuition
A faculty of mind distinguished from empirical observation and reasoning. This is commonly appealed to by ethical nonnaturalists in an explanation of how we can come to know ethical facts.

intuitionism
This is the view that we know ethical facts through a special faculty of intuition.

justifying reasons
These are the considerations (or facts) that legitimate an action (insofar as it is legitimate).

knowledge-first epistemology
A movement in epistemology based on the idea that knowledge is a more fundamental epistemic concept than justification or evidence, suggesting that we shouldn't try to analyze knowledge.

linguistic turn
This was a period in the history of philosophy (early twentieth century) when philosophers became increasingly interested in language and sought solutions to longstanding philosophical problems through linguistic analysis.

meaning fictionalist
Someone defending the view that the meaning of the sentences in some area of discourse is implicitly relativized to a fiction.

metaepistemology
The investigation into meta-level issues about epistemic judgments that parallels metaethics.

metaethical relativism
The view that there's no such thing as ethical right/wrong, full stop, but only ethical right/wrong relative to some culture, morality, social agreement, etc. (Contrast anthropological relativism.)

metaethics
This is the area of the philosophical study of ethics where we move to a more abstract level to ask about the first-order practice of making ethical judgments, which leads to various questions in metaphysics, epistemology, philosophy of language, and philosophy of mind.

metanormative theory
The extension of meta-level questions from metaethics to normativity in general.

metaphysics
This is the area of philosophy concerned with what exists and the nature of reality.

minimalist theory of truth
The view that the truth predicate does not carry heavy duty metaphysical commitments but rather figures in any area of discourse with contentful declarative sentences.

missionary and cannibals example
Hare's famous example meant to motivate the idea that ethical terms prescribe and evaluate rather than pick out the empirical or factual characteristic of things.

moral disagreement
This is when two people's views about morality stand in tension and that tension is not due to some underlying factual disagreement.

moral psychology
This is the area of philosophy concerned with the psychology involved in motivation to act, especially in contexts where one has made an ethical judgment about the action.

moral skeptic
Someone who doubts that we have any moral knowledge.

Moral Twin Earth Thought Experiment
The thought experiment where we imagine a twin world, exactly like the actual world, but different properties casually sustain the use of our ethical terms. This was introduced by Horgan and Timmons (drawing on a similar example Putnam used in a different context) to argue that a posteriori naturalism is problematic.

motivating reasons
These are the mental states that explain why someone did what they did in the sense of *rationalizing* it.

motivational externalism
This is the view that ethical judgment alone cannot play the role of a motivational state of mind but rather requires the support of some further state of mind (such as a desire or preference) to generate motivation.

motivational internalism
This is the view that ethical judgment can play the role of a motivational state of mind.

naturalism
This can refer to a general view in metaphysics that the only facts that obtain are natural facts or the more specific view in metaethics that ethical facts are natural facts.

naturalistic fallacy
The supposed fallacy of identifying something's ethical qualities with the natural qualities in virtue of which it has those ethical qualities. Moore argued that views like Utilitarianism commit this because they identify being good with causing pleasure.

naturalistic worldview
The idea that all that exists is what is natural.

natures
Neo-Aristotelians argue that facts about things' natures might be viewed as natural facts capable of underpinning ethical facts.

Neo-Aristotelians
Philosophers such as Foot and Hursthouse who try to revive ideas from Aristotle in arguing for a kind of metaethical naturalism.

network-style analysis
A kind of conceptual analysis that seeks not to break concepts down into their component parts but rather identify the network connecting a class of concepts. Jackson used this to develop a new form of a priori naturalism, not subject to Moore's open-question argument.

noncognitivism
This is the view that ethical judgment culminates in some nonbelief attitude such as a desire, intention, plan, or preference.

nonnaturalism
This is the metaethical view that holds that ethical facts are not reducible to facts of some other sort (such as natural or supernatural facts).

norm-expressivism
The view Gibbard defended according to which ethical statements express commitments to norms which rule some actions in and other actions out.

normative epistemology
The epistemic analog of normative ethics.

normative ethics
This is the area of the philosophical study of ethics where we attempt to come up with general theories to classify things as ethically right/wrong, good/bad, virtuous/vicious, etc.

normativity
Involving norms, rules, or reasons.

objectively prescriptive
The idea that some facts provide reasons for agents to act irrespective of their desires, cares, or concerns.

ontological commitments
What a theory is committed to about what entities are part of reality.

open-question argument
The argument first developed by Moore for ethical nonnaturalism based on the fact that one can wonder whether something that is N is good, for any natural property N, without displaying conceptual confusion.

original position
Rawls' term for the hypothetical choice situation where, behind a veil of ignorance about where in society one might end up, fair principles of justice might be chosen.

partners-in-crime response
A style of philosophical objection which suggests that if a critical claim about something (e.g., ethics) is correct then it would also have to be correct about something else (the "partner") that we are less willing to grant (e.g., mathematics).

permutation problem
An objection that network-style analyses are potentially open to based on the idea that some networks of concepts could be satisfied by different constellations of properties, each comprising a systematic permutation on the others.

philosophy of language
This is the area of philosophy concerned with explaining how language has meaning and characterizing various aspects of the use of language.

philosophy of mind
This is the area of philosophy concerned with all phenomena mental. In metaethics, the relevant mental phenomena are the psychology of motivation and the connection between our minds and having reasons to act.

practical ethics
This is the area of the philosophical study of ethics where we attempt to reach practical conclusions about what someone should do in the face of particular ethical questions.

pragmatics
This is the study of the way language is used for various effects.

pragmatism
The movement in philosophy emphasizing our practices with words and concepts rather than what they refer to in reality.

predicative adjective
Geach's label for a term such as 'red' that contributes freestanding meaning in particular sentences rather than depending on the way it modifies some other term. (Contrast attributive adjective.)

prescription
This is a category of speech-acts involving telling someone what to do (for instance, commanding, entreating, suggesting, advising, etc.). Sometimes this term is also used to refer to vehicles (e.g., imperative sentences) that are distinctively usable to perform the related speech-act.

prescriptivism
Hare's theory of ethical language according to which ethical statements do not describe matters of fact but rather make "universalized" prescriptions.

principle of charity
The counsel to start out with the presumption that most of what someone says is true, requiring explanation for false beliefs rather than true ones.

principle of parsimony
The idea that, of two explanations of some phenomena, the one appealing to fewer sui generis things is preferable, all other things being equal.

projectivist
Someone defending the view that ethical statements "guild and stain" reality rather than track features existing independently of human interaction with reality.

quasi-realism
Blackburn's program of earning the right for expressivists to use terms in conjunction with ethical discourse that had traditionally been assumed to be markers of representationalism and cognitivism, such as 'true,' 'believes,' and 'fact.' It involves adopting a minimalist stance towards these terms.

radical skepticism
The view in epistemology that there isn't and couldn't be knowledge (and/or justified belief).

rationalism
A way of developing ideal observer accounts of ethical truth, where it's the observer's ethical beliefs that matter.

realism
It is difficult to define this precisely, but realism about X is roughly the view that X facts obtain objectively (or equivalently, that X properties are objectively instantiated). So *moral realism* is the view that ethical facts obtain objectively.

representationalism
This is the view that an area of discourse (e.g., ethical discourse) purports to be about something in reality.

representations
Various linguistic and mental items can be vehicles for depicting or standing for something assumed to be real; doing so is to be a representation.

scientism
A derisory term for those who think science is the ultimate arbiter of what's real.

semantics
This is the study of the meaning of words and the sentences they can be used to form.

sentimentalism
A way of developing ideal observer accounts of ethical truth, where it's the observer's moral sentiments that matter.

speech-act fictionalist
Someone defending the view that the statements made in some area of discourse aren't really assertions expressing beliefs in some matter of fact, but rather the performance of some other speech-act such as pretense or loose speak.

subjectivism
An extreme form of relativism that holds that ethical right/wrong are relative to individual subjectivities.

sui generis
This Latin term means "of its own kind" and it is used in metaethics to characterize the views of nonnaturalists who think ethical facts are of their own kind (and not reducible; e.g., to natural or supernatural facts).

supervenience
The relation holding of two domains of facts or properties when there cannot be differences in the first domain (e.g., ethics) without differences in the second domain (e.g., facts about benefits and harms). Although every domain trivially supervenes on itself, supervenience is weaker than identity or reducibility.

theoretical cost–benefit analysis
This is one of the main methods of metaethics, whereby one evaluates the relative attractiveness of various theories by tallying their costs and benefits along fixed dimensions of one's theoretical concern.

truth-apt
A sentence is truth-apt when it can properly be said to be true or false, i.e. it can be used in such a way that it makes sense to embed it in "It's true/false that…"

veil of ignorance
Rawls' term for the suppression of personal and individual8istic information that will put one in a better position to choose fair principles of justice.

verificationist principle
The principle that the meaning of a sentence is its verification conditions.

index

action theory 8–11, 29, 93
adjective, attributive vs. predicative 66–67
akrasia 48
Anscombe, G. E. M. 9
antirealism 4, 12, 32, 107, 114
  metaepistemological 133–136
antirepresentationalism 6–7, 12, 99, 111–112
Aristotle 66–68, 100, 130
Ayer, A. J. xvii, xx, 5, 33, 36–48

belief–desire psychology of motivation 9–10, 93,
  101; see also Humean theory of motivation
Blackburn, Simon 35, 41–48, 126, 134–135
Boyd, Richard 78, 83

Canberra plan 79
causal theory of reference 76–78
characteristic ways of living 67–71, 130
Chrisman, Matthew 136
cognitivism 8–10, 29, 65, 84, 93–94, 102
  hybrid 103–105
coherentism 5, 26, 91–94
compositionality assumption 45–47
constructivism 108–111
Copp, David 105
correspondence theory of truth 43

directions of fit 9, 83
disagreement, moral xviii, xx, xxi, 5, 53, 56,
  103, 126, 129, 136
  in arguments for expressivism 38–42
  in arguments for error-theory 53–56
  as a problem for relativism 75, 78
divine command theory 52, 108
Dreier, James 74

empirical investigation xviii, 18, 76, 109;
  see also knowledge, a posteriori
Enoch, David 22–23, 110
epistemic modal 112
error theory xxi, 12, 52–61, 88, 92–97, 121,
  126–128
  conservationalist 127

expressivism xx–xxi, 12, 32–49, 52–54, 88, 94
  ecumenical 101–105, 114, 124–125
  hybrid see ecumenical expressivism
  global 113
  epistemic 134–136
externalism see internalism

fallacy of equivocation 46
fiction, convenient 52–53
fictionalism xxi, 12, 52–61, 126–128, 136
  meaning 59, 88
  speech-act 59–60, 88, 94
Finlay, Stephen 105
Firth, Roderick 107
foundationalism 5
Frege–Geach problem 45–49, 102
functional kinds 67–68

Geach, P. T. 45–47, 66–67
Gettier problem 133
Gibbard, Allan 41–48, 134–136
Grice, H. P. 103

Hare, R. M. xvii–xx, 35, 40–41, 47–48, 71, 75, 78
Harman, Gilbert 5, 22–24, 73–75
Horgan, Terrence 78
Hume, David xvii, xx, 41, 106–107, 111,
  128–129
  Hume's Law 19, 29, 33, 122–124
  Humean theory of motivation i, 9–10, 34–35,
    93, 100–101, 125
Hursthouse, Rosalind 69–71, 100

implicature 103–105
indexical 74
inference to the best explanation 20–22, 36
internalism 27, 93–95
  about justifying reasons 11, 57, 128
  motivational 10, 34–35, 48, 54, 74, 101–103,
    125
intrinsically motivating 54–57, 94, 126
intuition, faculty of xi, xviii, 4, 25, 55, 90–92,
  95–96, 130

Jackson, Frank 79–82

Kalderon, Mark 60
Kant, Immanuel xvii, xx, 23, 78, 109, 111, 131
knowledge, ethical xi–xii, xv, xvii, xxi, 1, 4–5,
    10, 26, 65, 84, 90–91, 100–101, 113
    a posteriori 75–79, 90, 123
    a priori 76, 79–83, 91, 123
    challenge for expressivism 45, 57–58
Korsgaard, Christine 110–111
Kripke, Saul 76–77

Lewis, David 108

Mackie, John 53–58, 126–127
    argument from queerness 54
    argument from relativity 53
McDowell, John 100–101, 114
meaning xi, xvii, xviii–xxix, xx, 1, 6–7, 55,
    59–60, 67, 82, 112, 122, 132
    emotive 36–39, 47
    semantic 20, 35, 40, 45–46, 76, 99, 102–103
metaepistemology 119–120, 131–137
metanormative theory 120–130
minimalist theory of truth 44–45, 92, 94
missionary and cannibals example 40–41, 71,
    75, 78
moral psychology xvi, 8–10, 34, 93–94, 129
moral skeptic 5, 91
Moral Twin Earth Thought Experiment 78
Moore, G. E. xvii–xx, 2–3, 16–21, 25, 55, 76,
    123, 133–134

naturalism xxi, 2–3, 17–18, 33, 52, 65–66,
    89–90, 100–101, 128–130
    a posteriori reductive 75–79
    a priori 79–84
    Neo-Aristotelian 66–71
    relativistic 71–75
naturalistic fallacy 20
natures 66–70, 130
Neo-Aristotelians see naturalism,
    Neo-Aristotelian
network-style analysis see naturalism, a priori
noncognitivism 8–10, 102
nonnaturalism x, 2–3, 16–29, 94, 122–124
norm-expressivism 42, 136
normative ethics xv, 120–121, 131–132
normativity 17, 24, 120–121
    all-things-considered 121–137

ontological commitments 21–23, 38
open question argument 20–21, 33–34, 76, 79,
    123, 133
original position 109–110, see also constructivism

partners-in-crime response 26, 58, 113
permutation problem 82
Plato xvi–xvii, 16, 53, 68
practical ethics xv
pragmatics 6, 14, see also implicature
pragmatism 112–114
prescription xviii, 40–41, 47, 135
prescriptivism 39–41
Price, Huw 113
principle of charity 56, 60, 127
principle of parsimony 24, 33
Prinz, Jesse 108
projectivism 42
Putnam, Hilary 77–78

quasi-realism xxi, 42–45, 91, 94, 102, 126, 135

Rawls, John 109–110
rationalism 107–108
realism 4, 12, 21, 44–45, 72, 88, 100, 108, 114,
    132–133
reasons xix, 17, 23, 57, 70, 110–111, 122,
    128–130, 136
    justifying 9–11, 27–28, 74, 126–127,
        see also internalism, motivational
    motivating 9–11, 27–28, see also internalism
        about justifying reasons
relativism 15n1, 53–54, 71–75, 95, 103, 106,
    129
    anthropological 71
    metaethical 71
representationalism 6, 8, 32, 40, 92, 95, 99,
    106
response-dependence 106–108
Ridge, Michael 118n2

scientism 100
skepticism xvi, 91
    radical 55, 136
Smith, Michael 80–82
Street, Sharon 24, 110–111
subjectivism 15n1, 71–74, 103, 106–107, 129
supervenience 26–27, 35–36, 55, 89, 123–125

theoretical cost–benefit analysis xix, 18, 29, 33,
    89, 95–96, 115, 121
Timmons, Mark 78
Tresan, Jon 105

veil of ignorance 109
verificationist principle 37
virtues, ethical 2, 70–71

Yablo, Stephen 83